Italianità

The Essence of Being Italian and Italian-American

William Giovinazzo

DARK RIVER

An imprint of Bennion Kearny Ltd.

Published by Dark River, Bennion Kearny Limited
6 Woodside
Churnet View Road
Oakamoor
Staffordshire
ST10 3AE

www.BennionKearny.com

With love to my sister Judy,
My second mom

Italia Mia

My Italy, though words cannot heal
the mortal wounds
so dense, I see on your lovely flesh,
at least I pray that my sighs might bring
some hope to the Tiber and the Arno,
and the Po, that sees me now sad and grave.
Ruler of Heaven, I hope
that the pity that brought You to earth,
will turn you towards your soul-delighting land.
Lord of courtesy, see
such cruel wars for such slight causes:
and hearts, hardened and closed
by proud, fierce Mars,
and open them, Father, soften them, set them free:
and, whatever I may be, let your Truth
be heard in my speech...

Il Canzoniere 128
Petrarch

Foreword

I started The *Italian American Podcast* and wrote my book *Forty Days in Italy Con La Mia Famiglia* because I believe it is important for all Americans to discover and record their history. Record it for themselves, for their families and for their communities. It matters.

In this book, William Giovinazzo did just that. He cataloged his past and the past of many Italian-Americans. From *Sunday Dinners* to the *Jersey Shore, Bella Figura, Little Italies, Catholicism,* and he even touched on *Nuns with Rulers* (it brought back some not so good memories for me).

He went deeper though. He gave a history of how our people came here. The poverty, diaspora, immigration, Garibaldi. The layers in this book are many and are important, but above all, they are our origin.

You are about to take a ride from the poverty-stricken farms of southern Italy to Italian-American neighborhoods of the 1950's and 60's. A ride that all Italian Americans should take, at least once, in their lives. Buckle up.

C'e la luna mezz'o mare

Mamma mia me maritari,

Figghia mia, a cu te dari

Mamma mia pensaci tu…

Anthony Fasano
Host of *The Italian American Podcast*
Author of *Forty Days in Italy Con La Mia Famiglia*
ItalianAmericanExperience.com

Table of Contents

Chapter 1: The Awakening

Midway through our life's journey
I awoke to find myself within a dark forest
For the straight path had been lost
Ah me! How hard a thing it is to tell
This forest wild, rough, and hard
The very thought of it renews the fear.
So bitter it is, death is little more;
But of the good which I found there
I'll also tell …

Inferno 1: 1-8

A Dantesque Love

Just as Dante awoke to find himself lost midway through his life, I too had a similar awakening. Unlike Dante, however, I know how I came to such a state. In the pages to follow I will tell you what I have learned.

You see, I am in love. For most of my life, I have cherished this love. While I love my wife dearly, this love is the love of another. How this other love began I cannot say. My love's presence has always been part of my life; it permeated my existence in subtle ways. In the food I ate, in the words I spoke, in the music I heard; my love was always there. When I was a child I never really thought of it. It was a way of being, as normal a part of my existence as breathing air.

Then something changed in me.

I became aware of this presence, this quality of life that was absent for most other people.

When did this happen? When did this awareness first stir in my heart?

It was August the 20th, 1972.

Che La Luna

My parents wanted to go the drive-in to see a movie, *The Godfather*. This was unusual for my parents. My mother's cousins, Nick and Florence, had come by for a visit. It was a typical Sunday dinner with the relatives. My mother made her famous lasagna. The centerpiece of the dinner table in our home was not a vase of flowers, but my mother's white enamel sauce pot where the sausage lay half sunk in the deep red sauce. The sauce was as thick as lava which, in a certain light, had a faint shimmer of gold along the contours of its surface.

After the main course had been cleared away, the adults began to talk about *The Godfather*. The film had captured the attention of most Italian-Americans. In the film, there were many things reminiscent of the old days in the Italian-American community, of the days when my parents were young. When my mother heard they sang *Che La Luna* she could not believe it. In a Hollywood movie? Incredible! It was scandalous. As I sat there listening to them speak, I didn't understand why they would care. So, they sang some old Italian song in a movie. What was the big deal?

Growing up, I heard *Che La Luna* often. It was usually on sleepy mornings when my mother, after working most of the night in the local textile mill, would sing from the washroom outside my bedroom door:

Lazy Mary, you better get up
We need the sheets for the table

She would replace "Mary" with "Billy" while the remainder of her morning serenade was delivered in Italian. I can still hear the sound of the washing machine as an accompaniment to her singing. My mother had spent most of her life working, working hard, both in and out of the home. She didn't have the soft hands of mothers from more prosperous families. I can still feel those rough hands caressing my face once she came into the room to rouse me out of my bed.

At the time, I did not speak Italian so I never really understood what the song was about. Never really gave it much thought, either. It was only another one of those silly Italian songs my mother used to sing. I now understand. The song is a dialog between a mother and daughter discussing who the daughter should marry. A typical song verse is:

There's the moon in the middle of the sea
Mother, I must get married
My daughter, to whom will I give you
Mother, I'll leave it up to you
If I give you the farmer
He will come and he will go
But he will always hold his plow in his hands
If He likes the idea

He'll plow you oh my daughter
La la la, fried fish and baccala
We don't want any calamari

Each verse discusses men of varying professions. If you marry a policeman he will always have a rifle in his hands, a baker will have cannoli, a musician will have a trumpet…

Well, you can imagine the rest.

It is actually quite a long list. Each tool is a phallic symbol of some sort that the prospective husband would like to use on the girl. In the movie, a skinny old Italian man sings the song during the wedding reception. He gestures with his hands and thrusts with his hips as he sings. There is a great shot of Carmela Corleone, the Godfather's wife, laughing with obviously faux embarrassment as the old man does his routine.

The song is something really embedded within Italian-American culture. Years later I was talking with an acquaintance who ran a Bed & Breakfast place. I suggested she name the place "Mama Bacciagalupe's Bed & Breakfast – you can't sleep late because we need the sheets for the table." Although she laughed at the reference, she didn't think it was the branding she wanted to establish; most non-Italians wouldn't quite understand.

Returning to the dinner, hearing they sang *Che La Luna* in *The Godfather* was enough of a draw for my parents. The decision was made; we were off to the New Hartford Drive-In.

So, there I was in 1972, my 16-year-old self, sitting between my mother and father with Nick and Florence in the back seat, watching *The Godfather*.

As anyone who has seen *The Godfather* knows, Michael, the war hero son of Don Corleone, flees to Sicily after murdering a rival Mafioso and a corrupt police chief. There he meets, courts, and marries his first wife, Apollonia. How I remember those scenes of Sicily! Perhaps it was a genetic memory or the overactive imagination of a 16-year-old boy, but I could feel the warmth of the Mediterranean sun on my neck as I approached the rustic cantina of Apollonia's father. I heard the crunch of the unpaved road beneath my feet. As I sat with Michael and his bodyguards, I knew the taste of the wine and the sharpness of the provolone. Why did those places seem so familiar?

My entire existence had been in a small city in upstate New York; a place as different from Sicily as Vermont is to Hawaii. Yet there was something on the screen with a resonance I could not describe. I longed for Italy. I wanted to walk in the steps of my ancestors, to eat the fruit of the trees that once fed them, to pray in the churches where they once knelt. I wanted to rediscover what had been lost to me when my grandparents came to this country.

You see this was, and is, my love, Italy. ITALIA!!!

It is the place of my ancestors; a land one can easily describe without exaggeration as having shaped western civilization. I am not certain if I love Italy because of my Italian heritage, or if Italy is objectively as wondrous as I believe it to be. Regardless of the cause, the effect is I love Italy. Despite the multiple trips to the *old country* I have made over the years, the same yearning stirs in me whenever I see pictures of Italy. Whether it is the fecundity of the voluptuous Tuscan countryside or the sun-washed Greek ruins in Sicily, I long for the land of my forefathers.

I should point out this was not the awakening to which I referred at the start of this chapter.

At the age of nine, Dante fell in love with Beatrice when he saw her at a party. Although over his entire life he had only seen her four times, he never stopped loving her, even after her death. He never knew her, really knew her; he loved her from afar. She was a concept to Dante. At the end of *Purgatorio*, he is finally reunited with her, although the term reunited may not really be an appropriate word since they had never been united. She scolds him, telling him he only loved the concept of her. He did not actually love her.

Similarly, for most of my early years, I did not know Italy, really know her, I loved the concept of her. Many Italian-Americans love Italy, but they love only the concept of Italy, much as I had. Italy to them is a black Venetian gondola, Saint Mark's Square, cypress trees on Tuscan hills at dawn, and the houses of Amalfi clinging to cliffs above the sea. To them, the people of Italy are black & white images of women stomping grapes, *nonne* (grandmothers) dressed in black, and old men sitting in a *piazza*. The concept of Italy is aimlessly strolling down a cobblestone *via* eating *gelato* with Gina, an Italian girl who laughs easily and kisses passionately. Italy, the concept, is wine and cheese, pasta and pizza. It is the sea, and vineyards, and ancient ruins.

The reality of Italy is somewhat different. When you get to Italy, you do see the gondolas, but you also experience the crowded train stations. When you get to Italy, you do see the cypress trees on the Tuscan hills, but you also experience the filthy streets of Naples. When you get to Italy, you do see the previous generations who are reminiscent of those old photographs, but you also see the young Italians who are more like the kids back home than they are of *Dondi*.[1] When you get to Italy, you get to eat all the pasta and drink all the wine you like, but you will also see a McDonalds off Saint Mark's square or a Kentucky Fried Chicken in Rome.

The reality of Italy is of Europe's battlefield; a place where secular and religious powers have contested with one another for not just supremacy on the boot-shaped peninsula, but greater Europe. The reality of Italy is of a people who have struggled for millennia against foreign invaders. The reality of Italy is a country plagued with government mismanagement and corruption. The reality of Italy is a people who, despite these challenges, have – with great dignity and grace – led the world in science, philosophy, art, and literature.

What I did know of Italy and being Italian was based on her children and grandchildren as well as the culture they created in the United States. Italian-Americans know Italian-American culture, something which has evolved over the past one hundred years. It is not less than Italian culture, just different.

Growing Up Italian

I was raised in an Italian neighborhood with neighbors whose names were Brittelli, Custodero, Tringo, Vallelo, and Visconti. When we went out for dinner, we ate at Ventura's Restaurant or Basile's. Saturday afternoons were spent at the Rialto Theatre. Our mothers cooked in their cellar kitchens listening to Frank Sinatra and Dean Martin while our fathers tended to the tomato and pepper plants in the family garden.

Although our way of life evolved over the years, it was based on the customs our parents and grandparents brought with them *on the boat*. I cannot say we were necessarily proud of our ethnicity. I don't believe many of us gave it much consideration. We didn't think we were eating this or saying that because we were Italian, we simply lived in a way that was natural to us. It was a rich life, though not necessarily a prosperous one.

---

[1] Dondi was a comic strip that ran in the United States from 1955 to 1986. The main character, Dondi, was an Italian war orphan who was brought back to the United States by two U.S. soldiers who spoke Italian. He had dark hair and big soulful eyes.

The people who were *other* to us, who lived an alien lifestyle, were the people on the screen at the Rialto. To us, being Italian was the normal state of the world. It was these other people – who ate meat on Friday and had casseroles for dinner – who were odd.

Typically, the old folks, when encountering these strange Northern Europeans, would simply roll their eyes and say "American." Now, the pronunciation here is very important. It wasn't simply "American," with the flat English pronunciation of the word, but *A-mar-i-ghan*. The *mare* bit sounding like the word for a female horse with a rolled R and the emphasis on the last syllable. I remember my mother would say with a slight tossing of her head, "What do you expect? She's A-mar-i-ghan,[2] she keeps her butter in the cupboard." I don't really understand what she meant, the butter part, but that is what she used to say.

It seemed as if all women over 60 were short, round, and dressed in black. Even their shoes were black; thick-soled, man-like shoes. The only deviation from the blackness of their attire was the beige orthopedic stockings that seemed eternally bunched around their ankles. Though they had been in the United States for decades, most barely spoke English, while they all maintained their old-world traditions and superstitions.

I remember a friend's grandmother who would not allow her picture to be taken. She thought it would steal a piece of her soul. Of course, my friends and I thought it was hilarious to try to take her picture to upset her. I never said I was a good kid. When I think of some of the things I did as a boy… if my father had ever found out, oh *madone*!![3]

The short round seriousness of these *nonne* was in contrast to their husbands. Most of these men had made their way in life through hard physical labor; their hands were gnarled and frequently missing part of a finger or two. They were men with salt and pepper grizzled chins, who always seemed to have a smile for the kids in the neighborhood.

When these old guys spoke Italian, they did not just speak Italian. They SPOKE Italian.

The language is highly emotive, but even more so in the mouths, and hands, of these weathered old-timers. The emotions were amplified not

---

[2] For simplicity, going forward I will simply spell A-mar-i-ghan as Amarigahn

[3] Madone – Italian-American pidgin for "Oh, my God!" See Chapter 8.

only by their tones of voice, but their facial expressions and hand gestures. When they spoke, everything about them seemed given over to making their point. It was a laugh to watch them argue with one another, hands flailing, voices raised. I didn't understand what they were saying, but it sure seemed like they were arguing. I was to learn later, most of the time they were just talking, passing the time of day.

I remember walking into Tony's Sweetshop on Bleecker Street in Utica, New York. My father, who drove a truck at night, would frequently stop there on the way home in the morning for a cup a coffee and to *shoot the shit* with some of his friends.

The image you already have in your mind is probably not far from what it was like.

When you walked into Tony's, there was a long counter running down the right-hand side with red stools mounted on the floor in front of it. Down the left, there was a row of booths with aluminum-banded red Formica table tops. I can still see the old men standing around in groups talking with one another, face to face and nose to nose. It is one of many pleasant memories I have of my hometown. As they spoke, their little black Italian cigars were balanced between their first and second fingers.

If you have never been assaulted by the stench of one of these cigars, count yourself blessed. Although I have always described them as old man cigars – since they were the only ones who seemed to smoke them – they were Italian stogies. About as long and wide as your index finger, they were knobby and black like a stick pulled from the ashes. A less delicate description of these things is of the droppings of a small dog left in the summer sun. In my opinion, their smell was far worse than those droppings. Then again, I suppose they were an acquired taste, but I am not quite sure how anyone could develop a fondness for such a thing.

Nothing Went to Waste

Italian immigrants brought with them more than the way they spoke or dressed. They also brought the remembrance of poverty and starvation.

When I was a child, there was an old man who lived in the neighborhood who helped my father whenever there was a home repair project. Let's call him Mr. Bacciagalupe. He didn't ask for payment, he did it to merely help out his neighbor. He was as kind-hearted a man as you could ever hope to know.

Years later, I heard that when Mr. Bacciagalupe was back in Sicily, he had killed a man who was his friend. The story I had been told was that people had a difficult time getting enough to eat back then. So, to survive, they would catch small game. Mr. Bacciagalupe had gone into the countryside with a friend and had the luck to catch a rabbit. Both men were on the verge of starvation. Well, there isn't a lot of meat on a wild rabbit, certainly not enough for two starving men to share. A fight broke out between the two, leaving the friend dead. I was told Mr. Bacciagalupe, when asked about the incident, would look down, breathe a heavy sigh and say, "It was either him or me."

I don't believe Mr. Bacciagalupe was simply referring to the fight.

That was Southern Italy back in the early 1900's. Sometimes a rabbit could mean the difference between life and death.

These people knew hunger. So many of the things practiced by our *nonne* and *nonni* (grandfathers) in the old neighborhood were done in memory of the clawing existence of Southern Italy. It was not unusual to see the old *nonne* out picking dandelions. We could see them in vacant fields, in parks, or along the ramps of the freeways. Today, I suspect they would be objects of ridicule; that wasn't the case for us. We saw them and accepted it as simply what they did. As children, we didn't understand how the memory of starvation marked them so deeply that it drove them for the rest of their lives.

Nothing went to waste.

There was a time when pigeons infested the eaves of the library across from our home, my father caught them and wrung their necks. Although we did not eat pigeon, we had friends who did. After dressing the birds, Dad gave them to these friends. They ended up as a tasty meal for someone.

Nothing went to waste.

Most backyards in the old neighborhood had large barrels used by the old men to collect rainwater. Today, in Southern California, we are happy to see it rain because it cleans the air. We would never dream of drinking rainwater because of the pollutants. In those days, we thought rainwater was the purest water we could get. The Italians remembered the dryness of the *Mezzogiorno* (Southern Italy). They would use rainwater to water their gardens.

Nothing went to waste.

Every backyard had a vegetable garden; tomatoes, peppers, basil, oregano, escarole. It was not uncommon for there to be multiple fruit trees, but I loved the grape vines the most. These were grapes the old folks would use to make wine; small, and juicy, and sweeter than grape soda. There was nothing like stealing a handful on a hot summer day. Sometimes I would simply pop them whole into my mouth where they would explode in purple chrysanthemums. At other times, I would peel off the bitter skin, exposing the vulnerable, almost translucent, meat within. It was a sticky, messy affair, but well worth it to a kid on a summer afternoon.

We knew where all the grape vines were in the neighborhood; we also knew which ones had the best grapes. The Custoderos had well-tended vines that ran along trellises next to their grandfather's garden, but you didn't touch them. Frankie, the grandson, was one of the guys. It wouldn't be right. There were also wild vines that grew in the vacant lot behind The Rialto, our neighborhood movie house. The grapes were delectable, but those vines could not be counted on for any decent supply.

Now that I am an adult, I can't believe I did what I did. If some kid in my neighborhood today were to raid my garden as mercilessly as we did back then I would feel justified in skinning the little hooligan alive. Fortunately, the one time we did get caught, the old guy was much kinder than me. He probably remembered his days back home in Italy.

Although he was angry with us at first, he ended up paying us to harvest some of the fruit trees in his yard. We were small enough to climb to the top of his pear tree to get the fruit from the branches he could not reach. So, we walked away from the mess with a couple of bucks and a small bag of pears. Some may say we should have been punished more severely. If my father had known about the incident, I certainly would have been. No punishment was really necessary, however, the kindness of the old man made us feel so guilty afterward we never did it again.

Italian-American Life

We were mostly Catholic, but not too Catholic.

On Sundays, we attended mass, and on Fridays, we ate fish. Each home had either a picture of the Blessed Virgin or the Sacred Heart. Frequently, there would be one place in the home, typically atop a dresser in the master bedroom or bureau in the living room, which would act as a small altar with statues of various saints and a candle or two. For some families, this devotion would spill into the front yard. It was not uncommon to see a shrine in front of your neighbors' homes. These shrines consisted of a bathtub stood on end, buried half deep in the lawn. They would then cover the exterior with brick or plaster. In the tub, they would place a statue of their favorite saint, surrounding the entire thing with flowers. The Virgin Mary surrounded by lilacs was a popular choice.

Many of us attended Catholic School where we were subjected to the infamous nuns of lore. Nuns hidden beneath layer upon layer of black; rosaries of black walnut-sized beads hung from black cord belts like a gaucho's bola.

Black. Black. Black.

We said a Hail Mary and an Our Father to start the day. "Bless us, oh Lord, in these thy gifts which we are about to receive, from thy bounty through Christ our Lord, Amen," was our grace before lunch which signaled a precious 30 minutes of freedom was about to begin.

At the end of the school day, we said our Act of Contrition, "Oh my God I am heartily sorry for having offended thee…" I guess the nuns thought we couldn't get through a day without doing something to piss off God. Then again, as I mentioned before, I never said I was a good kid.

When I say we were not too Catholic, we had faith, but we didn't get crazy about it. It might seem we got a bit carried away with our religion with all the altars and such, but the idea was if you did these things you were pretty much covered. Religion had its place. The priests and nuns had their world and we basically had ours. We simply didn't get in each other's way.

If only my words had the power of Dickens' ghost of Christmas past so I could transport you back to that time. You would see there was not a Mafioso on every street corner. You would see the young men did not walk around with their shirts half open to display excessive numbers of gold chains. You would hear we did not say "dem" when we meant "them." I have asked others of my generation if they had ever used or heard the phrase "For-ged-aboud it." All seem to agree it was an invention of Hollywood Mafia movies. I suspect the phrase was popular within a few groups and later projected onto all Italian-Americans. While we may have had our own way of doing things, we were not the hackneyed images of popular media.

This is what life was like in an Italian neighborhood in the United States in the 1950's and 60's. It was a wonderful time and a wonderful place to live. It was a culture derived from the culture of the *Mezzogiorno*. So, when I saw those images on the screen at the drive-in that night with my parents, there was something that resonated with me. As I said above, I had a dream to visit those places. I am sure it comes as no surprise, however, that the dreams which a 16-year-old boy dreamt on a warm summer evening faded. Like many of the things dear to me then, the dream of Italy was put in the back of my closet with my guitar. For many years, the dream of Italy was as likely to be realized as my career in music. Yet, every now and then, taking that beat up old guitar out of the closet I would strum, dreaming of standing in front of cheering crowds. In the same way, taking those vague old dreams of Italy out of the closet I would talk; dreaming of wandering down through ancient ruins.

Nothing serious, just talk.

For Christ's sake, Go!

When I say I talked about going to Italy, I mean I talked about going to Italy a lot. So much so that people got sick of hearing about it.

If I saw something about Italy on television, I would bore co-workers with it, dominating the lunchtime conversation. I had to see any movie even vaguely related to Italy, only to rave about it the following week. At family get-togethers, I would say I wasn't going to end up like my father. He always talked about going to Italy when he retired, but he got sick and never made it. I said it so often that one evening, while having dinner with my nephew's family, he moaned in frustration; "For Christ's sake go already and stop talking about it."

On the way home that evening, my wife said to me, "You know we can do it."

"Do what?" my mind was in caloric shock. My nephew's wife is a good cook and I should have stopped eating long before I actually did.

"Go to Italy."

"You're crazy."

I couldn't believe my wife, the daughter of a banker, was suggesting such an extravagance. One of the many virtues for which I love my wife is her frugality, so how could she be making such a suggestion? We had recently enrolled our two kids in private school. "With the kids' tuition and the mortgage payment, we can't afford it," I said, dismissing the idea. But, as I said, I married a banker's daughter and she knows her way around a household budget. In the week that followed, she found a way for us to go.

The decision was made; we were off to Italy.

Coming Home?

So, there I was in 2004, my 48-year-old self, sitting between my wife and the emergency exit, our two kids sitting in the row behind us. We were on our way to Rome.

In the weeks leading up to the trip, I imagined what Italy would be like. I expected to be welcomed with open arms when I arrived, that I would be adopted as the Italian-American returning to the land of his ancestors. My joy would be matched only by their joy in discovering I was a fellow Italian who had found his way home. I expected them to see I was exactly like them. It did not take long for reality to set in.

Our plane arrived at Leonardo da Vinci airport in Rome in the mid-afternoon. As our feet touched Italian soil for the first time, all four of us cheered in unison: "Eureka!!"

We had found it. We had found Italy.

As the other passengers pushed past us, I could see the irritation on some of their faces. "Tourists." This was the first indication I had that things were not to be quite as expected. I didn't understand at the time why they weren't as thrilled as I thought they should be. I had come home. Why didn't they realize my love for Italy not only included the land but them as well? I brushed it off simply as a few people who didn't get it; you find people like that everywhere. Some people are just spoilsports. They probably kick puppies.

Later, I realized I was the one who did not understand. A significant portion of Italy's economy is based on tourism. Travel and tourism contributed 11.1% of Italy's GDP and 12.6% of its employment in 2016.[4] This means a lot of visitors; a lot of people planting their feet on Italian soil and cheering their arrival. Years later, an Italian friend, Enrico, explained to me that as the average Italian goes about their daily

---

[4] World Travel & Tourism Council, *Travel & Tourism Economic Impact 2017 Italy*, pg. 8

lives, they often need to navigate around and sometimes through groups of tourists. One could easily imagine the frustration of having a difficult day, only to be blocked at every turn by tourists gumming up the works. Enrico told me of a time when, as a student in Venice, he was late for class but stopped to help some confused Americans. They asked him if he could direct them to the exit. The exit? Venice has an exit? Did they think they were in Disneyland? Although he was irritated by the comment, he had the grace not to show it and provided assistance.

My enthusiasm for Italy did not weaken in spite of encountering the real city of Rome where people worked and lived; where they dealt with reality not the romanticized dream I had developed over the years. As we walked through the airport, we were walking through not just any airport; it was THE Leonardo da Vinci airport in ROME. The cab drivers were not just any cab drivers; they were ITALIAN cab drivers. The same rush hour traffic getting into Rome, that I saw as delightful and interesting, would have been an intolerable frustration if it were between Los Angeles International and my home.

We passed a billboard where a watermelon was cut to resemble the Colosseum. How clever it was! How funny! My wife rolled her eyes when I pointed it out to her. To her, the traffic was traffic, Roman or otherwise. It had been a long trip. Both she and the kids were ready to be at the hotel.

When we arrived, my wife asked if the concierge could make dinner reservations for us at a nearby restaurant for 18:30 that evening. "I am sorry Signora," he said with remarkable politeness, "No one starts serving dinner until 20:00 at the earliest." We had heard the Italians ate later than Americans, but we thought we could surely find someplace that served dinner early. He then explained. "You see before the staff serve you, they have to eat. After all, how can they serve you a meal when they themselves have not eaten?" That has always struck me as being a civilized way of looking at things.

That night we ate later than we normally ate. After dinner, we wandered down to the Trevi Fountain to throw in our coins, as all good tourists must. I think there is a law requiring it. We learned the pleasure of a simple meal and a *passeggiata*[5] through Rome, about giving things the

---

[5] *Passeggiata* – the literal interpretation of the word is a walk or a stroll. It is actually a tradition in Italy to stroll slowly through the main streets of

proper priority. Back home in the United States, we ate early, so we could get up early and get to work. We rushed through our meal to get to our emails that were piling up. We spent our evenings plowing through social media with the television blaring in the background. We didn't have time to savor our microwaved out-of-the-box factory-stamped meals. We had important things to do, like tweeting our most profound thoughts on Twitter whilst watching *Dancing with the Stars*!

As we wandered back to our hotel, we stopped for gelato and relished being in Italy. Once back in our room, I stood on our balcony looking down at the street below. The Venetian windows were open; the curtains billowed with the evening breeze. From where I stood, I could hear the laughter coming from the diners of the *trattoria* across the street as they enjoyed their meals *al fresco*. They were totally oblivious to the *Vespas* whizzing by. A feeling of contentment warmed me.

After all these years, I was in Italy. And it was good.

It was at this point that I had my *Dante-esque* awakening. The realization set in that I had been lost in a dark wood, *una selva oscura*. I had lost the way, the way of Italian life. Dante's realization that he was lost in a dark wood was the beginning of a journey for him. In the same way, that night was the beginning of a journey for me. It was a journey of discovery, the discovery of the real Italy and the true Italian way of life.

The Case for the Italian-American

I am proudly Italian-American. There are some who don't believe this type of thinking is a virtue. Some people tell me there is no room for hyphenated Americans, which is a term first used by President Theodore Roosevelt. On Columbus Day in 1915, while addressing the primarily Irish Catholic Knights of Columbus, Roosevelt said:

> There is no room in this country for hyphenated Americanism. When I refer to hyphenated Americans, I do not refer to naturalized Americans. Some of the very best Americans I have ever known were naturalized Americans, Americans born abroad. But a hyphenated American is not an American at all... The one absolutely certain way of bringing this nation to ruin, of preventing all possibility of its continuing to be a nation at all, would be to permit it to become a tangle of squabbling nationalities,

town – typically on pedestrian thoroughfares – greeting neighbors, socializing, or even having a drink with a friend.

an intricate knot of German-Americans, Irish-Americans, English-Americans, French-Americans, Scandinavian-Americans or Italian-Americans, each preserving nationality, each at heart feeling more sympathy with Europeans of that nationality than with other citizens of the American Republic… There is no such thing as a hyphenated American who is a good American. The only man who is a good American is the man who is an American and nothing else.[6]

Personally, I think Teddy Roosevelt is perhaps one of the greatest presidents in American history; but, no one is always right. The multicultural character of American society is one of those areas where Roosevelt was quite often wrong, not just wrong but very wrong. In a letter to his sister Anna, shortly after the lynching of 11 Italian-Americans in New Orleans, Roosevelt said, "Monday we dined at the Camerons; various *dago* diplomats were present, all much wrought up by the lynching of the Italians in New Orleans. Personally, I think it rather a good thing, and said so."[7] Note the use of the pejorative *dago*.

Roosevelt was a product of his times. In the United States, increases in immigration fuel American xenophobia which in turn drives a greater emphasis on assimilation. This was certainly the case for the Italian diaspora as we entered the 20th century. American institutions, as we will discuss in the upcoming chapters, pressured Italian immigrants to abandon the traditions of their ancestors in favor of an American way of life. The children of immigrants, succumbing to these pressures, sought to be like everyone else, to lose their ethnic *otherness*. In so doing, however, they lost their connection to the past.

Establishing a connection with the past has a substantive benefit for both the individual as well as society. In cutting ourselves off from our past, we have lost what Robert Bly, author of *The Sibling Society*, describes as vertical integration. Bly argues that we have replaced this structure with a horizontal integration: we are all siblings. We are all leveled. Parents proudly proclaim they are friends with their children, not conventionally parental. In these sibling societies, we not only lose the traditions of our ancestors but the values that have evolved over the centuries. It is these values, tested by previous generations, which provide a structure for leading a good life while giving us an understanding of what truly is of value.

---

[6] Roosevelt Bars the Hyphenated, *New York Times*, 1915

[7] Letter from Theodore Roosevelt to Anna Roosevelt, March, 21, 1891

Confucius is quoted as having said, "If your plan is for one year, plant rice. If your plan is for ten years, plant a tree. If your plan is for one hundred years, educate children." This epitomizes the difference between horizontal and vertical integration. Sibling societies plan for a year, maybe ten. Societies that are vertically integrated, however, educate their children. This education is not simply in functional skills, but of their history, literature, and music. They educate their children in the culture of their people.

You might argue there is no need to look beyond the United States, the vertical integration discussed by Bly need only extend to American history and American values. This, however, misses the very essence of what it means to be an American. In 1782, Congress adopted the Seal of the United States. On that seal was "E Pluribus Unum" which in Latin is "Out of Many, One." This is the essence of the United States; a single people derived from many cultures and beliefs.

You will hear people speak of the United States as the great melting pot. I disagree. I see the United States as a great stew where each group that immigrates to this country brings with them their own flavor. As we live and work together, those flavors infuse to make something which is truly unique. No one flavor is ever really lost but becomes an element of the American blend.

Think of things that are truly American. A Super Bowl party's menu is a celebration of American multiculturalism; German bratwurst, Italian pizza, Irish Guinness Stout, and Mexican tortilla chips and guacamole. African-Americans brought with them the music that eventually evolved into the Blues and Rock & Roll. Our system of Government is based on the Romans and Greeks. Of course, we cannot forget our closest and dearest ally, Great Britain, whose culture was the very foundation of our own. Today, Indians are migrating to the United States bringing with them a new vitality, a new energy. Vietnamese and Bahraini, Icelanders and Emirati, are all coming to the United States adding new flavors to the American stew.

One of the things that made Rome a great empire was its ability to incorporate other cultures into its own. If you were to look at the Roman pantheon of gods, you would see how Rome embraced other cultures and religions. Even Mithras, a god whom Constantine considered in preference to Christianity, was a god the Romans had adopted from the Persians. In adopting these other cultures, Rome was able to take the best of what they had to offer, continually looking at the world in a new and different light. This is why we must maintain our connection with our ethnic past, not to replace being an American but to enhance it.

At the heart of the argument against hyphenated Americans is the misconception that we somehow have an allegiance to a country other than the United States. Although for a brief period of approximately ten years during the World War II era there was some division between Italy and the United States, from Columbus to Cuomo, the two nations have shared a close, symbiotic relationship. Even while we were put in concentration camps and had our businesses taken away, Italian-Americans fought for the United States. We are American, a particular type of American, but American none the less.

Rediscovering Italianità

While there is a justification for retaining our status of hyphenated Americans, as noted earlier many of us have not retained our connection with the past. Years after my first trip to Italy, I was discussing my expectations with a friend who had immigrated to California from Sicily. I told him how disappointed I was that Italians did not see me as one of them. He laughed, saying it happens all the time. "Americans come to Italy and say 'Hey, I am Italian!' What do you mean you are Italian? You don't speak our language. You don't know our history or customs. Even the food you eat is different from the food we eat. So, how are you Italian? Your grandparents, they were Italian. You? You're an American."

What my friend was describing was Italian-America's loss of *Italianità*. *Italianità* is the essence of being Italian. It is living the Italian spirit; the language, the food, the music, the art… All those things make Italians Italian.

There are many Italian-Americans who mourn what we have lost, our *Italianità*. Many Italian-Americans who are the children of the generation that sought to lose their ethnicity are now trying to reclaim it. They are hoping to find what was lost. While there are many universities and Italian-American associations who have a formalized approach to the study of Italian-American culture, much of what passes for Italian-American is an amalgam of phantoms of Southern Italian customs and an *invented tradition*.

Many of the differences we will discuss in this book can be attributed to the differences in Italy itself. The icons of purely Italian culture are those of the north. The vast majority of Italian immigrants who traveled to the United States, however, came from the south with their unique regional culture. It is from these regions that Italian-American culture has evolved. Many of the differences we will discuss in the following chapters are a result of these regional differences.

Another important influence on Italian-Americans is *invented tradition*. The term *invented tradition*, first coined by Eric Hobsbawm in 1983, refers to traditions thought of as having ancient origins but which were actually invented quite recently. In reference to Italian-American culture, many Italian-Americans who have lost touch with their *Italianità* have adopted traditions that were either created in the movies to fulfill a stereotype, or customs developed by specific Italian-American communities that have been attributed to all Italians. An example of an invented tradition is the use of the phrase "For-ged-aboud it" which I discussed earlier.

Let me conclude with an alternative view. If *Italianità* is the essence of being Italian – the essential attribute of Italianism – then it can exist in many forms. It can have a variety of implementations. Certainly, as we shall see going forward, even within Italy itself, there is a great deal of cultural diversity. I see *Italianità* as a flowing river. Just as a river's path is shaped by certain geographical forces, so has the path of Italian culture been shaped by historical ones. As Italians immigrated to other parts of the world, the river formed new branches with their own paths. Each of these paths have their own unique character. Some are churning rapids, others deep and wide waterways, others still placid streams through lush forests. Despite their differences, they are all still part of the same river, fed by the same sources.

I would like to examine two particular branches of *Italianità*, Italian and Italian-American. I would like to explore what has been retained, what has evolved from our immigrant forbearers, and what have we adopted as part of an invented tradition. The culture of Italy I see as our North Star, the thing from which we derive our bearings. This reference point will tell us not only what we have in common, but where we have deviated so far, and where we are in jeopardy of losing our *Italianità*.

Chapter 2: Italy! What a Concept!

Italy, Concept and Reality

I ended the previous chapter by describing *Italianità* as a river with many branches. Just as the course of a river is determined by geographical forces, the course of a culture is influenced by historical ones. In this chapter, we will briefly discuss the aspects of Italian history that have shaped both Italian and Italian-American culture. Understanding even a high-level summary of Italy's history would take hundreds of pages; I focus on the most relevant points to lay the groundwork for the comparison of the two cultures in later chapters.

I also want to show the symbiotic relationship between Italy and the United States. Italy has had great influence on American culture which has, in turn, greatly influenced Italian culture. In this symbiosis, we find commonality between not just Italians and Italian-Americans, but Americans as a whole. I hope to demonstrate the two nations as more than allies, but sister states with great mutual love and respect. To demonstrate these points, however, we have to go back in time...

Beginnings

Think back 3,000 years, past Berlusconi, past Mussolini, past the Renaissance, past the Romans. Even think past the *Magna Graecia* when the Greeks were the power in the Mediterranean with colonies on the peninsula to their west. Much of the world, and the workings of our universe, was unknown; man populated this cloud, the unknown space beyond the familiar, with terrors and monsters. It was a time when the natural world was personified in various gods, gods as flawed and vain as the mortal men whose fates they controlled; mortals who the gods used in their petty rivalries.

In this time, the jealous goddess Hera persecuted Hercules son of her unfaithful husband, Zeus, and a mortal woman. As part of her revenge, she put upon the Greek hero a fit of madness during which he killed his family. As he awoke from this fevered state the grief, the death of his wife and children at his own hand drove him to seek forgiveness from

Apollo. The god's oracle told Hercules that he must serve Eurystheus, the king of Tiryns and Mycenae, for 12 years as penance for his sins.

In these 12 years, Hercules was tasked to perform 12 seemingly impossible feats. The tenth of these sent him into the western Mediterranean to steal the Geryon's cattle for Eurystheus. The Geryon, the grandson of Medusa, was a terrible giant with three bodies all joined at the waist; three sets of legs, three torsos, three sets of arms and three heads.

Hercules killed this fearful monster and stole its cattle, but this was only half the task. In bringing the herd back to Eurystheus, Hercules fought the sons of Poseidon who tried to steal the cattle. Then, at Rhegium, a bull got loose and jumped into the sea. It swam to Sicily. Hercules pursued the bull as it crossed the island and then made its way to the nearby country. In these lands, the native word for bull was *"italus."* Since then, the country across which Hercules chased the bull came to be called *Italy*.

Although the story of Hercules is colorful, a more likely explanation is that the name originates with a tribe living near the bay of Naples, the *Osci*. Since they were known for the quality and quantity of their cattle, their country became known as *Víteliú* which in Oscan, means *calf-land*. The implication was the land was well suited to the raising of cattle. Later, the name, which had evolved to Italy, was used by the Romans to apply to the entire peninsula.

The Land

In 1814, Count Klemens von Metternich, a leading European statesman at the time, said Italy was only a *geographic expression*. His point was that Italy was really an independent, and often warring, collection of regional principalities and city-states. When the Romans expanded the area to which the name Italy applied, they glossed over this diversity of land and people.

Historically, the *Mezzogiorno* has had very poor grazing land which was evident by the quality of livestock. The cattle were small and white with wide horns; typically, they were used for drawing plows and pulling wagons. In addition, the Apennine Mountains have significantly reduced the acreage for farming and grazing cattle. The south has a dry climate with little pasture land or fields of grain.

The northern end of the peninsula is very different; the beauty of the Tuscan countryside is the stuff of postcards and wall calendars. We are all familiar with the images of the lush, undulating hills. We have all imagined ourselves sitting in our villas overlooking those hills sipping the local wine and snacking on the region's cheese and fruit. Such *abbondanza*, abundant richness, is more appropriate to the north than the rest of Italy.

Much is made of the Alps and how they divided Italy from the rest of Europe. The reality is they were not as formidable as one might think. Of the approximately 20 passes through the mountains, the majority were already in use in Roman times. The *Tabula Peutingeriana*, a copy of a Roman fourth century map, shows nine of these passes. Indeed, northern Italians more easily interacted with the rest of Europe than they did with the *Mezzogiorno*. When visiting Milan or the Piedmont, you can see a much greater European influence than in Palermo or Bari.

The Apennine Mountains, which run down the center of Italy for virtually its entire length, did much more in creating divisions than the Alps. Speaking as someone who has crossed these mountains on a bicycle, they are most definitely a barrier to overcome. I did this on modern roads with a bicycle built with the most current technology. Even then, it was no easy task. The motivation of my ancestors to make the same trip without these conveniences would be low I would imagine. Resultantly, trade and cultural exchanges between the people in the east and those in the west were hindered.

Neither is the impact of this mountain range lessened by any means through navigable rivers. As opposed to North America, where the Saint Lawrence Seaway reaches deep into the continent linking the Great Lakes with the Atlantic Ocean, the waterways of Italy rarely travel across multiple regions. The exceptions to this are the Po and the Tiber. The Po, however, is mainly in the north. Although the Tiber does travel a respectable distance from east to west, it is relatively shallow.

The division of eastern and western Italy takes on a special significance when you consider two other prominent geographic features. First, Italy is in the center of the Mediterranean with Southern Sicily closer to North Africa than Rome. Second, Italy has over 4,000 miles of coastline with many natural harbors as well as soft sloping beaches. The distance from Lecce in Italy to Vlore in Albania is a mere 76 miles. With trouble-free access to the sea, it is easier to get from Brindisi on Italy's eastern coast to Albania, than from Brindisi to Sorrento in Western Italy. Even today, traveling from east to west is no simple task. When I took the train from Sorrento to Bari, it pretty much consumed the entire day.

This divide created a situation in which influences such as Byzantium, the Islamic threat to Christianity, and the eastern challenge to Catholic orthodoxy, impacted eastern Italy much more than the west. To see the Byzantine influence, compare the ornate architecture of Venice with western Italian cities such as Florence or Siena. Meanwhile, Western Europe was leaving its own mark on cities such as Rome and Naples. The political battles between the Catholic Church and the Holy Roman Emperor shaped much of northern Italy in the 14th century. The result of the Spanish and French incursions into Western Italy has had a significant and pervasive impact. Meanwhile, the Spanish rule of the kingdom of Naples created persistent poverty in the south which has in turn greatly affected Southern-Italian and Italian-American culture to this day.

Empires Come & Go

While the Spanish influence upon Italy may have been more current, the Greek influence is older and perhaps more embedded. The above-noted Greek colonization began as early as the 8th and 7th centuries BCE. Many forget that long before the foundations of Rome were laid, or Romulus and Remus were suckled by a she-wolf, Greece was already an old civilization. Prior to the Roman dominance of the Italian peninsula, the Greeks colonized the *Mezzogiorno*, especially around the coastal areas, leaving an impression on Italian culture that has not been worn away by time. While the majority of the settlements were in Calabria and Sicily, some settlements were established as far north as Naples. This created, in the south, a culture which was more Greek, more Hellenistic. The Romans referred to this area as *Magna Graecia*, Great Greece. While there is debate as to whether the term applied to Sicily, it most certainly encompassed Calabria and Apulia.

Although the influence of the Roman Empire is obvious, a less apparent effect of Roman rule is its contribution to the divisions within Italy. For hundreds of years, before the Romans, Italians were fragmented into regions because of the above described geographic obstacles. The center of their cultural identity was the local community. When Caesar Augustus divided Italy into regions, he took special care to have those boundaries reflect the various local loyalties that existed before Rome. In essence, he codified and preserved the differences between the various factions. After the fall of the Roman Empire, there was no unifying authority, so these groups returned to their original, divided conditions.

The historian Arnold Toynbee has suggested there were more city-states in Italy in the 1300s than there were in the entire world. This division, although not quite as severe as what is described by Toynbee, has continued through the time of unification up to today. Historian David Gilmour has questioned: "… whether the lateness of [Italian] unification and the troubles of the nation-state had been not accidents of history but consequences of the peninsula's past and its geography, which may have made it unsuitable territory for nationalism. Were there not just too many Italies for a successful unity?"[8]

Throughout most of its history, the land was divided by the city states or carved up between foreign powers. As I had mentioned earlier, Italy was Europe's battlefield, and this is by no means an exaggeration. The disruption of war and invasion with their associated alliances, as well as the stratagems of international politics, hardly created an environment in which the people could form a strong national identity. Arnaldo Momigliano, in describing Italian history wrote: "The presence of a foreign rule, the memory of an imperial pagan past, and the overwhelming force of the Catholic tradition have been three determining features of Italian history for many centuries."[9]

The Overwhelming Force of Catholic Tradition

Momigliano touches on the greatest power in fracturing Italian culture, *the overwhelming force of the Catholic tradition.* In 312 CE, Emperor Constantine reportedly had a vision prior to the Battle of the Milvian Bridge. Looking up to the sun, he saw a cross of light with the words *in hoc signo vinces* (in this sign you will conquer). Quickly, he commanded his troops to decorate their shield with the Christian symbol to which he later attributed his victory. Then in 313 CE, he issued *The Edict of Milan* stating: "It was proper that the Christians and all others should have the liberty to follow that mode of religion which to each of them appeared best." Except for the brief rule of Julian the Apostate, from that time forward, Rome and her emperors embraced Christianity. Catholicism, however, did not become the church of the Roman Empire until 380

---

[8] Gilmour, David, *The Pursuit of Italy*, Farrar, Straus, and Giroux, 2011, pg. 3

[9] Gilmour, David, *The Pursuit of Italy*, Farrar, Straus, and Giroux, 2011, pg. 49

CE, when Emperor Theodosius issued the Edict of Thessalonica. Although there is some debate concerning the sincerity of Constantine's conversion, his adoption of Christianity changed the course of Western Civilization and made an indelible mark on Italian culture.

While Constantine may have made Rome Christian, what so infused Christianity into Italian culture was what came afterwards. When the empire broke apart and Italy reverted to city-states, the only remaining powerful institution spanning the entire peninsula was the Catholic Church. Local bishops were able to parlay their spiritual leadership into civil authority. Later, in the 8th century CE, *The Donation of Constantine* provided formal justification for the church's civil authority. The donation was essentially Constantine's will which was supposedly written by the Emperor. It made Rome and the provinces, as well as the districts and towns of Italy, a present to the Catholic Church. Although later proven to be a forgery, its believed authenticity lasted for a sufficient time to enable the church leadership to establish and maintain its hold on major portions of Italy.

You might think such a large organization would ultimately unite the people, but the machinations of the church leaders to maintain power only further divided Italians. At the end of the Middle Ages, for example, multiple popes wrestled with the Holy Roman Empire for control of Italy. This broke Italy into two factions; the Guelphs who supported the pope and the Ghibellines who supported the Holy Roman Emperor. The battle between these two groups tore Italy apart. Each of the city-states battled with one another depending on with whom they sided.

The most infamous of these rivalries is the conflict between Florence and Siena. A competition whose reverberations still echo in the Tuscan hills. One of the key battles between these two cities was the Battle of Montaperti in 1260 CE. The defeat of the Florentines was so complete that the city was in jeopardy of being razed to the ground. Had it not been for the efforts of Farinata degli Uberti to preserve the city, the world would have been denied Florence's contributions to western civilization.

I should also point out the Florentines do not remember Farinata as a hero. He was a Florentine who, fighting on the side of Siena in the battle, was largely responsible for the Sienese victory. His objection to the destruction of the city was not out of a sense of loyalty, but a desire to rule. He argued for the city's preservation so he might make it his own. Farinata is to Florentines what Benedict Arnold is to Americans.

As I had noted, the sound of these battles can still be heard. To this day, after more than 700 years, when the two cities confront one another on the soccer field, the Sienese fans chant "Montaperti! Montaperti!"

The Church & Temporal Power

Approximately 400 years before Thomas Jefferson, Dante in his work *De Monarchia* (The Monarchy) argues for the separation of church and state. He maintained that while both the church and state derived their power from God, the church should have no earthly power. The state was to rule over the earthly kingdom while the church acted as the watchdog over men's souls. Dante points out that only the emperor can keep peace on earth while the role of the church is spiritual – providing moral instruction.

Dante realized something that Machiavelli would write about in *The Prince* some 200 years later. There are times when a prince, if he wishes to rule well, cannot be good; he cannot always act according to the Gospel. This, of course, means the church cannot both rule well and fulfill its spiritual mission. Dante recognized how the Catholic Church, in his day, was just another political faction; just another empire, vying for the control of Italy. It was these factions that kept the people divided.

Despite Dante's criticism of the church, it would be incorrect to think he opposed Catholicism. Dante correctly saw a distinction between the Catholic Church and its leaders. Something we should remember as we look at the church's participation in Italian history. Dante places many popes and cardinals in hell, but he does so not as an indictment of the church. He places them in hell for the abuse of their authority within the church. They had their gazes down toward the earth, rather than up toward heaven.

The Catholic Church itself, for example, cannot be held responsible for the enormous negative impact of the political aspirations of Cardinal Giuliano della Rovere.[10] In the 15th century CE, Cardinal Rovere was contending with Pope Alexander VI (Rodrigo de Borja) for the papacy. Along with Ludovico of Milan, the cardinal urged Charles VIII of

---

[10] With the assistance of Cesare Borgia, Cardinal Giuliano della Rovere would later become Pope Julius II following the death of his nemesis Pope Alexander (Rodrigo Borgia).

France to march on Italy to press his claim to the throne of Naples. Rovere hoped to use Charles to remove his rival Alexander as the head of the church. Charles VIII marched through Italy virtually unopposed. He was openly welcomed by some, such as Girolamo Savonarola of Florence and took Naples without a fight.

There were others, however, who were not as happy to see the French. To expel them, Northern Italian states united with the Spanish and the Holy Roman Empire in what was called the League of Venice. This could have been a turning point in Italian history. For the first time in centuries, the Italians were united; for the first time since Rome they acted to expel a foreign power. This could have been the time when *Italia* could have risen from its knees, with a straightened back and a sneer of cold vengeance to forbid further excursions into its homeland. Sadly, this was not to be. As the French retreated, the League of Venice met them near the village of Fornovo on July 6th, 1495, CE. Some claim the French had won the battle since Charles escaped. Others claim the Italians were the victors. If it was an Italian victory, it was an expensive one; they lost two-thirds of their troops.

More important than the death toll was the long-term effect the battle had on the psyche of the Italian people. Luigi Barzini said it well when he wrote; "Fornovo is the turning-point in Italian history. The distant consequences of the defeat are still felt today. If the Italians had won, they would probably have discovered then the pride of being a united people, the self-confidence born of defending their common liberty and independence… Nobody would have ventured lightly across the Alps, for fear of being destroyed."[11]

Since Fornovo and its effects on Italian unification, various world powers have all taken their turns adventuring in Italy. As Barzini points out, a united confident Italy would have led to a very different world than the world today. Many, such as the Spanish, who have ravaged the country, might not have done so. Be that as it may, John Greenleaf Whittier reminds us how, of all words of tongue or pen, the saddest are "it might have been." The sad reality is that the French invasion and the battle of Fornovo left their mark on Italian history and the psyche of many Italians.

---

[11] Barzini, Luigi, *The Italians*, Simon & Schuster, 1964, pg. 287

To list all the conspiracies of Catholic Church leadership would be a retelling of all Italian history. Let us simply say that, for much of Italian history, the church leaders hardly acted as you would imagine the Prince of Peace would have. Although Raphael's portrait of Pope Julius II is as a contemplative, old man with a gray beard, he is known as the Warrior Pope who had no qualms about going to war to defend the property of the church. And so, it goes. From the middle ages through the Renaissance and unification, the popes and cardinals have struggled with earthly principalities, not for the salvation of souls, but the preservation of power. The result was often a divided Italy.

I'm not Italian, I'm Sicilian

As a result of the fracturing of Italian society, the Italian identity is not *sono Italiano* (I am Italian), but *sono Romano* (I am Roman), or *sono Napolitano* (I am Neapolitan).

Italians have a strong sense of loyalty and pride, first to their individual birthplace or region, and then to greater Italy. This loyalty to your local town is known as *campanilismo*. The term, *campanilismo*, comes from the word for bell-tower, *campanile*. Bell-towers have a special significance in Italy in that they serve as the symbol of the town or village. The suffix -*ismo* in Italian is the equivalent of -*ism* in English. For example, in Italian *turismo* is tourism. By the same token *campanilismo* is "bell-tower-ism" which roughly translated is "town-ism" or patriotism to your town. In some cases, *campanilismo* can apply to your individual neighborhood.

Although Dante is credited with having been one of the earliest proponents of a unified Italy, the disunity of the world in which he lived is evident in *La Divina Comedia* (The Divine Comedy). While traveling through the various domains of the afterlife, when he encountered a fellow *Italian*, they identified themselves by their local city or region, not by their Italian identity. At the very beginning of the Inferno, when Dante first meets Virgil, his guide, the Roman poet does not identify himself as an Italian, or even a Roman. Virgil first identifies himself as a Lombard and his parents as Mantuan. The irony is Virgil has been called by some the first, and possibly the last, Italian for another 1,800 years.[12]

---

[12] Gilmour, David, *The Pursuit of Italy*, Farrar, Straus, and Giroux, 2011, pg. 44

The various shades (the dead) that Dante encounters throughout *The Divine Comedy*, recognize Dante as a fellow Florentine by his speech and clothing. As Dante crosses the burning plane of the sodomites, he is recognized by Brunetto Latini as a Florentine by his clothing. Latini does not see Dante as an Italian but as a Florentine. As Dante passes between the oven-like coffins of the heretics just inside the walls of the City of Dis he meets Farinata degli Uberti (who we discussed earlier) who recognizes Dante as a Florentine by his speech.

This particular encounter highlights Dante's own *campanilismo*. First, Farinata's great sin to Dante is that he betrayed Florence. Although he is in the field of heretics, it is clear Dante places him in hell for his disloyalty. Second, the discussion between the two is about Florentine politics. Stop and think about this for a moment. You are in the midst of hell, literally in the midst of hell. Any earthly gain or loss is irrelevant, the game of life for Farinata is over. So, what do they discuss? The meaning of life? The lessons learned from living a life that resulted in eternal damnation? Nope. They argue politics; loyalty and disloyalty to Florence.

Sicilians are excellent examples of *campanilismo*. Whenever I said I was *full-blooded* Italian in front of my dear sainted Sicilian mother, she would quickly correct me saying I was only half Italian and the other half was Sicilian. Sicilians are fiercely proud of their ethnic identity, pointing out they were Sicilian before they were Italian – which is a point that has more than a little merit. Beginning as a Greek colony as mentioned above, Sicily was eventually held by the Carthaginians until 260 BCE when they were evicted by the Romans. So, when Sicilians claim they were Sicilian before they were assimilated into the larger Roman/Italian identity – they have a point.

While the *Risorgimento* (Italian unification which we will discuss shortly), created more of an Italian identity, there is still a very strong sense of *campanilismo*. Today, this feeling of disunity is kept alive by The Northern League and the political faction it represents. Since 1991, when they formed from a number of conservative groups in the north, they have opposed a strong centralized government. Xenophobic and racist, in many ways, they are similar to the Tea Party in the United States. The Northern League has turned its attention to Southern Italy. They are of the opinion that Italy stops at the Garigliano River which is the traditional northern boundary of Naples. They joke "Garibaldi did not unite Italy, but divided Africa" referring to Calabria with such pejoratives as *Calafrica* and *Saudi Calabria*. The Northern League has made the *Mezzogiorno* the scapegoat for the problems of Italy in general. David Gilmour tells of a conversation with a former history professor:

> ... *I was astounded by the next words of Signor Rossi, who twenty years earlier had been the minister of education. "You know, Davide," he said in a low conspiratorial voice, as if nervously uttering a heresy, "Garibaldi did Italy a great disservice. If he had not invaded Sicily and Naples, we in the north would have the richest and most civilized state in Europe." After looking round the room at the other guests, he added in an even lower voice, "Of course to the south we would have a neighbor like Egypt."*[13]

In the north, some maintain that Southern Italians have only themselves to blame. As is the case all over the world, the victims of poverty are blamed for their situation. The claim is that their condition is because they are either immoral, ignorant, lazy, or some combination thereof.

Campanilismo is a significant difference between Italians and Italian-Americans. In the United States, we talk about Italians as if we are all one monolithic group. When two Italian-Americans meet, there is an assumption we have something in common. I cannot count how many times in a business meeting or social gathering another person hearing the name 'Giovinazzo' almost immediately replies with a smile, "I am Italian, too." Typically, my response is to ask from which part of Italy their family came. More often than not, they don't know. (Except Sicilians, Sicilians always know they are Sicilian.) Beyond knowing they are of Italian heritage, few know the province and a much smaller minority the town of their family's origin. In the minds of most Italian-Americans, however, we are all one group. This unification of Italians is a result of the evolution of Italian-American culture. We will look at how this came about in the next chapter.

The Dream of a Unified Italy

Although Italy was not unified into a single nation until the 19th century, there were prior efforts to create an Italian nation. At the dawn of the first century BCE, there was an attempt to establish a state independent of Rome within the central Apennines. The state was called *Italia* with the capital city named *Italica*. Interestingly, their enmity with Rome was

---

[13] Gilmour, David, *The Pursuit of Italy*, Farrar, Straus and Giroux, 2011, pg. 2

so strong that they stamped on their coins the Italian bull (remember the origin of the word *Italia*) goring and raping the Roman wolf. National symbols certainly have become tamer over the centuries. In retrospect, perhaps it was not the best strategy to antagonize the powerful empire that surrounded you. As you might guess, the Romans, being Romans, crushed the first Italia with such brutality no one tried anything like that again.

Dante recognized the negative impact that warring between the different factions and cities had on the Italian people. In the first canto of The Divine Comedy, he attempts to ascend to heaven under his own strength, without relying on the grace of God. He is turned back by three beasts: a leopard, a lion, and a she-wolf.

While Danteists debate the specific meaning of the first two beasts, there is no confusion concerning the third. Although to the Romans the she-wolf nurtured Romulus and Remus, in a Christian context the she-wolf is contemptible and unclean. The description is of an insatiable animal that is never satisfied in its desires. This is the biblical image of a dog, an unclean vermin that would wander the countryside and city streets devouring dead bodies and their offal. This is how Dante saw the various Italian city-states of his time. Like a dog devouring a corpse, the city-states with their wars consumed one another as well as the wealth and potential of Italy.

The symbol of the she-wolf is especially significant in its connotation. Dante uses the word *lupa*, which is a synonym in Italian for *puttana* or whore. Dante confirms this imagery when he writes: "Many are the animals, with whom she mates, / And more they shall be still ..." The factions within Italy mated in their making of political alliances both with one another and foreign powers. Their political intrigues knew no boundaries; their ends justified their means. Like a whore, they sold themselves for gain.

Later, Dante predicts the coming of The Greyhound in a reference to Proverbs 30:31 that says: "A greyhound; a he goat also; and a king, against whom there is no rising up." Unlike a dog, The Greyhound is a noble creature. It will put down the she-wolf and establish a new order.

The Renaissance

It is ironic that Italy has had such a significant impact on civilization, yet it still feels what Barzini described as "distant consequences of defeat." According to the United Nations Educational Scientific and Cultural

Organization (UNESCO), Italy has more world heritage sites than any other country. Of Italy's 53 sites, 48 are cultural, and five natural. The next closest nation is China with 52 sites, but of these, only 36 are cultural. While Italy, since the fall of the Roman Empire, has not led the world in military conquests or colonization, it has led in the arts and sciences. It is most probably because we have not expended our energy and resources on military pursuits that Italy is such a cultural leviathan. Be that as it may, it is no exaggeration to say Italy is responsible for leading Europe into the Renaissance.

The meaning of the word *Renaissance* is rebirth or reawakening. The first way Italy brought about the Renaissance was to reawaken or reintroduce the wisdom of the ancient world. This began with Petrarch who, in the 1330's, reconstructed Livy's *History of Rome*. He also reintroduced Europe to the writings of Cicero and Propertius. Petrarch's success and subsequent fame launched other Italians into similar searches. When I think of this resurgence I am reminded of the *dot com* craze of the 1990's. One success generated a host of imitators.

Among those inspired by Petrarch was Poggio Bracciolini who recovered Lucretius' *On the Nature of Things*. The work is an epic poem describing the physical theories of Epicurus. I began this chapter by describing how people once populated the 'unknown' with gods who controlled the motions of the universe. Lucretius' epic poem changed that way of thinking. Lucretius presented the world as a natural place, governed by natural causes. Great thinkers as diverse as Galileo and Jefferson were inspired by Bracciolini's discovery to see the world with this different perspective. It changed not only how the world was seen, but it changed humanity's understanding of our place in the universe.

Many of these scholars recovered these texts by searching the libraries of monasteries and churches. Other works were reintroduced to Europe through trade with the Arab world. The Arabs, not succumbing to the superstitions of the Dark Ages, preserved many ancient Greek texts destroyed in Europe. This included such works as Plotinus' *Enneads* as well as Proclus' *Elements of Theology* and Aristotle's *Metaphysics*. Italy became a gateway for Europe's access to the thinking of the ancients.

Trade also made 14th and 15th century Italians fantastically rich. Florence was to Europe what New York City is to the financial world today. Being the center of banking and commerce, the leading families of the north were as affluent as their modern-day Fifth Avenue counterparts, if not more so. With wealth came patronage for the arts and sciences. A significant percentage of the UNESCO World Heritage sites mentioned earlier were funded by these moneyed families.

The greatest of these patrons was Lorenzo de' Medici, *Il Magnifico*. The incredible contributions made to our world by this one individual are breathtaking. Lorenzo de' Medici's patronage gave this world Botticelli, Michelangelo, Verrocchio, and Raphael. Absent his investment, Italy would not be the Italy it is today; the western world would not be what it is today, both in terms of cultural depth and richness. Which of these artists could the west afford to strike from its galleries and museums? Beyond the arts, he expanded the Medici library, retrieving from the east many classical works which he then had copied in a large workshop. These copies were then disseminated throughout Europe. His retinue included such philosophers as Giovanni Pico della Mirandola as well as Marsilio Ficino and Poliziano. These were all people who were part of his household at one time or another.

When I think of what dinner must have been like in the Medici home, I am reminded of the Pazzi Conspiracy. The plot was devised by the Pazzi family, in league with Pope Sixtus IV, to assassinate Lorenzo de' Medici and his brother Giuliano. On the pretext of wanting to see the famed Medici art, a number of assassins stayed in the Medici home. Their real intent was to discover any Medici vulnerabilities that would enable them to kill the two brothers. As one of the mercenaries hired for the task got to know the Medici, he soon realized he could not bring himself to carry out the crime. He was swayed by the Medici graciousness and intellect as well as Lorenzo's famed charisma. Amateur murderers (two priests with a grudge against the Medici) replaced the mercenary and botched the attack. Although Giuliano was killed, Lorenzo survived.

How incredible that household must have been to turn a paid assassin, a mercenary, into a friend. I often try to imagine what it must have been like to dine in the Medici home at that time. Long candlelit tables piled high with the delicacies of the day. On the walls would hang what today would be priceless masterpieces, while in the various corners of the room stood sculptures crafted by expert hands. As the wine was poured, conversation would inevitably turn to weighty matters of science and philosophy. Long into the night, some of the greatest minds of the time would debate the nature of things.

Italian American Symbiosis

The origin of the symbiotic relationship between Italy and the United States began when Italians, in reawakening Europe to the ideas of the past, planted the seeds of the Enlightenment. Without this change in thinking, it is doubtful the American Revolution would have occurred. If it had, it certainly would not have had the same philosophical basis. In return, the American Revolution inspired a new spirit that ultimately led to the *Risorgimento* – Italian unification – and the empowerment of the common Italian, the *contadini*.

We have already discussed how Italian philosophers such as Dante promoted the idea of the separation of church and state long before Luther and Locke. While it cannot necessarily be proven that *De Monarchia* contributed to influencing the thinking of the Founding Fathers, we do know Jefferson and others studied Dante's work.

A key American value, perhaps the most basic of all American values, is individuality. This concept, individualism, began with the Italian poet Petrarch. Professor of History and Renaissance Studies, Dr. Kenneth Bartlett, differentiates Dante as a man of the Middle Ages and Petrarch as of the Renaissance. Although their lives overlap, this distinction is based on Petrarch's emphasis on a person's struggle for self-actualization, although the term itself did not appear until centuries later. In his *Familiar Letters and Life of Solitude*, Petrarch argued that a person must live a life in keeping with who they are, with their own morals and personality.

This new thinking challenged the biblical view of the world described by the Apostle Paul in the book of Romans, where God granted authority to a monarch from whom power and authority flowed down. This older biblical perspective had a neatly ordered world where each person had their place and they stayed in it for the common good.

In his book, *The English Village Community and the Enclosure Movements*, W.E. Tate describes how in the 18th century, the lower classes bettered themselves by working to expand the wealth of the upper classes. This was based on the belief that peasants were poor because of some inherent flaw in their characters. Given this fact, they were better off working for the aristocracy who would order society and ensure the proper distribution of wealth.

While the Founding Fathers certainly studied the classics, such as Petrarch and the Italian humanists who followed him (education at the time would not have been considered complete without them), Italy's

33

influence on the Founding Fathers went beyond mere philosophical and poetic writing. Indeed, individual Italians were actively engaged in the American Revolution, men such as Filippo Mazzei.

A good friend of Benjamin Franklin and Thomas Jefferson, Mazzei was one of the first Italian-Americans. When the revolution came to the colonies, he wrote extensively on the rights of free men and how the colonies should break away from Britain. Since he wrote in Italian, Jefferson would translate Mazzei's work into English for publication in the colonies. The influence his writings had on Jefferson is undeniable. Jefferson, in creating a constitution for the state of Virginia, used parts of Mazzei's *Instructions of the Freeholders of Albemarle County to their Delegates in Convention.* Jefferson also solicited input from Mazzei on the Declaration of Independence, providing him with an early rough draft for comment.

When revolution did come, Mazzei worked closely with Benjamin Franklin in Europe to acquire aid for the revolutionaries. Meanwhile, some 2,000 Italian-Americans fought for independence from Britain. Among them was the fur trader Francesco Vigo who fought alongside George Rodgers Clark in securing the Northwest Territory. In addition to providing Clark with much-needed funding, Vigo led Clark and his army through the wilderness to Fort Vincennes which was held by the British. Ultimately, Clark's victory in evicting the British from the fort secured the Northwest Territory, protecting Washington's western flank.

In recognizing the contribution of Italians and Italian-Americans to the United States, we should also note the contribution of William Paca.[14] In addition to signing the Declaration of Independence, Paca also contributed to the writing of the Bill of Rights. Recognizing Paca as one of the Founding Fathers of the United States demonstrates Italian-Americans not as a people who are alien to Americanism (newcomers if you will), but full partners from its very inception.

As men such as Mazzei returned to Italy, the Italian people were provided with first-hand accounts of the American Revolution. Along with these accounts came discussion of the ideals that drove it. Italians, through America's example, saw it was possible to overturn the

---

[14] Paca's Italian heritage has been the subject of debate. While the Paca family themselves claim Italian ancestry, historians have not been able to conclusively prove him to be of Italian descent.

institution that had oppressed them for so long. Italians sought a society which was based on such principles as the equality of all men, reason, and the elimination of ignorance.

We will see, as we continue our exploration of history, how Mazzei was the first of many who shuttled ideas back and forth between Italy and America. In addition to individuals, many institutions straddled the Atlantic with one foot planted in the United States and the other firmly in Italy. One such institution was Freemasonry.

At the time of the American Revolution, in both the American Colonies and Italy, Freemasonry was spreading values such as the brotherhood of man. It has been confirmed that eight of the 56 signers of the Declaration of Independence were Freemasons, while approximately another half-dozen were rumored to be so. Washington reportedly said it was from Freemasonry that the United States should expect to find its leaders. There are a good many conspiracy theories about the involvement of Freemasons in the American Revolution. While entertaining, the truth is much more mundane. Freemasonry's part was one of spreading ideas; ideas of equality, freedom, and democracy. Although this was a significant contribution, it is not nearly as romantic as some of popular culture's hypotheses.

Just as many of the leaders of the American Revolution were Freemasons, so too were many of the *Risorgimento*. Like Washington, Giuseppe Garibaldi, who was to Italian unification what Washington was to the American Revolution, was a Freemason. In Italy, however, Freemasonry gave rise to a number of other groups, the most significant of which were the *Carbonari* (Charcoal Burners) who were also called the Freemasons of the Woods.

Not the French, Again!!

In 1796, the French, shortly after their revolution, invaded Italy yet again, this time under Napoleon. This invasion, however, is of particular interest to our understanding of Italian culture. Although their stay was relatively brief, roughly 17 years, it was significant in setting the stage for Italian unification in a number of ways. First, the image of Italians as decadent cowards and morally corrupt – an image held by many since the defeat at Fornovo – had less potency as Italians proved their worth in Napoleon's army. Many a European experienced, firsthand, the quality of the Italian soldier whether it was shoulder to shoulder or face to face. In either case, the Italian soldier proved their mettle; renewing their belief in themselves which set the stage for unification.

Second, and more importantly, when the French brought down the old power structures, the Italians were given space for constitutional experimentation. The groups who had been suppressed by the aristocracy and church were given greater freedom with self-government. Along with the inspiration of the American and French revolutions, Italians began to think of the possibility of Italian unification. Several Italian states were consolidated into republics, giving the rising middle class an opportunity to participate in government.

The third change came with the French ending the feudal system. As we have discussed throughout this chapter, Northern and Southern Italy have distinct cultures. One of the many differences between them is that of the feudal system. In the north, even before its official ending, the feudal system had begun to fade. Land (and the power that went with it) was used as a means of accumulating wealth while operating within the law. In the south, at the time of the French invasion, however, the feudal system was still very much alive. The *Mezzogiorno* had its own unique perspective on land and power. The latter was seen as a means to exercise your will regardless of the law. While this may sound harsh, understand the perspective of the *Mezzogiorno*. For much of their history, they had been ruled by foreign powers; powers to whom the Southern Italians felt little loyalty. There was no Rousseau-like social contract between the populace and the ruling class. To Southern-Italians, the law was simply a foreign power attempting to dominate them.

The freeing up of southern land did not benefit the peasantry as was hoped, though. Instead, it was snatched up by the middle class, often at prices much lower than what the land was actually worth. Although a strong middle class is associated with a more democratic society, in the south the newly-propertied gentry was absent from the land they purchased; they used their newfound wealth as a means to buy their way into the ranks of the aristocracy.

In the north, however, a prosperous middle class gave rise to an intellectual class which was concerned with the well-being of *the people*. One such member of the intelligentsia was Giuseppe Mazzini who was the son of a university professor. Mazzini and his views on Italian nationalism established a way of thinking in Italy that survives to this day. The future of Italy was not in each man as lord of his own lands, but in the community working together for a greater tomorrow for all. While the movement towards Italian unification certainly was a movement towards individual freedom, it also saw freedom in the context of society as a whole.

In Mazzini's time, this sense of community was just as much an American value as it was an Italian one. A reading of Alexis de Tocqueville's *Democracy in America* clearly discusses this American communal spirit. In his travels through the United States in the early 1800's, de Tocqueville saw in Americans a sense of unity, a sense of working together. Civic-minded social groups formed to better the community with active participation in local government. There were groups that worked for the beautification of their towns, or literary groups that promoted a better-read community. Both Italians and Italian-Americans felt they were all working together towards a common end.

This has since changed in the United States. I am not sure how or when this change occurred, but this is no longer the American spirit. Robert Putnam writes of this collapse of the American community in his book *Bowling Alone*. A prevalent (although not universal) feeling within the Italian-American community, is consistent with the rest of American society. Many see American culture as focused not on being part of a community, but of *rugged individualism* born out of a libertarian philosophy. The image is of strong, self-reliant, lords of their own domains, no matter how small that domain may be. It is the bronze image of the coonskin-capped, buckskin-clad frontiersman staring steely-eyed onto the horizon.

In the 2012 presidential campaign, President Obama was pilloried for suggesting people were successful not solely through their own efforts, but by building on a foundation laid by others. This inter-dependence is no longer seen as a virtue, but as symptomatic of a society of *takers*. In this way, many Italian-Americans are in conflict with Italian values. They no longer share the sense of being part of something but place a greater value on libertarian self-reliance.

Risorgimento!!!

As I noted above, France's stay in Italy at this time was brief. In 1815 they were evicted by forces basically in support of the conservative regime. The first half of the 19th century, however, was by no means peaceful. Foreign powers such as the Austrians, Spanish, and British, in addition to the French, continued to venture into Italy. Of course, thrown into the mix, were the Italians themselves; politicians, popes, and patricians all fought to carve out a piece of the pie for themselves as well.

There were also a number of revolutionaries, such as the *Carbonari*, the Italian version of Freemasonry described earlier. Unlike American Freemasonry, however, the Carbonari were actively engaged in revolution. They enlisted the aid of foreign governments to fund clandestine activities against the conservative factions who controlled the country after the expulsion of the French. Many were imprisoned for their political activity. As we shall see in Chapter 10, *The Beautiful People of Palermo's Prison*, imprisonment had such long-term effects on Italian society that they are still felt to this day.

Then, in 1831, Giuseppe Mazzini, a Carbonari himself, frustrated by the lack of success, started his own secret society, *Giovine Italia* (Young Italy). It was here he first formed an association with Giuseppe Garibaldi, who would later lead Italian troops against the Spanish. The objective for Young Italy was "independence, unity, and liberty for Italy." I will not go into the details of the events leading up to the *Risorgimento*. There are too many successes and failures, battles with foreign powers, and competition between rival factions to sort through, while not really helping us develop a deeper cultural understanding. What I do want to communicate is how the feeling of this time rallied the people; there was renewed energy and strength.

The spirit that had romanced the country is described in the Italian national anthem. Written in 1847, in the heat of *Risorgimento*, it begins:

> *Brothers of Italy,*
> *Italy has awoken*

More importantly, in the second verse, the anthem acknowledges the historical divisions of the Italian people as well as how factionalism held the nation back. Despite those rifts of the past, it calls on Italians to come together.

> *We were for centuries*
> *downtrodden, derided,*
> *because we are not one people*
> *because we are divided.*
> *Let one flag, one hope*
> *gather us all.*
> *The hour has struck*
> *for us to unite.*

I love the imagery in these words. When I hear them, I see the Italian flag – *Il Tricolore* – fluttering over hills populated by the *contadini*, the common Italian worker. Their heads are downcast and shoulders rounded due to centuries of oppression. Fornovo echoes in the distance. Then, as dawn breaks over the hills, their heads rise and their backs straighten. As they march forward in history, to a new Italy, I see the painting *Il Quarto Stato* (The Fourth Estate). The *contadini*, working men with calloused hands, and women still carrying their infants in their arms, are on the move; going forward to the Italy of tomorrow.

This was a period of revolution and every revolution has its bards. The labor movement of the early 20th century had Woody Guthrie and the cultural revolution of the 60's had The Beatles. The Italians had Giuseppe Verdi, *il maestro della rivoluzione Italiana*. His operas were considered a call to the people to rise up. They were, in essence, the musical scores of the *Risorgimento*.

The two operas that best fit this mold are *Nabucco* and *Attila*. The opera, *Nabucco*, premiered in the famed *La Scala* opera house in 1842, and is set in the time when the Jews were exiled from their homeland by Nebuchadnezzar II. Long seen as a metaphor for the Italian people, in the Chorus of the Hebrew Slaves titled *Va Pensiero* (Fly Thought), the Jews long for their homeland. They sing:

> *Fly thoughts on golden wings.*
> *Go and rest on the densely wooded hills,*
> *Where warm and fragrant and soft*
> *Are the gentle breezes of our native land!*
> *The banks of the Jordan we greet*
> *And the towers of Zion.*
> *O, my homeland, so beautiful and lost!*
> *O memories, so dear and yet so deadly!*
> *Golden Harp of our prophets,*
> *Why do you hang silently on the willow?*
> *Rekindle the memories of our hearts,*
> *And speak of the times gone by!*
> *Or, like the fateful Solomon,*
> *Draw a lament of raw sound;*
> *Or permit the Lord to inspire us*
> *To endure our suffering!*

Italians heard, in those words, the longing they had for their own nation. When sung properly, these words stir the heart, they envelop the listeners in the desire to breathe free in their homeland. As I listen to them sing, I close my eyes to see the cypress trees on green hills at dawn, the waves crashing against Apulia's shores, and the Amalfi hills softly rolling to the Tyrrhenian Sea.

Equally as stirring to *Risorgimento* hearts is *Attila*. The opera, as the name makes obvious, is about Attila the Hun. At the outset of the opera, a Roman envoy, Ezio, in an audience with Attila, asks the Hun not to invade Italy. "You can have the world, but leave Italy to me," Ezio sings. Reportedly, this would evoke cheers of "Viva Verdi!!" from the audience. According to some, this was a demonstration of Italian patriotism where the name Verdi was meant as an acronym for *Vittorio Emanuele Re d'Italia* (Victor Emmanuel, the King of Italy). This was meant as open defiance toward the Austrians by declaring Victor Emmanuel as the rightful ruler of Italy, not these invaders.

It is not difficult to imagine the stirring of national pride that must have electrified the audience when it was first performed in 1846 in Venice. Imagine being in the audience; the mustachioed Austrian military officers sitting stiff and straight in their uniforms. The wives are seated next to them in their finery. Then Ezio sings: "You can have the world, but leave Italy to me." Those officers hear in the back of the theater an almost plaintive cry, "Viva Verdi!" Then another from the balcony, but this time with greater strength, and greater conviction. "Viva Verdi!!" This is soon followed by another, then another. The hairs on the backs of the officers' necks rise. A wife looks worriedly at her husband; another turns to the side to see who is calling out. The more disciplined officers continue to stare straight ahead, attempting to appear unconcerned as the cheers from the audience drown out the performance.

Lately, there has been some debate as to whether the spontaneous demonstrations at *Attila* occurred. Some have also questioned if Verdi was as much of a revolutionary as some historians have given him credit. In either case, the Italian people at his death must have recognized him as a hero of the *Risorgimento*. For his funeral procession, they sang *Va Pensiero*.

This passion swept Italy and there were many battles in which men such as Garibaldi led inexperienced troops against professional soldiers. In this way, the Italian Revolution was similar to the American Revolution. For many years, unfortunately, these attempts at freedom failed. Then when King Ferdinand II of Spain died, the Italians saw an opportunity. The initial revolt in 1859, led by Francesco Crispi, evolved into an anti-government guerrilla war. Giuseppe Garibaldi came to Crispi's aid. Leaving Genoa with his *red shirts*, a group primarily composed of students who had very little military training, Garibaldi landed in Marsala Sicily and pushed east into Palermo. He and his men swept through Sicily crossing the Straits of Messina onto the mainland of Italy. He then turned to the north until he reached Teano, a town just north of Naples.

Garibaldi, as did the other leaders of the *Risorgimento*, had faith that Victor Emmanuel, the Piedmontese King, was a patriot who believed in a unified Italy. So, when Garibaldi reached Teano, he was met by Victor Emmanuel. There, in the famous "Handshake of Teano" Giuseppe Garibaldi handed over his authority in the south to the Piedmontese King. This was a great moment for the Italian people. Here was Garibaldi, the man of the people, the leader of the revolution, shaking hands and turning over the power that the people of the south had given him to the monarchy in the north.

Italy, the nation was born.

This handshake is significant, not only in what it means to the Italian people but to aid us in understanding the forces leading up to the difference between Italian and Italian-American culture. It is important to note the king was in the north, the Piedmont. For Sicilians, and much of the *Mezzogiorno*, this was further away than Africa. Many in the south felt the new government, despite it being *Italian*, was just another invader from the north. This sense only intensified as the promised benefits of unification failed to be realized.

A common expression of Italian anti-government sentiment is the phrase *piove, governo ladro* (it's raining, thieving government). Even the rain was just another scheme for the government to steal from the *contadini*. There are several alleged sources for this expression. Some say that when the northern Italian farmers – under Austrian occupation – looked at the rain, they would curse the government for the increase in taxes the additional harvest created (rather than being happy about the increased harvest it implied). There are other stories about how taxes on salt were levied on rainy days which increased the weight of the salt which increased the taxes. Regardless of the origin of the expression, the sentiment was the same – the government stole from the *contadini*.

Catholicism & Unification

The Catholic Church's opposition to the *Risorgimento* is not at all surprising. In addition to taking away the Papal States, it was a direct challenge to its authority. The *Risorgimento*'s empowerment of the *contadini* put priests and the pope at the same level as farmers and fishermen. These common people, whose daily mass was with cow manure and fish offal, had the same access to God as those who drank their wine from a golden challis. As part of this awakening of the masses, they recognized the Papal States "were a medieval anachronism legitimated through outdated absolutist conceptions of sovereignty."[15] Indeed, the debate concerning the earthly power of the pope over the once Papal States in the new Italy became known as the *Roman Question.*

The *Risorgimento*'s confiscation of the Papal States was not out of some vindictiveness towards the church. The Papal States were in poor condition, economically backward and poorly administered. Examination of these regions throughout Italy revealed how the Church had mismanaged the governance of these areas. The conditions in these regions were far worse than the rest of Italy. The restrictive control of the Church inhibited many of the innovations that science was bringing to the rest of Europe such as modern farming techniques and the modernization of production. Rome, the city itself, had faded. The one-time hub of the western world was nothing more than the home of the Church.

Just as the Catholic Church was no supporter of the *Risorgimento*, the leaders of the *Risorgimento* had no great love for the Catholic Church. While in Verdi's opera *Nabucco*, which was described earlier, the enslaved Jews were a metaphor for the Italian people, the high priest represented the Catholic Church. In the opera, he was depicted as inflexible and complicit with despotic rulers.

Neither was Verdi alone in his feelings towards the church. In his memoirs, Garibaldi's visceral hatred of the church is apparent. He complains how Italy is "overrun by priests and thieves."[16] He clearly saw the Catholic Church as the enemy of the people. At another point in his memoirs, he writes: "It is time for the Pope with his tiara, the foreign bullies, and the domestic tyrants to pack their bags and leave."[17] Garibaldi's animosity towards the church, however, would not be satisfied with mere banishment. He declared in a speech, "Death to the Priests! [...] Who deserves to die more than this wicked sect which has

---

[15] Connell, William J., & Gardaphé, Fred, (Eds), *Anti-Italianism, Essays on a Prejudice*, Palgrave Macmillan, 2010, pg.33

[16] Garibaldi, Giuseppe, *My Life,* Hesperus Press Limited, 2004, pg. 5

[17] Garibaldi, Giuseppe, *My Life,* Hesperus Press Limited, 2004, pg. 62

turned Italy into *un paese di morti* (a country of the dead) into a cemetery?"[18]

After unification, the church found itself stripped of its lands and any real earthly power. Describing the church in the latter half of the 19th century as having a *bunker mentality* is no mere metaphor. After the 1860's, popes described themselves as *prisoners of the Vatican*. They saw the liberal world as an attack on their authority, which it was. The liberals saw the church not as an organization working for the betterment of humanity and the salvation of souls, but an organization which lived off the sweat of others.

The Pope, as had so many popes before him, used his authority to punish those who opposed him, excommunicating the leaders of the *Risorgimento*. Neither did he recognize the new government as legitimate, forbidding any Catholic to participate in it. This included everything from voting to holding any national office. At the same time, he reached out to Catholics around the world and to foreign governments to pressure and destabilize the newly-formed Italian government as well as putting them into conflict with the republican movement.

Taking measures to ensure their hold on the faithful, Pope Pius IX issued the *Quanta Cura* and the *Syllabus Errorum* in 1864. The *Quanta Cura* condemned such principles as the will of the people being supreme. It also rejected the idea Catholics were under no obligation to obey church law unless ratified by the state, and that the state has the authority to take the property of the Church. The *Syllabus Errorum* condemned such things as rationalism, socialism, and liberalism while affirming the rights of the church, Christian marriage, and the civil power of the Pope in the Papal States.

It was also during this period that the church held the First Vatican Council. Although other councils had been held in the past, this was called specifically to deal with the wave of liberalism washing over Europe. The most famous (infamous?) teaching to come out of the First Vatican Council is of Papal Infallibility. While most people think of this as saying the pope can never be wrong, it is a bit more complicated. First, Papal infallibility is that the pope, with divine assistance, defines faith and morals. It is not so much that the pope is not wrong, but that he establishes the correct manner of Christian life. Also, the pope has

---

[18] Garibaldi, Giuseppe, *Clelia, Il Governo dei Preti, Fratelli Rechiedei*, Milan, 1870, pg. 229

43

full and supreme authority over all of the Roman Catholic Church; all fall under his authority. We should also keep in mind, although challenged throughout the centuries, the First Vatican council merely codified a level of papal authority many in the church took for granted.

The Catholic Church continued to support the same social order it had since the time of Rome. The expectation was that if you were a master, an employer, any person with authority over others, you were to use your authority in a Christian manner. The other side of that teaching is reminiscent of what Christianity taught the Roman slaves. If you were a servant, you accepted your station in life. It is God who made you a dirt farmer who hadn't enough to feed his children or have the basic comforts of life. It was his divine will. Don't resist it, but embrace your lowly position. As one author put it: "For the wealthy, their property confirmed that they were among the privileged, and hence that they had a responsibility to husband it with care. For the poor, lack of property was proof of their humble station, and hence of the need to practice humility, which was likely to secure their salvation in the afterlife... A woman's role was that of mother and husband's helpmate, with the attendant virtues of modesty, submission, and sacrifice."[19]

The church hijacked themes from philosophers such as Rousseau for their own purposes. Invoking *the noble savage*, they attempted to sell the *contadini* on the nobility of their lowly station in life. Their lack of education and social sophistication left them unspoiled and closer to nature. Seeking material wealth, industry, and technology separated the individual from the spiritual enrichment of a simple agrarian life leading to moral degradation. The response on the part of the *Mezzogiorno contadini* was a resounding *"vaffanculo."*

Garibaldi

Earlier, I noted how men such as Mazzei who were active in the American Revolution, shuttled ideas back and forth between Italy and America. Of these men, Giuseppe Garibaldi is one of the most important. Although he came along after the American Revolution and his freedom fighter activities were in South America, Garibaldi is among

---

[19] Baranski, Zygmunt G., & West, Rebecca J., (Eds), *The Cambridge Companion to Modern Italian Culture*, Cambridge University Press, 2001, pg. 103

a group of Italians that lived and worked in the United States although they never settled there. Admittedly, Garibaldi may seem to be a bit of a distraction from our main purpose which is to compare and contrast Italian and Italian-American culture. However, Garibaldi is the personification of the shared values of these two cultures.

As Italian immigrants and their children adapted to life in the United States, many of the icons of their adopted home took on almost saintly status. Two of these civil saints were George Washington and Abraham Lincoln. Garibaldi was, in a very real way, a swashbuckling combination of the two. In addition to being a Washington-like general, Garibaldi's commitment to equal rights exceeded those of Lincoln.

It is said that Washington was the "indispensable man" and a "modern day Cincinnatus." Without Washington there would have been no United States; the American Revolution would have failed. It was his personal strength and ability to draw men to him, to motivate them to fight for a cause that seemed unattainable, that made the American Revolution a success. Washington led an army of farmers and tradesmen against professional soldiers from the world's greatest military power.

Just as Washington defeated the British with amateurs, Garibaldi faced the Spanish with common men who were not trained in the art of war. Garibaldi was able to forge, from the different social classes, a united Italian army, or more appropriately a militia. Garibaldi's *Red Shirts* – the men he led against the Spanish – were primarily students. As they marched through Sicily and Southern Italy, common men and women along the way joined them in their fight. It is important to recognize that Italian women fought for a free Italy as well.

More importantly, just as Washington was the indispensable man of the American Revolution, Garibaldi was the indispensable man of the *Risorgimento*. When he and the *Red Shirts* landed in Sicily, the people rallied to him. They did not see him, as they had so many others, as just another foreign invader. He, like Washington, was the hope of the people.

Both Washington and Garibaldi were the Cincinnatus of their times. Like Cincinnatus – the Roman farmer who after serving as the Roman dictator[20] to repel an invasion, returned to his farm – each willingly

---

[20] The Romans had a somewhat different concept of a dictator. A Roman was given power to act without the normal constraints that were

handed over power they had fought hard to win. Washington, after serving his nation, returned to his farm when he could easily have been crowned king by popular consent. Garibaldi, meanwhile, after the famous handshake at Teano, retired to the Island of Caprera. He did not ask for or accept any reward for his service to Italy. Both men did not seek power because they shared a similar ideology, a commitment to equality. The extent to which they supported equality, however, is where Garibaldi differs from both Washington and Lincoln.

In 1861, Garibaldi volunteered to fight on behalf of the Union in the American civil war. In response, Secretary of State William Seward offered him a commission as a Major General. Garibaldi responded "that the only way in which he could render service, as he ardently desired to do, to the cause of the United States, was as Commander-in-chief of its forces, that he would only go as such, and with the additional contingent power – to be governed by events – of declaring the abolition of slavery; that he would be of little use without the first, and without the second it would appear like a civil war in which the world at large could have little interest or sympathy."[21] Garibaldi insisted on the power to free slaves, and made his service contingent on the authority of the Emancipation Proclamation well before Lincoln made any such declaration.

Prior to the civil war, Lincoln supported the return of runaway slaves to their owners. Although Lincoln is known as the "Great Emancipator," he not only would have allowed slavery to continue in the southern states to avoid a civil war, he was willing to support a constitutional amendment that would guarantee it. Although Lincoln supported the Thirteenth Amendment that abolished slavery, he did not recognize the equality of blacks, going so far as to suggest that whites and blacks could not live in harmony. At one point proposing they be repatriated to Africa.

Garibaldi had no such confusion. Beyond his support for equal rights for women, he also saw the humanity of blacks. While a freedom fighter in South America, he saved a black man from drowning when no one

---

placed on consuls and other Roman leaders, but the role was temporary. A dictator was typically appointed to address a particular task in times of crisis such as an invasion. Once the situation was resolved, their rule was over.

[21] Mack Smith, Denis, *Garibaldi*, Prentice-Hall, 1969, pg. 69-70

else would come to the man's rescue. In another incident, he encountered a number of slaves being beaten and, although he was greatly outnumbered, he attempted to rescue them, failing only because his friends pulled him away fearing for his life.

So why Garibaldi?

So why Garibaldi? I began this chapter before Italy was even Italy... when it was just a colony of Greece. We discussed the ebb and flow of the various tides of Italian history if you will forgive the cliché, only to end here at Garibaldi. Ultimately, I see in Garibaldi the essence of the subject of this chapter, a unified Italy which is a sister state to America. Where for so many centuries, millennia even, Italy was divided (as the Italian national anthem reminds us) we are now united. It is my sincere hope this unification will, in the future, be among all Italians throughout the world. Equally important are the common values that are shared between our two cultures such as individual human rights and equality, as well as the brotherhood of men and women.

Chapter 3: To Your Scattered Bodies Go

The Diaspora

At the round earth's imagin'd corners, blow
Your trumpets, angels, and arise, arise
From death you numberless infinities
Of souls, and to your scattered bodies go.

Holy Sonnet 17, John Donne

John Donne's sonnet evokes thoughts of the Italian Diaspora in me. Diaspora is a scattering of people from their homeland which well describes the mass migration of Italians from our homeland. When I read Donne's sonnet, I imagine the angels calling us all back, gathering us together, this scattered people, a virtual infinity of souls.

I can see, in my mind's eye, the bodies rising up, uniting with their spirits and gathering with angels above the earth. I think of Italians, both present and past, being called together. I see among them the *contadini*, peasants, of the south with wooden farm tools in hand; immigrants on Ellis Island dressed in homespun cloth; the Triangle Shirtwaist women whose resurrected bodies no longer bear the scars of the fire; and the Armani-suited lawyer equipped with requisite cell phone and Starbucks.

I do not only see those who came to the United States. Among the resurrected are those who made new homes in Canada, South America, and Northern Europe. I also see those who stayed, who waved goodbye to the sons and daughters who would never again feel their father's firm strong hand on their shoulder or mother's teary cheek on theirs. I see the subsequent generations of Italians who have long forgotten the ones who left, who fought the wars in Europe, who battled corrupt governments and organized crime, and who struggled against poverty while maintaining an enviable dignity and decency. In their faces, in their diversity, I see the story of Italians; how we evolved over generations and across geographies.

Today there are nearly 60 million people of Italian ancestry across the globe. It is ironic that there are nearly as many people with Italian ancestry living outside of Italy as there are Italians in Italy. The Italian government refers to us – Italians who were born and raised outside of Italy – as *Italiani Nel Mondo* (Italians in the World). Indeed, Mussolini said, "Once an Italian always an Italian." Contrary to what many Italians think today, it was felt – at the time – that you are Italian up to the seventh generation.

According to one study by the Vatican, 29 million of us left Italy between 1861 and 1985, with about 55% of that number leaving prior to World War I.[22] This seems to be a remarkable number. The destinations for these groups varied. Most Northern Italians sought out new lives in other parts of Europe. The majority of Italian immigrants, however, were from the *Mezzogiorno*, the south, and they headed for the Americas, but not only the United States. From 1876 to 1890, most Italian immigrants left for Argentina, then from 1891 to 1897, they began to find new homes in Brazil as well.

While Italians have been part of the history of the United States from its inception, the majority of Italian immigrants did not come to the States until the end of the 19th century with close to four million arriving between 1898 and 1930.

Immigrant Song

'Italian immigration' is a phrase which – to Italian-Americans – often sparks a melancholic remembrance of what was endured to be recognized as American. Perhaps it is best captured in the iconic image of Vito Corleone as a child in *Godfather II* where he is on Ellis Island looking out of the window at the Statue of Liberty. On one side is the statue reflected in the glass, on the other Vito, an expressionless boy alone. The *Godfather* movies have such resonance with Italian-Americans because these vignettes capture our romanticized past, our invented tradition. We project onto these images fantasies of our own grandparents coming here with hope for what could (and fear of what might) happen. We envision them in the rough dress of the Italian *contadini*; the women with their heads covered and the men in ragged

---

[22] Perego, Giancarlo, *The Migrants Report, Italians in the World 2011* http://banchedati.chiesacattolica.it/cci_new_v3/allegati/21532/introdu zione.pdf

suits. To many of us, Italian immigration is the Statue of Liberty, Ellis Island, and North-Eastern United States.

If you are fortunate enough to know an Italian-American family who has not lost their *Italianità*, you will see they love to tell their immigration stories. They hang on with great tenacity to that connection. Ask them. Try it. They will tell you about the grandfather who came here without any money in his pockets or the grandmother who worked in the sweatshops.

Although these stories may be more sentimental than factual, they are important to the family because those stories describe how they believe their family became who they are. When I was a child I heard my own family's stories over and over again. Typically, it was on Christmas Eve after we had gorged ourselves on what is known as *The Feast of Seven Fishes*. I never met my grandparents, they passed long before the sun ever shined on my smiling face, but I wish I could have met them. I wish I could have heard more of their stories, the stories that went untold or which were simply forgotten by my parents.

When in Italy, my error-filled, American-accented, attempts at speaking Italian immediately identify me as a non-native, but when they see the name they ask me from what part of Italy my family came. The response to my Calabrese/Sicilian heritage is always the same. *"Calabrese e Siciliano?* WOW!" they say, with a roll of their eyes.

I will sometimes get a *"Minchia!"*[23]

Of all the rivalries between the different regions in Italy, the one between the Sicilians and the Calabrese is one of the most infamous. So, the combination of the two in one family turns into quite a novelty.

When my brother told a Roman cab driver of our family's *mixed ethnicity*, he responded: "Oh, good, if they don't knife you, they hang you!" He then cocked his head to one side as if he had been hanged, with his tongue lolling out one side of his mouth; one hand was raised above his head in the air holding an invisible noose. Southern Italians are known for their volatile tempers, especially the Sicilians. There is also the obvious association with organized crime.

---

[23] The literal translation of *minchia* depends on the region; I think of it as being roughly translated as "Holy Shit." A word of advice… don't use this word unless you are in a situation where profanity is acceptable. In some regions, some people consider the word quite profane.

There are multiple variations on our family's lore. Although I am sure some will hotly contest this particular version, this is how I remember the story of my mother's family. My maternal grandfather first came to this country alone, temporarily leaving his first wife and children behind. To be near his sister, who had previously immigrated to the states, he settled in a small town in upstate New York, called Frankfurt. Eventually, his wife joined him there where they settled down to become an American family. But, as the saying goes, the best-laid plans of mice and men...

I am not sure which of my uncles was born in Italy and which in New York, but while giving birth to their last child, both my grandfather's wife and child died shortly after birth. One part of the story that is firmly established is that she and the baby were buried together in the same coffin. I can still hear my mother's voice ringing in my ears, even after all this time. "They buried them in the same coffin. In the same coffin! She was holding the baby in her arms."

This was my grandfather's first wife, not my grandmother. Although she is not really any sort of blood relative, the story has always had an emotional effect on me. It was repeated to me so often it has created a false memory. I envision her in her coffin surrounded by white lace, a river of long dark hair flows over her shoulders. In my mind, I see her cradling a baby wearing a satin baptismal dress. The child slumbers on his mother's breasts with closed eyes in a wakeless sleep. I don't think there was ever a time when I didn't have this image in my head. Is it the child who passed or my grandfather's lost love? It was said my grandfather loved her deeply.

Unfortunately, this was the beginning of his troubles.

The tradition back then was that, when a wife dies, an unmarried sister takes her place. This was how the Fates decided to bring about the coupling of my grandparents to create my mother. Unknown to my grandfather, this woman was in love with another man back in Sicily. Yet she still came to the States as tradition commanded. She and my grandfather had three children together, the youngest of which was my mother. Shortly after my mother's birth the man with whom my grandmother was in love made it to the US and they ran away together.

My grandfather, not wanting my mother to know she had been abandoned, told her his first wife (the woman who was buried with the infant) was her mother. Some may question my grandfather's wisdom, but consider the times. In those days, and in that culture, what had happened to him was something shameful. He also thought it less hurtful to tell my mother that her mother was dead rather than having abandoned her.

As the father of daughters, the stories of the halcyon days of my mother's time with her father have been inspirational. Often, when holding my own little girl, I would think of how my mother told me she would sit on her father's lap and they would eat from the same plate when they ate dinner. Although my wife would chide me for spoiling my daughters, I remember how my grandfather favored my mother, thinking: "Well, she turned out, OK." When I think of how, decades after his death, she would speak of his admirable character, I could only hope to have a shred of such admiration from my own girls.

The Fates, however, are cruel mistresses, cutting the thread of my grandfather's life when my mother was entering her teenage years and needed her father the most. My mother's life after her father's death was the stuff of melodramatic orphan stories. Unfortunately, the sensational overdrawn events of such fiction for her were realities. She had neither a permanent home nor people who cared for her. Dropping out of school when she was an adolescent, she began a life of manual labor that continued until her health failed her in her senior years.

It was the loss of her father that cut her the deepest. Being left, again, was a hurt from which I do not believe she ever recovered. She was, however, eventually reunited with her mother. Abandonment, though, is not something easily forgotten and whilst they interacted for a period, eventually my mother broke off the relationship with her. The stereotype of Sicilians carrying a vendetta to their grave is a truth I know all too well from my mother's example. I remember my mother would say of her own mother with as venomous a tongue as any Sicilian could ever muster: "Not even a dog on the street would have done what she did to me."

So Why Leave?

My mother's story is representative of the story of so many Italian-Americans. It is the story of a hard and, at times, lonely path. It was a Hobbesian existence in which life was truly solitary, poor, nasty, brutish, and short. It is the story of the tempering of a steely character in the forge of a foreign country. It was a demonstration of how being heated and hammered, heated and hammered, heated and hammered, strengthened their mettle. Men and women came here and suffered greatly in the hopes of sculpting a future which was better than what they had left behind.

I can't help but wonder what Italy might have been if they had not left. Surely, these were people of great courage, strength, and industry? What might have been if these people of such great resolve had not left, but rather applied their energies to building a better Italy?

So why did they leave? Why would people of such stern stuff risk so much for an unknown future in the Americas? Life was difficult in Italy after unification. The population increased by 14 million people in the 1800's burdening an already poor nation. While an increase of 14 million over a 100-year period may not seem significant by today's standards, think of that growth in proportion to all of humanity at that time. Remember the entire world population rose from 1 billion to 1.6 billion in that same time period. Such rapid population growth would have strained any nation.

For Italy, it was much worse. After centuries of being subjected to invasions, it entered the 20th century poor with a fragile infrastructure and tired farmland. Admittedly to say Italy had been hit by a series of plagues of biblical proportions would be hyperbolic, but not by much. First, there was the attack on the people; between the years of 1884 and 1887, there were a number of cholera and malaria epidemics. Then there was an attack on the crops; the vineyards were hit by phylloxera, a nearly microscopic insect that feeds on the roots and leaves of grapevines. Finally, there was an attack on the land itself; there were a series of natural disasters such as Vesuvius and Etna erupting in 1906, and earthquakes in Sicily and Calabria in 1908.

Still, we could ask why they left. What was so different about the period of the diaspora that would cause so many to leave? After all, Italians have been poor and starving for centuries. Would it not have been easier to stay where you spoke the language, and had a network of friends and family upon whom you could rely? Also, it is somewhat counter-intuitive for the diaspora to have begun *after* unification. Why leave Italy when the people were given a new hope, when they had finally seized their own destiny? One would think, given the reforms promised by the new government, they would want to stay.

Unfortunately, the reforms were promised, not realized; unification failed the *contadini*. Antonio Gramsci, an Italian politician and theoretician who was eventually imprisoned by the fascists, said the

Risorgimento was a passive revolution, in which the Piedmontese consolidated their power over the whole nation.[24] It was a matter of power sharing between the industrialized north and southern landowners. In the end, the average Italian, both the rural peasant and the urban factory worker, saw little improvement in their daily lives.

As mentioned when discussing the *Handshake of Teano* in the previous chapter, many in the *Mezzogiorno* saw the new *unified* Italian government as simply a new batch of invaders from the north, which is Gramsci's basic point. The south reacted to this new crop of occupiers as they had in the past – with resistance. Of course, the government responded the same way as every out of touch government responds to its people. They decided to get the great unwashed masses in-line through military occupation and mass arrests.

Forgive me for pressing the point, but you could *still* ask why the Italians chose that time to leave. Italians had suffered under oppressive governments since the fall of Rome. As I have said, the new unified government was simply another oppressor, nothing new, nothing unique. Why were they not immigrating en masse to America 100 or 200 years earlier when the New World was first colonized?

I believe the answer is that the *Risorgimento* created a new way of thinking. As discussed in the previous chapter, the political ideology that drove the *Risorgimento* was the emancipation of the mind. With liberated minds, the common Italian recognized their poverty wasn't the will of God. With liberated minds, Italians realized the old model of God granting authority to some ruler whose power then flowed down through the aristocracy wasn't true. With liberated minds, they could imagine a better life, a life in which they could shape their own destinies.

This independent view on life, this unwillingness to submit, is an essential element of Italian and Italian-American culture. The diversity of *Italiani Nel Mondo* makes it incorrect to say any one thing is universal to all Italians (many Italians, for example, are devout Catholics who stringently follow the dictates of the church, and many are not); Italians are not sheep. As we shall see, this is a key factor in many of the events of the Italian-American experience of the early 1900's.

---

[24] Baranski, Zygmunt G., & West, Rebecca J., (Eds), *The Cambridge Companion to Modern Italian Culture*, Cambridge University Press, 2008, pg. 83

California Dreaming

Despite the popular image of the North-Eastern United States as our primary destination, many of the 1.9 million pre-1900 Italian immigrants who found their way to North America made California's golden shores their home. Before California was a state and still part of Mexico, Italians came. Initially, they were drawn to the rich fishing grounds off the west coast which were untouched in comparison to those back in Italy. As early as the 1830's, Italians who had been working off the western shores of South America began to explore the California coast. They established fishing communities in places such as Monterey and San Pedro. Soon, word made it back to Italy about the richness of California, attracting even more immigrants.

These immigrants brought with them the crops they knew from back home: broccoli, bell peppers, eggplant, artichokes, and Sicilian lemons. Most importantly of all, they brought the knowledge of growing grapes and producing wine. By 1851, there were over 100 vineyards in the Los Angeles area exporting approximately 7,200 cases of wine annually by 1856. This number rose to nearly four million by 1869. Through the knowledge and hard work of these immigrants, the Southern California agricultural industry was established.

Prior to the great diaspora, there were more Italians in California than there were on the entire east coast. Settling throughout the state in the 1800's Italians established communities from San Francisco and Monterey to Stockton, San Pedro, and San Diego. They celebrated the richness of Italian culture with Italian opera in the 1850's and a number of Italian-language newspapers. In 1869, Italians held the first Columbus Day celebration in San Francisco. The Italians who first came to California were fortunate, finding acceptance from Mexicans who shared a common Latin heritage. They did not encounter, in the early 1800's, the bigotry that later immigrants experienced in other parts of the United States.

New Orleans

In the latter half of the 19th century, New Orleans was thriving. Being a major seaport, as it is today, its wealth was based on trade. Crops such as cotton and sugar cane were exported to Europe and South America while New Orleans received imports such as lemons and oranges from Southern Italy. Unfortunately, sugar cane and cotton were labor-intensive, which created a real problem for plantation owners. With the end of the civil war, many slaves – having obtained their freedom – set out for other parts of the United States. This left the former slave owners with a serious labor shortage.

The Southern States leveraged the close relationship with Italy that had developed through trade by bringing in Italian workers to replace the lost slaves. From the perspective of the Italians, this was an excellent opportunity for a better life. One of the unfulfilled promises of unification, described above, was a greater distribution of land. Without any farms of their own, the *contadini* had nothing to lose and a great deal to gain in leaving. When they came to America, they were given work they knew well. They were accustomed to working in the fields for long hours under a merciless sun. The Italian immigrant knew hard labor whether it was in Southern Italy or the Southern United States. So, they came, ready to work.

The plantation owners, in turn, were more than happy to accept the Italian immigrants. Southern Italians were considered an *in-between* race, called by some "*White Negros*"; they were not quite white and not quite black. Since they were thought of as partially white, they were marginally more acceptable than blacks. However, being partially white also meant Southern Italians were partially black. In the sugarcane fields of Louisiana, one Sicilian immigrant recalled, "The boss used to call us niggers" and "told us that we weren't white men."[25] This *otherness* hindered acceptance into *polite*, that is to say *white*, society.

The anti-Southern Italian bigotry was sustained by the government at the time. In 1899, the United States Bureau of Immigration divided Italians into two separate groups: Northern and Southern. The Northern Italians were considered white while Southern Italians were considered *partially* white. Recall from the previous chapter that this reflects the thinking of many Italians themselves, even to this day. As some of them say, *Garibaldi did not unite Italy, but divided Africa.*

The behavior of the Italian immigrants certainly did nothing to dispel the impression of *otherness*. When Southern Italians came to New Orleans, they did not segregate themselves from blacks as other European groups did. We lived in the same neighborhoods and worked shoulder to shoulder with African-Americans. This did not go over well in the south.

---

[25] Guglielmo, Jennifer, & Salerno, Salvatore, (Eds), *Are Italians White? How Race is Made in America*, Routledge, pg. 36

The southern way of life had strict rules, the most important of which was that races did not intermingle. For White America, it was unthinkable that a group of white people were willing to live and work with blacks. There had to be something wrong with the Italians as suggested by an 1899 Article in *The New York Sun* which described Southern Italians as, "willing to live in the same quarters with the Negroes and work side by side with them, and seem wholly destitute of that anti-negro prejudice which is one of the distinguishing features of all the white races in the South."[26] Putting aside for a moment that prejudice against the *negro* was seen as a virtue, it seemed totally alien to *The New York Sun* journalist that a white person would have no issue with blacks, no inherent prejudice.

To this day, Italians think of themselves as not having a racial bias which, when you consider what they say of Garibaldi, seems a bit ridiculous. Historically, however, the Italian word for race, *razza*, referred to social structures, not genetics or ancestry. So, when Northern Italians refer to Calabria as *Calafrica* or *Saudi Calabria*, it is not in reference to the genetic origin of the people as much as a social grouping of the two. Certainly, Italy has never codified racism into law as the United States had with *Jim Crow*. Having said this, the recent influx of immigrants from Eastern Europe and Africa is beginning to affect Italian attitudes.

Although there was an open-door policy in the United States in the late 19th century, the door was not opened quite so widely for some, especially for groups such as Southern Italians, who were seen as *other*. Liberty was seen as a wonderful thing, but it was really for whites only. There was a doubt that people of *lesser races* could truly assimilate, to become productive members of society.

The Southern Italian was one of those for whom liberty and inclusion in the American dream might not really work. In December 1890, *Popular Science Monthly* posed the question "What shall we do with the Dago?" The article maintained that jails were no deterrent since the conditions in the jails were better than what Southern Italians would find back home. They, like the Northern Italians, saw Southern Italians as barbarous and superstitious. If you could not intimidate them into behaving properly with jail, how could you ever expect them to appreciate the fruits of liberty? Thomas A. Guglielmo noted, "As one

---

[26] Connell, William J., & Gardaphé, Fred, (Eds), *Anti-Italianism, Essays on a Prejudice*, Palgrave Macmillan, 2010, pg. 26

local newspaper at the time wrote, 'when we speak of white man's government, they [Italians] are as black as the blackest negro in existence.'"[27]

Rather a Good Thing

Even while God-loving Anglo Saxon America fretted over the barbarity of these descendants of Rome, the Italian presence in New Orleans grew. By the close of the 19th century, there were more than 30,000 Italians in that one area. Worse yet, they were more than farm workers and laborers. They had expanded their ranks to include artisans, fisherman, and merchants. These *in-between* people started to dominate and, in some instances, control certain markets, particularly the fish, fruit, and oyster markets.

Now put yourself in the place of a southern white man at the time. You have lived in Louisiana all your life. Your pappy's pappy lived here all his life and you fought bravely in *The War of Northern Aggression*.[28] As you worked hard to scratch out a life for yourself, these *in-between* people started moving in. Worse yet they proved successful. More successful than you! They were opening businesses, even outright controlling some markets. How could you not hate these upstarts? How could you not resent their success?

Reading the newspapers of the time about Italians is like reading about immigrants coming to the United States today. Italians were said to be lazy, unclean, and came from the worst parts of society. Italy was not sending us their best. This, of course, generated the same hate and fearmongering towards Italians as we see against immigrants today. Between 1886 and 1916, 39 Italians were lynched across the United States. Admittedly, the number of Italian-Americans lynched is minuscule compared to the 3,311 African-American victims during that same period. Italians, however, have the dubious honor of being the victims of the largest single lynching incident in the history of the United States.

---

[27] Guglielmo, Jennifer, & Salerno, Salvatore, (Eds), *Are Italians White? How Race is Made in America*, Routledge, pg. 36

[28] The Civil War is described in former Confederate States as "The War of Northern Aggression."

The story of the lynching begins with the assassination of New Orleans Police Chief, David C. Hennessy. In 1890, the police chief was investigating a gang war between two rival groups of Italian longshoremen. On October the 15th of that same year, he was shot outside his home as he was returning from a meeting. His dying words were "The dagos got me." This was enough to send the city into a frenzy.

New Orleans' mayor ordered the police to arrest "every Italian you come across" which resulted in the detainment and interrogation of 150 Italians with nine being held for trial. When all nine were eventually found innocent for lack of evidence, the white majority of the city felt cheated. The mayor in his fervor fanned the flames of the angry white populace of the city saying, "We must teach these people a lesson that they will not forget for all time." With the blessing of New Orleans' white leaders, a mob formed to carry out the punishment they had decided the Italians deserved. In the end, nine Italian-Americans were shot and two hanged.

The mayor, when asked if he regretted the action of the mob, said, "No Sir. I am an American citizen and I am not afraid of the Devil. These men deserved killing and they were punished by *peaceful, law-abiding citizens*. They [the lynching victims] took the law into their own hands and we were forced to do the same."

Characterizing the men who carried out the lynching as *peaceful, law-abiding citizens* is indicative of the warped thinking of the time.

There is a myth that the Southern United States was different to the rest of the country; that they were somehow more racist. Unfortunately, they weren't. The mayor's reaction was echoed across the United States, both north and south. In Chapter 1, *The Awakening*, I made reference to Teddy Roosevelt's reaction to the lynching which he described to his sister Anna. If you will forgive the duplication, I believe it bears repeating. Roosevelt said, "Monday we dined at the Camerons; various *dago* diplomats were present, all much wrought up by the lynching of the Italians in New Orleans. Personally, I think it rather a good thing, and said so."[29] What is remarkable about this quote is that bigotry, which is normally attributed to the former Confederacy, was so common throughout the United States. Even a progressive such as Roosevelt shared it.

---

[29] Letter from Theodore Roosevelt to Anna Roosevelt, March, 21, 1891.

The lynching of Italians in New Orleans was distinct only in its size. Colorado, Illinois, Mississippi, and Florida also targeted Italian immigrants. A lynching of Italians in Tampa, Florida, was immortalized in postcards the next day. Rather than shame, lynching was something of which the perpetrators were proud.

We should be clear on the motivation of these lynchings. In today's language, lynching is an act of terrorism. Section 802 of the USA Patriot Act states that domestic terrorism involves acts dangerous to human life that are a violation of the criminal laws of the United States or of any State and appear to be intended to intimidate or coerce a civilian population. Back then, lynchings were the answer to the question which was posed by *Popular Science Monthly*. What do you do with the Dago? Lynch him! Jails are too good for him? Better than back home? Well, hang a few of them and those guinea bastards will get the message real quick. The Italian-American population will be brought into submission through fear.

One final point. Even today, it is reported that Hennessy was killed by *the Mafia*, by *Italians*, yet no one really knows who killed him. Certainly, there were others who had a motive. In 1882, although found not guilty, Hennessy was tried for the murder of New Orleans Chief of Detectives, Thomas Devereaux. Hennessy claimed it was a case of self-defense. Once he was appointed Chief of Police, Hennessy began to clean the department of corruption. Surely friends of Devereaux or those that profited from police corruption would have motivation equal to, if not greater than, any Italian? Yet, we are told with certainty *the dagos* did it.

Little Italy

As we transitioned from the 19th to the 20th century, immigration to the United States grew at such a phenomenal rate the government put much stricter regulations on the number of people allowed to enter the country. The majority of all immigrants who came to the States at this time were Italian. While there were many immigrants who came from Central and Northern Italy, nearly four-fifths of Italian immigrants came from the south. Although there was a small percentage of professionals, such as doctors, among the immigrants, most came with calloused hands. As a result, Italian-American culture is primarily a derivative of Southern-Italian *contadini* culture. Many of the ways that the Italian-American culture differs from Italian culture is based on the differences between the northern and southern regions as well as the differences in social class.

The Italians who landed in places such as New York, Boston, or Pittsburgh, had a very different experience from those who settled in the Western and Southern United States. These rural farm workers, many of whom were accustomed to a rustic life based on generations of tradition, suddenly found themselves in modern cities and intermingling with vastly different cultures. While immigrants to California mixed well with the Hispanic community, and Italians who resettled in New Orleans integrated with African-Americans, those who landed in the large cities of the North East clustered together, forming their own communities (described by some as Italian colonies).

It wasn't long until most major cities in the United States boasted of having their own Italian section of town, their own *Little Italy*. East Harlem, in the northern part of New York City, became known as Italian Harlem. Also, with cheap rents and easy access to the downtown garment industry, the area around Mulberry Street and the Lower East Side was especially attractive to Italian immigrants.

Some cities' Little Italies still survive, such as San Diego's with its excellent restaurants, *pasticcerie*, and Italian cinema. Others have faded as Italian-Americans moved to the suburbs where they learned to eat fettuccini Alfredo and pineapple & Canadian bacon pizza. Although the heart of Italian-American culture has been for so long New York City's Little Italy, even this enclave of Italians is not what it once was.

The fleeting existence of Little Italy, any Little Italy in any American city, began in the first half of the 20th century. The formation of these communities had a practical application beyond the convenience of retaining some semblance of a life left behind in Italy. Little Italy assisted the immigrants in establishing themselves. These communities provided the newly-arrived immigrant with an extended support system. If a baby decided to arrive sooner than expected, Rosa in the apartment upstairs was a midwife. If you needed to find work, Guido Bacciagalupe down the street, who was the cousin of your Uncle's *goombade*, could put in a good word for you on the construction site. And every *nonna e zia* (grandmother and aunt) acted as a member of the neighborhood watch, keeping vigilant guard against any mischief makers.

It is interesting that these communities were further subdivided, reflecting the factional nature of Italy itself. On one block, you might have Italians from Puglia, while on another block over you would have the people from Campania or Basilicata. The immigrants carried with them the regionalism of Italy, the *campanilismo* described in the previous chapter. Again, this was a practical consideration; your closest neighbors practiced the same food customs, followed the same traditions, celebrated the same holidays, and spoke the same dialect. Each of these could vary widely by region, especially language. There was no definitive common Italian language among the immigrants per se; mostly it was an Italian-American pidgin. The Italian my mother spoke, which was basically a mixture of Sicilian and Calabrese, was significantly different from what I learned in school which was Tuscan.

Chain migration was another factor that contributed to the regional divisions of Little Italy. In chain migration, once a family member is established in the new country, other members follow, settling in the same community. This is certainly nothing unique to Italians; I have seen this occur with immigrants to the United States even today. During the Italian Diaspora, the new family member or friend from the village would settle in Little Italy. Typically, not simply in the same general area, but on the same block and street of the already established relative. If possible, being in the same building was better yet.

Life in Little Italy

The stereotype of *Little Italy* is based on what these neighborhoods were during the diaspora. The idealized images of this time are of happy immigrants, children playing stickball, and laundry hanging on lines stretched between buildings. You could hear mothers calling their kids to dinner – *"Tony, su tavolo!!"* (Tony, it's on the table!!) Along the street, various mom & pop corner stores would be festooned with aged meats and cheeses as the pushcarts would roll along with fresh produce. "Come getta you tomatoes! Apples! ... Aye lady no squeeza da' tomatoes! Ah fa napala!"

The reality of these times was much harsher.

The Little Italy of this era was composed of tenement buildings; five or six-story structures that housed as many as 30 families. The buildings stood wall to wall with little or no space between. The crowded conditions were made worse by a lack of light and poor air circulation. Sometimes people would refer to these as railway flats, or railway apartments, because the layout was similar to a railway passenger car. The rooms were in a row with one hallway down the side providing access.

The typical tenement apartment consisted of three basic rooms: kitchen, main room, and bedroom. The main room served as a workroom, women would bring in piece work from the local textile factories. In the winter, this work would be done in the kitchen close to the stove, the source of heat. There was no central heating or even radiators; the apartments were typically warmed by a coal or kerosene stove. Although the tenements had no central heating, they did have central plumbing; by that I mean there was typically a common toilet at the end of the hallway or in a courtyard which was shared by multiple families.

The main room of these apartments served as the bedroom for the children at night. These rooms were not large, but they would squeeze in a couple of beds which would be shared by the kids. Being Catholic, it was typical for Italian families to have as many as eight to ten children. The parents' room was the furthest from the kitchen. With so many children in such a small space, no one had or even expected to have any privacy. Frequently, these children – due in part to the conditions in which they lived – died before reaching adulthood.

Little Italy vs. Italy

Now, these may seem to have been terrible conditions, and they were, but they were not so much worse than what the Southern-Italian immigrant had left behind. The homes of the *contadini* in Italy were reflective of the harshness of the lives they lived. They were tiny one-room structures, typically a mere 270 square feet or so. These dirt floor domiciles with unplastered walls were often shared with the livestock. Just as they did in the tenements of New York, a bed was shared among siblings. In Italy, however, these *beds* were simple heaps of straw.

If you were to travel to Alberobello in Puglia you can get a sense of what the homes were like for some of the *contadini*. There you can visit a *trullo* which is a small cone-shaped house, more accurately the main floor was circular with a cone-shaped roof. Being cone-shaped they could not be large. On average, the lower level had a diameter of approximately 15 to 20 feet with a height of around five or six feet. This was topped with a cone made out of limestone. At times there would be an alcove off the main room for a bedroom. A rough wooden floor would be laid at the base of the cone creating a loft often used for storage or a bedroom for the children.

Although some in Alberobello still live in *trulli*, it was primarily housing from the 14th to the late 19th century. One story (although the validity is suspect) is that the design of these unique structures enabled the homes to be taken apart easily to avoid taxes. When tax time came, you took your house apart and spread the stones around the field. Once taxes were over, you put it back together. If the *contadini* were poor, it was certainly not due to a lack of ingenuity!

Today, Alberobello is a tourist spot with most of the *trulli* stuffed with tourist items such as local olive oil, liquors, and small model *trulli*. While visiting, you may get a sense of the size of the home, but you will not get a sense of the poverty. Today, the buildings are well maintained with whitewashed walls and the paved streets are clean. The city is clean and thriving, far from the conditions of the previous century.

Hygiene

If you read some of the studies done at the time, you get a sense of how bad conditions were in the *Mezzogiorno*. An Italian Army doctor, Giuseppe Sormanni, reported how recruits from the *Mezzogiorno* between 1863 and 1876 had more occurrences of diseases caused by poor sanitary practices than soldiers from other areas of Italy.[30] For example, of the recruits rejected from the northern and central regions of Italy, 0.1% were for intestinal diseases while from the south 0.9% were rejected. Similarly, more than twice the number of southern recruits were rejected for ringworm than those from the northern and central regions.

The poor hygiene practiced in the south was brought to the United States. Maddalena Tirabassi in her essay, *Making Space for Domesticity*, describes the life of the Italian-American in Little Italy in the early 1900's:

> *"Macaroni is made in every block of the Italian neighborhoods of New York," one reformer reported. "In many streets, you will find three or four little shops in one block of houses, with the macaroni drying in the doorways and windows. The front room is the shop, the family living in the middle and rear rooms, and these are invariably overcrowded. The Italians not only have large families, but keep lodgers, and the front shop then becomes a sleeping and living apartment as well as the other rooms. The paste is mixed and pressed by a machine into long strings, which are hung on a rack to dry... A child lay sick of diphtheria in the back room where the physician visited her. The father manufactured macaroni in the front adjoining room, and would go directly from holding the child in his arms to*

---

[30] Zamagni, Vera, 'Istruzione e sviluppo economico. Il Caso italiano, 1861-1913', in Gianni Toniolo's *L'Economia Italiana*, 1973, pg. 158 - 62

the macaroni machine, pulling the macaroni with his hands and hanging it over racks to dry. '[31]

Nests for Birds of Passage

While boarding houses were common throughout the United States, they had a major impact on Italian-American culture. Unfortunately, boarding houses were seen as seedy, immoral, and promoting promiscuity. You can see it in the literature of the time. In Thomas Wolfe's *Look Homeward Angel,* the main character's family turns to running a boarding house when they are down on their luck. The connotation of proprietors having loose morals – as places where unchaperoned interaction between men and women can lead to trouble – is developed by James Joyce in *Dubliners.* Despite these negative connotations, boarding houses were common in Little Italy. They were a way for the Italian immigrants to make some extra income.

Most frequently, the boarders were *Birds of Passage.* A term applied to men who temporarily came to the United States with the intention of returning to Italy once they had built up some capital. By some estimates, 35% of Italian immigrants returned to Italy.

While, these proverbial birds typically flocked with those of the same feather – meaning they would seek out boarding houses run by people who were from the same region – they often took what was available. As I mentioned above, the *campanilismo* of Italy was retained when the immigrants arrived and settled in America. However, as we lived and worked with people from different regions, those divisions from back home began to break down. In Chapter 2, *Italy What a Concept,* I described how Italian-Americans haven't a regional bias, if you are Italian you are a cousin. It doesn't matter to us if you are from Bergamo or Bari. It was this intermingling in boarding houses that contributed to the breaking down of those barriers.

Birds of Passage also created a concentration of Italians in eastern cities. Unlike the Swedes who bought farmland in places like Minnesota, during the diaspora Italians primarily settled in the large cities, especially the growing cities of the east. A lot of us weren't here to stay. If your

---

[31] Cinotto, Simone, (Ed), *Making Italian America: Consumer Culture and the Production of Ethnic Identities (Critical Studies in Italian America),* Fordham University Press, 2014, pg. 61

intention was to make a few bucks and then go home, you didn't buy a farm, you worked construction. It was in the eastern cities where we were needed to build these burgeoning Gothams. The hands of these *sojourners* not only erected the skyscrapers whose spires poked through heaven's clouds, but dug the tunnels of the netherworld, and laid the track for subways. They were the hands that plumbed the water and sewer lines.

This was another place where *campanilismo* was broken down, at work. When you are guiding a girder into place, you weren't concerned with the region from where the crane operator came, you only cared about his ability to do the job. There may have been some initial sense of division. Familiarity, in this case however, did not breed contempt, but a sense of camaraderie. It was hard to believe a myth about another group of people when you spent most of your waking hours with them.

The Passeggiata

In addition to the workplace, the lifestyle Italians brought with them increased interaction between people from different regions. Italians in both Italy and the United States spent most of their lives out of the house. In Italy, the *piazza* was the Italian living room, a gathering place for the people to interact; children would be playing, friends would share an *aperitivo*, and the old women would sit gossiping.

When the immigrants came to this country, they brought this habit with them. A hundred years ago, in Little Italy, people would take to the streets in the evening. Some would bring out their chairs or sit on the front steps, others would go from building to building visiting with neighbors. This is the *passeggiata*. This was one of the traditions we brought with us from Italy. As you walked along, you would stop to speak with neighbors and friends you passed along the way. This custom stayed with Italian-Americans for many decades. In Little Italy, these social encounters also aided in the breakdown of old world divisions as well as building a sense of community.

I should point out that gathering in the *piazza*, as well as the *passeggiata*, is still something which is practiced in Italy today. Some of the most pleasant memories I have of Italy is sitting in a *piazza* in the evening. There I experience a delicious sense of contentedness. You can sit and breathe in the *Italianità*. Whether it was an espresso in the Piazza della Rotonda in front of the Pantheon in Rome; an Aperol Spritz in the Piazza Tasso in Sorento; or even a common Coke in a small unnamed *piazza* in Adria – in each place I experience the same peaceful appreciation of a summer evening reminiscent of my childhood summers in East Utica, New York. On such evenings, it is a challenge for my wife to get me to return to the hotel at a reasonable hour… well, a reasonable hour for an Amarighan.

When I was a boy, neighbors sat on their front steps on summer evenings and people visited with one another. I cannot recall one word that was said in all of those conversations, but I do remember how it felt. There was restful peace after a long day, something few of us feel any longer. We were not obsessed with the worries of the next day. Of course, we did not look at the text messages on our cell phones as friends spoke to us, nor did we scan social media while we were surrounded by people. We simply enjoyed one another's company and, when there was nothing to say, we listened to the quiet. I didn't understand back then how precious those moments were. It is unfortunate that this no longer seems to be the case; it is one of the things lost in our assimilation.

The Italian Community

How the community worked together, sometimes came through in ways that may seem a bit strange to Amarighans. One of those ways was *playing the numbers,* an illegal lottery which was popular in some communities. It was commonly referred to as the *Italian Lottery.* You may have heard, for example, that Joe Bacciagalupe was *running numbers.* This meant that Joe had an illegal lottery going. People would bet on numbers and a *runner* would take the bets back to where they conducted the lottery. There were various methods of picking the winning numbers, from drawing random balls to selecting digits from some regularly published numbers such as the last three digits of the balance in the US Treasury. Well, at least that is how it was supposed to have worked.

The way the system really worked was explained to me by someone who had been involved in running one of these games. Back in the day, I worked with a man who had recently returned from a government-funded re-education program, i.e. he just got out of jail. His job was basically to hang around the place; I think they gave it to him because he kept his mouth shut while he was *at the university.*

It was my first full-time job and we would have lunch together in a little break room in the back of a warehouse. It was a dimly lit corner with a few broken wooden folding chairs placed around a bench that served as our table. On occasion, he would tell me brief stories about the old days. I was a dumb kid, so it didn't really matter what he told me.

I had seen some Mafia B-movie where the characters were talking about running numbers. I didn't know at the time what they meant, so I asked him about it. After explaining the basic mechanics, he told me how they came up with the winners. "*You see, Billy, the way it worked was that we all knew who was having it tough. So, Joe Bacciagalupe lost his job – holy shit Joe's numbers hit. What a break for Joe. If the Nasto kid needed medicine – Nasto's numbers hit. Jesus isn't it great they got lucky! We just declared the winner to be the person who we thought needed it the most. We never had any drawing. Who has time to bother with that shit?!*"

Several years after this conversation, my elder brother told me about something that happened to my father long before I was born. It was a week before Christmas and the runner came around the house.

"Bill, hey Bill!" he called up to my father from the street.

"Get out of here," my father called back down. "I can't play this week. I don't have enough money to even buy my kids Christmas presents!" It was true. My mom and dad were caught short right before Christmas. The usual Christmas family feast had been canceled that year. Not only were there no gifts under the tree, there was no tree!

"No Bill, No!" the guy called back. "You're numbers hit! You won!"

My brother told me they had a great Christmas that year. There was the traditional family *Feast of Seven Fishes* and plenty of gifts for my two brothers and sister.

This was the Italian-American community. We were a close-knit group that had our own way of doing things. Those ways, those manners and customs, were quite different than the rest of America. This made us suspect. Of course, being a *secretive society* didn't help. You watched what you said to anyone outside the family, and you didn't speak at all to any Amarighan.

Added to the outside suspicion was the fact that we were growing in significant numbers. Now, more than ever, the question posed by the 1890 *Popular Science Monthly* article – "What shall we do with the Dago?" – needed to be answered. The solution was that the *Dago* had to be convinced to leave his backward foreign ways behind, in order to integrate into mainstream America. But, at the same time, voices from back home were calling on people not to forget their origins.

What ensued was a struggle for the hearts and minds of the Italian-American people.

Chapter 4: What Shall We Do With The Dago?

Turning Off the Spigot

What shall we do with the *dago*? Like the people of New Orleans, many across the United States were concerned about these exotic, secretive, and reportedly criminal Mediterraneans. Considering the birth rate, alongside the sheer number of immigrants coming to the States, the Italian share of the population was increasing alarmingly. Well, alarmingly to the established white population. Although we were passionate, we were also birth-control abhorring Catholics. The combination of the two made us very good at reproducing.

So, what *did* they do with the *dago*? The first step was to turn off the spigot, limiting the flow of people who did not fit into what white America saw as proper. So, Congress passed the Emergency Quota Act of 1921 and the Immigration Act of 1924. This legislation, while not affecting those arriving from Northern Europe, limited the number of immigrants coming from Eastern and Southern Europe. These acts restricted immigrants from the *Mezzogiorno* to no more than 4,000 per year. As has been described in the previous chapter, Italians from the north were considered a different race from those in the south; they were more European. The new restrictions, therefore, did not apply to them.

Correcting the Italian Diet

The next step in resolving America's *dago* problem was to deal with the ones already here. If they were ever to be civilized, the *dagos* had to be taught to live an American way of life, stripping them of their *Italianità*. Keep in mind, in this period of American history, racism was thought to have a scientific basis. The idea the Southern Italian immigrant was racially inferior was perfectly acceptable. School administrators and teachers saw it as their responsibility to educate these backward people in the proper way of life. Looking back on this attitude from the society in which we live today, one more accepting of multiculturalism, we may want to vilify these people. While some may have been acting out of *evil*

71

intent, many saw re-educating the Italian immigrant as their Christian responsibility, simple Christian compassion.

Unfortunately, this created a bias that attributed every ill faced by the Italian immigrant as the result of their *Italianità*. When Italian children went to school malnourished, the teachers blamed the traditions of Italian parenting rather than poverty. Even when the children were well fed, *what* they were fed was often seen as a problem. The *experts* of that era insisted Italians feed their children oatmeal and drink plenty of milk. They did not think it proper that children be given coffee to drink. They saw it as uncaring when children ate the same food as their parents, believing the young had more delicate digestive systems and different nutritional requirements.

This did not fit well with *Italianità*. Oatmeal was something you fed to the pigs, as some Italian immigrants would describe it. Despite my dear wife's best efforts to turn it into something palatable, I still can't stomach those thick gelatinous globs. If that is what is on the menu, I would prefer to skip the meal entirely in favor of a simple cup of coffee; black if it is a good blend.

Coffee brings us to another point of contention. As we shall discuss in Chapter 7, *At the Table No One Grows Old*, Italians do not see milk as the ambrosia from the gods like many other cultures. It was gratifying when Jack LaLanne, the *Godfather of Fitness*, would decades later decry milk as fit only for a suckling calf. As a child, my siblings and I would have black coffee instead of milk with our cereal. There I was, four years old, with a big bowl of puffed rice swimming in a pool of black coffee. When I went to school, the nuns made us drink milk midway through the morning from little six-ounce milk bottles that were always lukewarm. They meant well, but again a little black coffee to start my day was all I needed, even back then.

These American ideas sprang from the concept children needed a diet different from their parents, which was antithetical to the Italian way of life. Italian families did not make one thing for the children and another for the adults. I first encountered this when, as a boy, my family and I were visiting some Amarighan friends. While the adults dined on steaks, the kids were given homemade burgers. You can imagine my parent's conversation in the car ride home. "What's wrong with them? Are they so cheap they can't feed their kids? Ah, what the hell… they're Amarighan. What d'you expect?"

Italian culture, especially at that time, was patriarchal. The meals were based on what the father, as head of the house, wanted. My home was pretty much like most Italian homes. My mother cooked for my father and we were welcome to eat what my mother made or leave the table hungry. With the exception of birthdays and special events, such as a first communion, what we wanted came after what my father and then my mother wanted for a meal. Honestly. It didn't matter, I never turned away from anything my mother put on the table. Like every son's mother, my mother was the greatest cook in the world.

Piove, Governo Ladro

As has been discussed multiple times in the previous chapters, Italians and Italian-Americans have always had a distrust of the government; remember *piove, governo ladro* (it rains, the government is a thief). In the eyes of the Italian immigrant, the education system's attempts to convince their children to abandon their Italian way of life was only further evidence of government thievery. This time, however, what they were attempting to steal was their children.

The attack on how Italian-Americans ate was an attack on one of the core aspects of *Italianità*. Food, more so than with most other cultures, is central to the Italian way of life. When our children were taught there was something wrong with how they ate, in essence, they were being taught there was something wrong with being Italian. Indeed, many Italians of that era speak of how they were ashamed of Italian food. The food they ate was a very clear indication of being something other than American. One Italian told how he would dispose of his lunch before he got to school, going hungry rather than being seen eating the ethnic food his mother had prepared. Simone Cinotto's *The Italian-American Table* describes a recollection of one Italian-American's experience:

> *The teacher had said that clean hands, clean clothing, and a toothbrush are essentials. And that plenty of milk should be taken in the morning. I felt so ashamed, so inferior, when I realized that my parents do not exemplify such things at home. My mother showed even opposition to the teacher's recommendation about food. She began ridiculing all my teachers for their ideas, and this made me very sad, for she ruined my dreams of becoming a real American. I felt that I needed milk in the morning more than anything else.*[32]

---

[32] Cinotto, Simone, *The Italian-American Table: Food, Family, and Community in New York City*, University of Illinois Press, 2013, pg. 37

In the battle for the hearts and minds of second-generation Italians, the Amarighans were winning. Inevitably, despite the resistance of their parents, the children were becoming Americanized. They were convinced by their peers and educators that Italian ways were backward. They were convinced being an American was better, and to become an American you had to abandon your culture. We became diluted in the larger sea of Americana. The irony is the children and grandchildren of many of these Italian-Americans are now searching to recover what their parents willingly and happily jettisoned.

We Don't Need No Education

Italian parents were challenged by the very idea their children were required to go to school. In Italy, the folk wisdom taught only a stupid man makes his son better than he is. This attitude was unchanged when Italians settled in the United States. In the 1920's, the Italian section of Harlem held the record for juvenile delinquency.

This attitude towards education is understandable when you consider the Italian immigrants were the *contadini*, the poor of the *Mezzogiorno*, who struggled simply to survive; Cavalcanti's verse was not as pressing as fending off starvation. When the Italian immigrants came to the United States they saw no reason to change. The idea children would waste their time in a classroom when they could be contributing to the family income was contrary to how they had managed to survive for generations.

It is sad to note in many parts of the Italian-American community today, there are still some who do not see the benefit of education. On more than one occasion I have heard many an Italian-American say an education wasn't necessary. "There ain't no point in going to college. I didn't go to college and I did fine. Why should my kid?" You might, at first, attribute this to the anti-intellectual undercurrent plaguing all communities in the United States. After all, it is not uncommon to hear non-Italian-Americans question the necessity of an education or even the economic wisdom of an investment in college. Although this is something new in general society, it is an opinion consistent with parts of the Italian-American community since we first arrived.

I don't know what percentage of my friends from the old neighborhood went to college, but many families did not seem overly concerned about education beyond high school. In her essay *Good Enough*, Joanne Detore-Nakamura's description of what it was like for an Italian-American woman to grow up in a community where a person with an education was suspect is reminiscent of my own experiences. She describes how she was considered odd for her love of books and chastised for preferring a book over television.[33]

In regard to education, Italian immigrants trailed Jewish immigrants who were much quicker to take advantage of the American education system. As Italians became more integrated into society, education was seen as a way of building a better life. Knowledge was a means to an end and that end was a good paying job. It wasn't until we reached the 1960's and 1970's that we saw college attendance begin to rise within the Italian-American community, although many still saw it as unimportant.

This was the case with my own family. In the 1960's, my older brother Frank was the first in our family to both graduate high school and attend college. He was supposed to be the smart one; he wore glasses and was quiet, so everyone assumed he was smart. Although he was an inspiration to me for much of my life, the phrase from Shakespeare "reputed as wise for saying nothing" comes to mind. He ended up in the computer business, traveling around the world and making a good living. My parents stressed the importance of education to me as a result. On days when, like any child, I would pretend to be sick, my mother would give me a kick in the seat of my pants with the words "What do you want to do... grow up and dig ditches?"

Although both my parents lacked even a junior high school education, I grew up in a house filled with books. In our den, there was a wall of books. Literally, one wall of the room was covered with bookshelves from floor to ceiling. On these shelves were almost every kind of book you can imagine: fiction, zoology, huge dictionaries, and compilations of the works of the masters. As a child, the writings of Kipling, Tolstoy, Wilde, and Emerson were all right there within my reach. There were several sets of encyclopedias as well as *The Book of Knowledge*[34] which my father purchased on a whim because my brother, the *smart one*, liked some of the color illustrations. I have benefited a great deal from my father's love of books. Although he was not what one would consider a

---

[33] Connell, William J., & Gardaphé, Fred, (Eds), *Anti-Italianism, Essays on a Prejudice*, Palgrave Macmillan, 2010, pg. 116

[34] *The Book of Knowledge* was a set of children's encyclopedias originally published in installments that were later bound into volumes and sold door to door.

literary man, he instilled a lifelong love of learning in both my brother and me.

Anti-intellectualism is a significant difference between Italians and Italian-Americans. I can think of nothing that demonstrates *Italianità* more than a love for the arts and sciences. Italy, according to UNESCO,[35] has a literacy rate of slightly more than 99% while the overall literacy rate of the United States is 86%. Look at Italian heroes. While most nations celebrate generals and great conquerors, the icons of Italy are poets, artists, and composers. Few towns, if any, lack a statue or monument to Dante. The Italian identity, Italian not Italian-American, is wrapped in the likes of Da Vinci, Michelangelo, and Galileo. As we progress from the Renaissance we pass through Verdi and Puccini, to Fellini and Umberto Eco. All are Italian icons who are celebrated for their contribution to the arts and sciences.

We should make note that while Italy does have a higher literacy rate and interest in the arts, this does not translate into higher levels of education. Italy has one of the highest high school and college dropout rates in Europe. Only 56 out of every 100 Italian college students complete their degree. One of the challenges Italy's youth faces is that a college education does not necessarily mean a path to a job. Remarkably, those with a college education in Italy are much more likely to be unemployed than those without a degree.[36]

Learning Revolution

Despite these poor statistics for higher education, Italy is still a leader in the arts. These intellectual pursuits are really a benefit of the *Risorgimento* and the socialist leanings of Italian society. In 1932, Bertrand Russell argued that "the gospel of work is the morality of the slave state." He defended a position where people in society should be freed to pursue their passions rather than overworking simply to survive. Italians understood this well before Russell gave it voice.

In the first decade of the 20th century, *Università Popolare* (Popular University or People's University) began to pop up throughout Italy.

---

[35] UNESCO – United Nations Educational, Scientific, and Cultural Organization.

[36] http://www.thedailybeast.com/articles/2013/01/06/italy-s-statistics-make-it-look-like-a-third-world.html

Modelled after similar efforts in Denmark, England, and Sweden, support for the various *Università Popolare* came from the middle class and politicians. Some of these *universities* charged for classes or were associated with public institutions, others were independent with no enrolment costs.

As evidenced by their continued existence even to today, they were important in the development of Italian society with classes on a wide range of topics. They dealt with practical matters such as hygiene as well as purely intellectual pursuits such as art and literature. They did not see education simply as a means to make a better living but as a way of enabling the *contadini* to rise above the slave existence described by Russell. This was a vision in which overall society improved through the moral and intellectual development of the individual.

As we have seen, a liberated mind is a dangerous thing. The idea people should be able to pursue their passions was one of the principles of the *sovversivi* (subversives). The term *sovversivi* was applied to the radical left; groups such as the anarchists, communists, and socialists. Although they were not in the majority within the Italian-American community, they were at the forefront of not only freeing the *contadini* from oppressive institutions but also worked for greater social justice and equality becoming a major force within the American Labor Movement.

To bring about a workers' revolution in the United States, the *sovversivi* recognized the need to provide education for Italian immigrants. To achieve this, they followed the example of *Università Popolare* in Italy. In the United States, however, students funded these schools themselves through membership fees or voluntary contributions. They were genuinely universities of the people, universities of the common working man and woman.

Beyond these schools, the *sovversivi* established newspapers and published books distributed through likeminded bookstores. They also organized a wide spectrum of cultural activities such as musicals and festivals. This gave workers a chance to listen to music or hear bits from an opera. A rare treat in the time before you could stream a symphony or watch an opera on your tablet. The experience of music, fine music, was outside the day to day existence of the average worker.

Since the *sovversivi* saw both the church and state as institutions that oppressed the worker, they replaced traditional national and religious holidays with their own revolutionary celebrations. Many of these events were picnics or outings that gave the worker an opportunity to get out of the suffocating confines of the factory and city. Although uprooted during the Second World War, an Italian-American culture that saw life as something more than survival began to blossom.

Most Italian-Americans today do not understand the appeal of socialism or anything with even a slight connotation of limiting capitalism. The *Reagan Revolution* as well as the popularity of right-wing commentators and the writings of Ayn Rand, has fed the growth of libertarianism. There is a strong belief a government rules best when it rules least. Eventually, the forces of the free market will resolve all social ills. There is no need for the government to get involved.

In Italy, however, socialism had a resonance with the post-unification culture. Leaders of unification, such as Mazzini, envisioned an Italy as an educated society working together as one, eliminating caste, privilege, and inequality. Granted, unification did not achieve this envisioned goal, but it was the goal. It was (is) the vision to which Italians ascribed.

Sacco & Vanzetti

As noted earlier, the diversity of Italian culture makes it impossible to say Italians felt one particular way or another. Italians then, as well as today, are far from monolithic in their thinking, especially when it comes to political radicalism. Although there was a percentage of immigrants who were part of the *sovversivi*, many were not; many were simply common workers who were seeking a better life. Many others were similar to Bartolomeo Vanzetti, of Sacco and Vanzetti fame, who initially had little involvement with any sort of activism. When Vanzetti arrived in the United States, however, discrimination and exploitation made him, and many others, ready recruits for anarchists and socialists.

Vanzetti became a follower of the anarchist Luigi Galleani who believed the United States government was violent and oppressive. Galleani published a subversive newspaper, *Cronaca Sovversiva* (Subversive Chronical), that openly advocated violent revolution. Although Luigi Galleani had been deported in 1919, Galleanists who had remained in the United States continued their terrorist activities.

On April the 15th, 1920, the Slater-Morrill Shoe Company in Braintree, Massachusetts was robbed and two men were killed. Sacco and Vanzetti were two of four Galleanists suspected of committing the crime. While the other two escaped to Italy, Sacco and Vanzetti were left to stand trial. Ultimately, they were found guilty and executed. There was, however, strong evidence the two men had been framed. Even at the time of trial, many doubted the court had acted justly.

A cause célèbre for decades, the Sacco and Vanzetti trial was important in American history beyond its significance to Italian-Americans or the labor movement. The abuses of the prosecution in the trial, as well as an appeals process that hindered justice, spurred a judicial reform movement in Massachusetts. Despite these reforms, it took another 50 years for the restoration of the reputation of the two men. In 1977, the Massachusetts Office of the Governor's Legal Counsel submitted to Governor Dukakis the *Report to the Governor in the Matter of Sacco and Vanzetti* which advised the trial was not conducted fairly and evidence later surfaced that would have cleared the two men. Subsequently, on August the 23rd, 1977, which was the 50th anniversary of the Sacco and Vanzetti executions, Governor Dukakis declared "any disgrace should be forever removed from their names."

In order to understand their motivation, we need to stand in the shoes of our Italian-American forebears. The American dream, then as it is now, is the belief that if you work towards your goals you can improve your life. Today, if you listen to political speeches you will hear them describe this dream as "if you work hard, and play by the rules, you'll be rewarded." As we have seen many times throughout the history of the Italian immigrant, this is far from what they found when they arrived. Factory owners had little concern for the safety of their workers. The *dago* was a disposable commodity.

Triangle Shirtwaist Fire

One of the most infamous examples of the disregard owners had for their workers was the Triangle Shirtwaist Factory Fire of 1911. The Triangle Shirtwaist Company exemplified the sweatshops of that era. The majority of its workforce was composed of young immigrant girls who could not speak English, most of whom were Italian.

The factory conditions were so appallingly dangerous they did not even meet the lax safety requirements of that time. In addition to there being no sprinkler system despite past fires in the factory, the number of exits was not sufficient for the size of the workforce. The one working elevator of the four in the building could only be reached by filing down a long corridor. As is sadly the case in so many fires, stairwell exits were locked. The owners were fearful the girls might steal scraps of cloth.

The owners, Max Blanck and Isaac Harris, had little concern for the workers who provided them with their wealth. The women worked 12 hour days for $15 a week. When the Ladies Garment Workers Union went on strike in 1909, Blanck and Harris fought back. They hired police as muscle who would jail the women and greased the palms of politicians to look the other way. Although there was no evidence of arson in this particular fire, it is not unreasonable to speculate on the owners' motivation in not installing a sprinkler system. Blanck and Harris are known to have set fire to other factories they had owned in order to collect on insurance policies. When the time came to torch this place, they certainly did not want to risk the fire being extinguished.

The 18-minute Triangle Shirtwaist Factory fire claimed the lives of 145 workers; 36 in the elevator shaft, 58 jumping out of windows, 45 either burned or suffocated and 2 more who died after the fire from their injuries. Perhaps it is incorrect to editorialize at this point, but how can anyone not feel outraged? The corridor that led to the elevator was lined with the bodies of women who had suffocated. Young girls died because these two wealthy men were concerned they would steal scraps of cloth. These were young women who were simply trying to survive in their new home. They were the wives, mothers, and sisters of our parents and grandparents.

The tragedy of the Triangle Shirtwaist Factory is well known and well-remembered. Every year, on the anniversary of the fire, the names of the dead are read out and a bell is rung in memory of the event.

The conditions created by men like Blanck and Harris were the conditions that led Italian-Americans and other immigrants to become anarchists and socialists. The women who worked in the sweatshops, the men who labored on the docks, the construction workers who built the towers in Manhattan, all realized they were nothing more than grist to the mill of unregulated capitalism. They worked hard, but it wasn't enough. The game was rigged against them.

Bread and Roses

In January of 1912, the *Crusade for Bread and Roses* broke out in Lawrence, Massachusetts. Mary K. O'Sullivan described the conditions that led up to this strike.

> . . . *It must be understood that the Lawrence strike was not caused by the Industrial Workers of the World or by the reduction of the working week from fifty-six to fifty-four hours with the ensuing loss of pay. The reduction was only the last straw in a situation that the workers could not endure any longer. The many injustices of the section boss with his personal discrimination against men and women who refused to submit to his*

*standards helped to bring on a rebellion. The rise in the cost of living
during the last two years, including increased rents, had reduced the mill
hands to an extremity where the loss of a few cents weekly in their wages
became a calamity in hundreds of homes. At the turn of the year, then, the
strike began spontaneously without recognized leadership.[37]*

At the time of the crusade, 86% of the population of Lawrence
Massachusetts were immigrants. The crusade has long been considered
one of the most important and successful events of the labor
movement. The workers in Lawrence were from a dozen different
nations. The strike began in the Lawrence Duck Mill of the American
Woolen Company when Angeline Rocco of the Italian branch of the
Workers of the World announced all the Italians would strike on Friday
evening. The Polish weavers (mostly women) of the Everett Mill,
however, began the strike on Thursday when they received less pay than
expected.

Although the Polish women in the Everett mill were the first to go on
strike, Italian immigrants were quickly propelled into leadership roles.
As the New Orleans Italians' lack of racial bias enabled them to work
and live with African-Americans, the Italians in the North Eastern
United States were able to put aside cultural difference to form alliances
with other oppressed immigrants.

Today in the United States, strikes are relatively peaceful, the strikers
walking the picket line holding signs. Most times, you hardly even notice
them. This is a slight wisp of the smoke from the fires Italian-Americans
set in the labor disputes of the early 19th century. The strikers of *The
Crusade for Bread and Roses*, like the Galleanists and other anarchists, were
not averse to resorting to violence. John McPherson described the strike
as follows.

*"From the Washington Mill the crowd, composed of largely of Italians,
surged toward the Wood Mill, where the pay envelopes had not been
distributed, "rushed" the gate, broke open the doors, damaged the
escalators, pulled girls from their work, cut off the electric drive, stopped*

---

[37] O'Sullivan, Mary K., The Labor War at Lawrence, *Survey*, 6 April
1912, pg. 72-73

the machines throughout the mill, and threatened to kill any person daring to put the machinery in motion ... '[38]

In modern terminology, we would call these people terrorists. The Galleanists, Sacco & Vanzetti, and the Industrial Workers of the World which was the labor union at the heart of the *Crusade for Bread and Roses*, all advocated the use of violence to achieve a political end. To be clear, they were more than glad to unlawfully use violence and intimidation in the pursuit of a political aim. Most often, the targets of violence were civilians, factory owners, capitalists, and scabs which is a pejorative term referring to workers who come in to replace those who are on strike.

However, when it comes to the labor movement, we should remember they weren't playing softball, as the expression goes. This was a bloody battle on both sides. The owners had no concern for their workers. The laborer on the factory floor was less important, to them, than a beast in the field. If the workers should rise up, the owners had no qualms about breaking the strike with brutal violence, often with the help of the local government. In many ways, these workers were fighting a literal life and death battle.

The history of Italian-American involvement in the American Labor Movement would fill a library. In such a library, you would read of men like Joseph Ettor who was a leader of the Industrial Workers of the World. He was critical in holding together the *Crusade for Bread and Roses*. You will read the poetry of Arturo Giovannitti a union leader who authored *The Walker* and *O Labor of America: Heartbeat of Mankind*. You will also learn of how such men as Agosto Bellanca, and Eduardo Molisani, and Salvatore Ninfo organized garment workers in New York. Italians such as Luigi Antonini, Margaret DiMaggio, Emilio Grandinetti, Anzuino Marimpietri, and Angela & Maria Bambace united Italian-Americans in a fight for justice.

We should also understand much of this radicalism came from what they had been learning in Italy after unification. Many, already members of transnational political groups, understood the tactics of militancy. They had been educated on the parched slopes of the southern Apennines in their struggle against the Italian aristocracy. By applying this knowledge to their fight in the United States, they took on a leadership role within the movement.

---

[38] McPherson, John, *The Lawrence Strike of 1912*, Rockwell and Churchill Press, 1912, pg. 8

The Italian-Americans' involvement in the labor movement was more than being the angry muscle of the working class. The American Labor Movement's objectives, which were more than economic, fit well into the overall culture of the *sovversivi*. In practical terms, the goal of the labor movement was for better wages, safer working conditions, and reasonable hours. Looking at it in broader terms, the movement's goal was societal recognition of the dignity of the laborer while developing a world in which the need to survive did not trump the pursuit of one's passions and self-actualization. In the end, the labor movement succeeded in ending child labor, providing safer working conditions, health benefits, and aid to workers who were injured or retired.

Italians & Catholicism

Italian-Americans had no greater love for the church than they had for the state. As discussed in Chapter 2, *Italy What a Concept*, the leaders of the *Risorgimento* were openly hostile to the Catholic Church. While there were regions where the majority of the populace were devout, following the teaching of the church, there were others who were not so contrite. Those least likely to be devout were the *Mezzogiorno* Italians. Their rebellious attitude, an attitude inherited by the Italians of the diaspora, towards the institutions that had suppressed them for generations included the church.

On the one hand, you have the socialists telling the people they need not accept their lot in life. God did not ordain the authorities over them. On the other hand, the church was telling them God's wisdom made them impoverished. Their resistance was a rebellion against God. Southern-Italians were having none of this *accept your station in life*. In her book, *Living the Revolution*, Jennifer Guglielmo wrote of one woman saying, "We want everybody to work as we work. There should no longer be either rich or poor. All should have bread for themselves and their children. We should all be equal… Jesus was a true socialist and he wanted precisely what we ask for, but the priests don't discuss this."[39]

Many Italians, as well as Italian-Americans, felt while they were simply trying to survive, the priests were living off the sweat of the poor.

---

[39] Guglielmo, Jennifer, *Living the Revolution: Italian Women's Resistance and Radicalism in New York City, 1880-1945 (Gender and American Culture)*, The University of North Carolina Press, 2012, pg. 10-11

Cristina Melone wrote of priests in *La Questione Sociale*, "You don't even work... All of your work can be reduced to singing psalms for a half hour mass every morning... You are born lazy and you will die lazy... I don't have any children, but I hope to have them, and when I do I will educate them to rebel against all the laws of oppression and obscurantism. If all mothers were to open their eye and imitate me the Catholic Church would have to close and you would have to earn an honest living like my husband."[40]

The priests, themselves, did not help matters any, living lives that fell far short of Christ's example. Priests fathering children was common and open in many parts of Italy. Neither did the people so easily accept the church's teaching that to be happy with their lot was what was best for the spiritual well-being of the *contadini*. "Roma Cimma grew up in Italy during the 1910s and related with bitterness, the priests were the richest people in the parish. They deliberately resisted educating the people so that their corrupt power could continue."[41] Such comments are consistent with many Italians' feelings toward the church. As the Old Italian proverb reminds us; if you want to be rich become a thief, policeman, or priest.

The complexity of the relationship between Italian immigrants and the Catholic Church is captured in the Italian-American classic *Christ in Concrete*. Having lost his father on Good Friday due to a construction accident, the main character, Paul, appeals to the local priest for help. The boy's family is desperate; his brothers and sisters are without food and his family has no income. At first, he is turned away because the priest is eating his dinner. A starving child is turned away because the priest's meal can't be disturbed. When he persists, he is granted entry where the lone priest is eating at a table laden with food. The priest does nothing for Paul and his family other than to give the boy a slice of strawberry shortcake.

The novel captures the variety of attitudes Italians had toward the church. On the one hand, we see Paul, who in rejecting the church and God comes to the realization he must depend on himself. On the other

---

[40] Melone, Christine, Lettera aperta: Ai preti della Chiesa di San Michele di Paterson, *La Questione Sociale*, 1907

[41] Guglielmo, Jennifer, *Living the Revolution: Italian Women's Resistance and Radicalism in New York City, 1880-1945 (Gender and American Culture)*, The University of North Carolina Press, 2012, pg. 32

hand, we have Annunziata, Paul's mother, who encourages her son to put his faith in Jesus.

Italians are very adept at recognizing the distinction between God and those who run his church. "Similarly, while the priests were demonized, Jesus was glorified as a rebel and outcast: 'Christ was born poor and died poor,' wrote *Il Proletario*, 'the priest may be born poor but dies rich.'"[42] One commentator also noted how *Christ in Concrete* "points to the failure of American Catholicism as a force that controls and subdues the immigrants' reactions to the injustices of the capitalist system that exploits as it maims and kills the Italian immigrant."[43] This, of course, leads us to the other side of this relationship, which is the Catholic Church's attitude toward the Italian immigrant.

Catholicism & Italians

You would expect the *Roman* Catholic Church to be welcoming towards newly arrived Italians, but this was hardly the case. One of the institutions most biased against Italians was the church. There were two root causes for this prejudice. The first came directly from Rome and the Vatican. As I described in the previous chapter, unification challenged papal authority. When the pope reached out to Catholics around the world to put pressure on the Italian government, he created a hostility towards Italians on the part of non-Italian Catholics. When the Italian diaspora occurred, the Irish dominated the American Catholic Church. To them, we were *the Italian problem*, challengers to the faith. Even Italians who were faithful to Catholicism were suspect.

As a way of dealing with *the Italian problem*, the American Catholic Church forbade Italians to worship with the other Catholics in the main sanctuary. This was common throughout the country. Even in the small town of Frankfurt, New York, where my grandfather had settled, the Irish-controlled Catholic Church required Italians worship in the basement. In the late 1800's, the Italians of East Harlem, desiring an alternative to New York City's Saint Patrick's Cathedral, built *Our Lady of Mt. Carmel*. They built it, with their own hands, yet they were exiled to worship in the basement. To make matters worse, the East Harlem

---

[42] Bencivenni, Marcella, *Italian Immigrant Radical Culture*, New York University Press, 2011, pg. 82

[43] Donato, Pietro di, *Christ in Concrete*, Signet Classic, 1993, pg. 26

Italian community imported a statue of Our Lady of Mt. Carmel from Italy whose vestments were made of donated jewelry. Of course, since she was Italian, she was relegated to the basement with the rest of the *dagos*.

Although Italian and Irish immigrants had much in common, there was the inevitable friction between two different cultures, in addition to the prejudice that filtered down the hierarchy from Rome. The Irish were another group that hated us when we got here. Once Italians became more accepted in the United States after World War II, many Italians and Irish intermarried, but there are still pockets of bigotry in the states.

Some years ago, I was laughing with a Boston-Irish co-worker about the biases of the old days. She warned me her mother still carried a very hot flame of hatred towards Italians. To quote her, "my mother told me she would rather see me bring a god-damned n*gg*r into her house than an Italian."

In the old days, the Irish simply did not know how to deal with Italians or our method of devotion. Other Christian faiths, including Catholicism practiced by non-Italians, are more cerebral, conceptual. They are about theology and catechism. Italian Catholicism, however, is a full body contact faith. Pietro di Donato, author of *Christ in Concrete*, when describing his Catholic experience says, "I'm a sensualist, and I respond to the sensuality of the Holy Roman Catholic Church, its art, its music, its fragrances, its colors, its architecture, and so forth – which is truly Italian. We Italians are really essentially pagans and realists."[44]

As we consider di Donato's description of Italian faith, remember the culture of the Italian immigrant. We are not talking about a people, who in their leisure, studied the theological nuances of the Didache or debated the Platonic influences on the writings of Augustine. Southern Italians were simply trying to survive. Theirs was a very practical faith, based on their daily life experience, not on abstract concepts. The art and architecture of the church and basilica gave them a sense there was something greater than themselves. It was the images and stories of the saints, saints who stood against oppressors and powerful institutions who gave them faith in God's grace. They looked for God and his miracles in the substance of their daily lives, not the intellectual musings of dried up old men.

---

[44] von Huene-Greenberg, Dorothee, *A Melus Interview: Pietro di Donato*, *Melus XIV*, 1987, pg. 33-52

It was the sensuality of Italians' faith, the earthiness, the engagement of faith in daily lives in a way that did not come through the head but through the heart, the physical, palpable experience of faith that caused the American Catholic hierarchy the most pain. Simply look at what Peter R. D'Agostino in his essay *Utterly Faithless Specimens* writes:

> *Herbert Hadley, in the Jesuit magazine America, offers a typical example of this harsh rhetoric in an attack on Italian religiosity published in 1914: "Thousands upon thousands of boys and girls beyond the age of sixteen know nothing of their prayers, nothing of their catechism and have never even been instructed for or made their First Communion or Confession. The Italian ... outside of a display at baptisms, marriages, and funerals... has little attachment to the Church, its services or its sacraments. Piety," Hadley catechized, "does not consist in processions or carrying lighted candles in prostrations before a statue of the Madonna, in processions in honor of the patron saints of villages." Instead "... true piety consists in daily fulfillment of the religious duties extracted of us by God Almighty and His Church and it consists in a love for that Church and her ministers. In these points... the Italian immigrant seems very deficient.'*[45]

Make Italy Great Again

In the conclusion of chapter 1, I described Italian culture as a river. As Italians immigrated to different parts of the world, they formed different branches of this river. Up until the period between the two world wars, the flow of Italian and Italian-American cultures ran mostly in parallel to one another. Then came World War II. The impact of Mussolini and the fascists took Italians in one direction, while the response of the United States to Mussolini's alliance with the Nazis took Italian-Americans in a completely opposite direction. For a brief period, two nations who were so closely aligned for so much of their history were divided. I want to emphasize here it was the American response to Italy's alliance with the Nazis that was the origin of the division, not fascism per se.

As the 20th century dawned, Italy was economically prosperous, but after World War I the liberal Italian government could not repeat this

---

[45] Connell, William J. & Gardaphé, Fred, (Eds), *Anti-Italianism, Essays on a Prejudice*, Palgrave Macmillan, 2010, pg. 37

economic success. Military demobilizations at the end of the war caused unemployment to soar. There was approximately a 50% increase in the wholesale price index. Meanwhile, the Bolsheviks' success in Russia emboldened the militants within the Italian Socialist Party to foment unrest within the factory workers and the day laborers in the north. This led to violent strikes, factory occupations, food riots and looting. The same turmoil taking place in the American Labor Movement was happening in Italy as well.

Italians began to feel things were out of control. The factory owners and the landlords looked to the government for help. Rather than clamping down on the militants, the government sought compromise. As part of this friendlier approach to labor, it declined to send troops to assist when workers took over and occupied factories. The government also proposed radical pro-labor legislation, such as allowing labor unions to review company books.

When events become tumultuous, when society seems to have lost its values, when different factions seem to rise up in challenge of long-held beliefs, it is easy for bombastic demagogues to puff out their chests and pontificate on how the United States, or England, or Italy, or Kuala Lumpur for that matter needs to return to the traditional values that made them great. The people look for a strong man who can seize control. In Italy, this strong man came in the form of Benito Amilcare Andrea Mussolini, *Il Duce*, who came with an entourage of futurists and nationalists.

Luigi Barzini writes of Mussolini, "If he was not the great statesman he wanted to appear, he certainly was a good politician..."[46] Mussolini was smart and charismatic, a politician who understood the mood of the Italian people in a difficult period of their history. He could not have come to power in a more peaceful time but needed the insecurity of post-World War I Italy in order to establish his political dominance. He gave the populace a simple solution to a complex set of problems while stroking their overly inflated sense of self. You are the sons and daughters of Rome! Your destiny is to recapture the greatness that was once ours! His message was to make Italy great again.

---

[46] Barzini, Luigi, *The Italians*, Simon & Schuster, 1964, pg.145

What Might Have Been

Although Mussolini started his career as a socialist, his good political sense told him he needed to differentiate himself and his party from the socialists. He needed to step out of the battles between the various political factions. By doing so, he was able to offer stability to a populace who were uncertain about their futures. He presented fascism as a pillar to which Italians could cling in uncertain times.

Italian Fascism promoted Italian nationalism and veneration of Italian tradition. The Italian male was seen as strong, disciplined, and resolute with a clear sense of purpose. Italian Fascism embraced *old world* traditional values, condemning as deviant sexual behavior such as pornography, birth control, homosexuality, and prostitution. Mussolini had a Spartan-like view of the roles men and women were to play in society stating, "War is to man what maternity is to the woman."[47]

Italian fascism ascribed to a *corporatist* economic system. In the minds of most Italian-Americans, there is little difference between communism, socialism, and fascism. They are all dismissed as totalitarian forms of government that oppress individual liberty. In actuality, it would be difficult for the three to be more different. Where communism believes the government should own everything, especially the means of production, socialism advocates the means of production are owned by the people or the workers through cooperatives. In principle, under fascism corporations and government merge, although, in reality, corporations take over the government.

Ideally, in a fascist state, the employer and the employee work together. The ideal was not the real. Again, Mussolini was a sharp politician who knew to align himself with the corporatists and landowners. He knew this was his political base; a base which expected him to get the labor unions under control. Not only did this make his primary supporters happy, a crackdown on labor unions was a blow against his political rivals, the anarchists and socialists. As a result, many of his opponents fled to the United States, further fueling Italian-American radicalism.

Fascists used nationalism as a tool to overcome the many competing factions within Italy whether they were political, regional, or social. This was a true nationalism, supplanting previous generations' *campanilismo*

---

[47] Bollas, Christopher, *Being a Character: Psychoanalysis and Self Experience*, Routledge, 1993, pg. 205

with a single national identity: one Italy, one people. Mussolini described the fascist state as:

> ... *a will to power and to government. In it, the tradition of Rome is an idea that has force. In the doctrine of Fascism, Empire is not only a territorial, military or mercantile expression but spiritual or moral. One can think of an empire, that is to say a nation that directly or indirectly leads other nations, without needing to conquer a single square kilometer of territory. For Fascism, the tendency to Empire, that is to say, to the expansion of nations, is a manifestation of vitality ... Fascism is the doctrine that is most fitted to represent the aims, the states of mind, of a people, like the Italian people, rising again after many centuries of abandonment of slavery to foreigners.*[48]

By claiming fascism would complete the unfinished work of the *Risorgimento* which would recapture the glories of Rome, the fascists were able to overcome many of the divisions that had thwarted Italian progress for centuries. The Fascists saw themselves as establishing a New Rome, an Italian Empire.

I admit at times I see, and mourn, Mussolini as a lost opportunity. As I have written, Garibaldi was to Italy what Washington was to the United States. They were both charismatic leaders who, by their personal magnetism, were able to lead a group of people to nationhood. Italy, however, has remained what the United States was after the American Revolution, a collection of states.

In the United States, however, we had a Lincoln who came along when the nation was about to split apart. Lincoln not only held the United States together but transformed the United States into a single nation. Prior to the Civil War, people would say the United States *are*. After the Civil War, we say, the United States *is*. The term is no long plural, but, as the Pledge of Allegiance initially said, *one nation with liberty and justice for all*. It is almost sacrilegious to say, but while Garibaldi was Italy's Washington, Mussolini could have been its Lincoln. Unfortunately, his flaws prevented him from a greater destiny for both himself and Italy.

In speaking of Mussolini's flaws, one of his most fatal was his brand of nationalism. There is a form of nationalism in which one nation sees itself as superior, not through an adherence to a moral code or some valued set of principles, but as an inherent element of their being. In

---

[48] Cohen, Carl, (Ed), *Communism, Fascism and Democracy: The Theoretical Foundations (2nd. Edition)*, Random House, 1988, pg. 328-339

essence, what they do, whatever it is they do, is good because they were the ones doing it. This is a destructive form, the form Mussolini preached. It is the nationalism of which George Orwell said, "is the worst enemy of peace."

There is a constructive form of nationalism, however, that unifies a people in a common heritage. It ascribes to an inviolable set of values. While there may have been Italian-American anarchists, there were many who were (are) patriotic Italian-Americans, myself included, whose patriotism is based on a commitment to these values. Even many of the *sovversivi*, radical Italian-Americans, were not opposed to the principles of the United States, but stood against institutions and individuals they felt prevented the fulfillment of those aspirations.

Recently, I was fortunate enough to be invited to attend a graduation ceremony at the United States Air Force Academy in Colorado Springs, Colorado. Each of the cadets took an oath to "protect and defend the Constitution of the United States against all enemies foreign and domestic." While other nations' officers and ministers swear loyalty to a monarch or people, in the United States the oath is to a set of ideas. Although the United States may not always live up to these principles, what makes us good, exceptional in my opinion, is these are the principles to which we aspire.

If Mussolini had established this form of nationalism, if he had embraced the virtues of *Italianità*, perhaps many of the issues that plague my beloved Italy would not be a problem today. It is stunning the opportunity lost. I am yet again reminded of the adage: of all sad words of tongue or pen, the saddest are these; what might have been.

The Admirable Italian Gentleman

Despite its faults, Mussolini's message moved the masses in Italy drawing their Italian-American relatives along with them. Fascism's nationalistic bent was enticing to Italian immigrants who nostalgically looked back on Italy with yearning hearts. As their children were being told in American schools their way of life was backward, Mussolini's message of traditional values – *La religione, la patria e la famiglia*, (religion, fatherland, and family) – was a welcome validation of their cultural identity.

Of course, Mussolini's political acumen instructed him how to best leverage the Italian-American community. The Italian government supported Italian language schools in the United States that would validate their ethnicity. Mussolini's message of nationalism supported Italian-Americans' sense of a single Italian identity. It was the message we had referenced earlier, the idea Italians, regardless of time or place, were always Italians. From the time you left the olive groves of the south or the vineyards of the north down through each generation, you were Italian, always Italian; not Tuscan, not Calabreze, but Italian.

Mussolini's popularity was not limited to Italian-Americans. Mussolini's message of a return to traditional values with the three basic principles of order, discipline, and hierarchy appealed to conservative America as well. The fascist regime's promotion of discipline, industriousness, and hard work was very much in line with the Puritan work ethic. Between 1923 and 1943, Mussolini was featured on the cover of *Time* magazine eight times, with him being named *Man of the Year* on August the 6th, 1923. There were many articles in the *Saturday Evening Post* concerning Mussolini, including a serialized autobiography. In November of 1923, the *New York Times* wrote of him, "[he] has many points in common with that of the men who inspired our own constitution – John Adams, Hamilton, and Washington." Even President Roosevelt wrote, "... I am much interested and deeply impressed by what he has accomplished and by his evidenced honest purpose of restoring Italy ... I don't mind telling you in confidence that I am keeping in fairly close touch with the admirable Italian gentleman."[49]

Not all Italian-Americans were fascist supporters, however. Approximately, ten percent of Italian-Americans stood in opposition to Mussolini.[50] The *sovversivi* in the United States were at the forefront of this resistance. *Il Duce*, in driving many of the radicals out of Italy, provided the United States with a new highly motivated first-hand set of witnesses to the excesses of the fascists. Together, with liberal intellectuals and labor unions, some Italian-Americans spoke out against fascism, forming the *Anti-Fascist Alliance of North America* as early as April of 1923, long before the rest of the United States turned against the Italian leader.

Despite the efforts of the *sovversivi*, Mussolini remained popular in the United States until his invasion of Ethiopia in 1935. From that point

---

[49] Weber, Mark, *America's Changing View of Mussolini and Italian Fascism*, http://www.ihr.org/jhr/v15/v15n3p6_weber.html

[50] Bencivenni, Marcella, *Italian Immigrant Radical Culture*, New York University Press, 2011, pg. 30

forward, the relationship between Italy and the United States began to cool considerably. Although Italy attempted to minimize its relationship with Germany, as the two nations grew closer the United States became less and less enthusiastic about the fascists and *Il Duce*. The Italian government, however, continued its outreach to Italian-Americans who continued to support Italy. In order to help the war effort in Ethiopia, Italian-American women contributed their wedding rings. Then, when the United States government embargoed copper, Italian-Americans circumvented the embargo by sending copper postcards to Italy which totaled an approximate eight hundred tons.

A Man Sent by Providence

The Catholic Church, for good reason, was one of *Il Duce*'s biggest fans. Although Mussolini was not a person of faith, as a student of Machiavelli he bore in mind Machiavelli's admonition *everyone sees what you appear to be, but few experience what you really are*. So, in public he embraced the Catholic Church, preaching a return to conservative values. Remembering Machiavelli's lessons on the power of the church, Mussolini said, "There is no need to get all tied up with anti-religiousness and give Catholics reason for unease. A fight … between Church and State, the State would lose."[51]

Contrast Mussolini's attitude with the 1920's liberal social values as well as the rise of *godless* communism, both of which threatened not only the Catholic Church's temporal authority, but its very existence. As a result of Mussolini's more *Christian* attitude, the animosity the Catholic Church felt toward the Italian government subsided as the Fascists' power rose. Pope Pius XI saw Mussolini as a man "sent by Providence" and fascism as a vehicle of "moral regeneration."

Finally, in 1929, the Concordat and Lateran Accords resolved the *Roman Question*. With these treaties, in return for papal recognition of the state of Italy, the pope was given Vatican City as a fully independent state. The church recognized Rome as the capital of the Italian government while the government recognized Rome as the center of the Catholic world. All bishops were to take an oath of loyalty to the Italian state which included being able to speak the Italian language. This was only

---

[51] Price, R.G., *Fascism Part I: Understanding Fascism and anti-Semitism*, 2003, www.rationalrevolution.net/articles/understanding_fascism.htm

logical since the clergy were essentially made into salaried and pensioned public employees.

The big win for the Catholic Church, however, was Catholicism became the de facto religion of the Italian state. In addition to a law requiring a crucifix to be placed at the front of the classroom, which we discuss in a later chapter, it also made the Catholic religion a compulsory subject in school. This was a major shift in Italy. Recall the *Risorgimento* was a secular movement with leaders who felt the church acted more often in its own best interests and not those of the common man. Mussolini recognized, as did Constantine 600 years before him, religion as a powerful political tool to solidify support; something also discussed by Machiavelli who Mussolini faithfully studied.

At first blush, this might seem like the Catholic Church, in surrendering their claim on the papal lands, gave up a great deal in return for the 44 hectares (109 acres) that make up Vatican City. The reality is, however, they were not going to get those lands back no matter what they did. Pope Pius XI was actually quite wise in accepting this reality, for by giving up something he didn't have, he was able to shape Italian attitudes in a way he wouldn't otherwise have been able. All other non-fascist groups were banned. The Catholic Church not only survived but thrived, expanding the practitioners of the faith, *The Pope's Army* as it was called, to two million people.

What is most interesting is the pope inadvertently proved Dante correct in the separation of church and state. By losing temporal power, under the fascists, the pope was able to focus on social issues he felt were neglected by the secular government. Rather than dealing with the intrigues necessary to hold power over territories, maneuvering that often undercut the message of the Gospel, the pope was able to focus specifically on moral issues. The church pursued establishing the Kingdom of Christ on earth in which Catholic culture addressed the complete life of believers.

Remembering *Il Duce*

Growing up in the United States, the only thing I knew of Mussolini was he was one of the bad guys, one of the Axis leaders. From the Three Stooges to the Marx Brothers, he was presented as Hitler's apish lackey. In many of the wartime Hollywood films or political cartoons, he was a gorilla dressed up in a military uniform with a chest covered in meaningless medals. I was to learn later some of these images originated with the *sovversivi* artist Fort Velona. When I was a boy, if the subject of

Mussolini came up, my mother would say in an upraised voice and a wag of her finger, "He got the trains to run on time!"

Given this background, while cycling through a small town in the Po region of Italy, I found several shops selling Mussolini *swag;* small busts of *Il Duce*, bobble-heads, and plaques with his image next to a quote, for example. I got the distinct feeling from several residents that Mussolini was perhaps not remembered as quite the villain he is seen as in the United States. That evening, after dinner with our chairs pulled away from the table, sipping anisette, I took the opportunity to ask a friend about what I had seen that day, and what the people thought about Mussolini today.

"So, what do they say about him back in the States? What did your parents tell you?" he asked.

I stammered. I didn't really know what to say. Since I did not really know his opinion, I was concerned I might offend him.

"Wait, I know..." he said slapping my knee. "He got the trains to run on time."

My face lit up, "How'd you know?"

"That's what they all say. It is a common statement." Then he got serious. "Look, there are a lot of things Italians don't agree about. Some say he was a good leader who made a mistake when he sided with Hitler. Some say he was terrible. The thing you have to learn is no one is all good or all bad. You told me you look up to Lorenzo Medici and I can understand that. People talk about all the art he supported, but a lot of that was for propaganda's sake. He also did some pretty terrible things. Mussolini wasn't all bad and he wasn't all good. He did a lot of things that were good for Italy. The Mafia hated him because he was doing a good job in getting rid of them. He was getting the country to move forward. And..." my friend said with a smile, "he got the trains to run on time."

Mussolini is a good case study in the difference between Italians and Italian-Americans. Italian-Americans, like most Americans, have a binary view of historical and political leaders. They are good guys or they are bad guys. Either you are a conservative or a liberal, which of those two is bad is the opposite of what you are. Most Italians I know, however, seem to accept the complexity of historical figures. So, Italians take the good with the bad, willing to give people who are not necessarily the heroes of history credit for what good they did, while accepting some of history's golden boys were simply gold plated.

A Knock on the Door at Night

While Mussolini was delivering a message of a single unified Italian national identity, Italian-Americans were being told to forget... forget they were Italian. We learned to be accepted as citizens of the United States we were required to abandon our heritage. In the introduction to *Una Storia Segreta*, Lawrence Distasi describes an exchange during the Tenney Committee hearings. The Tenney Committee was part of the California Senate Fact-Finding Subcommittee on Un-American Activities which was, roughly, the Californian equivalent of the House Committee on Un-American Activities. The committee was not only ineffective in its investigations of communist activities but was known for its violations of due process. In one hearing, Dr. Jesse Kellems, a committee member, specifically stated the only way for Italian-Americans to be happy is for them to forget. Distasi summarized the exchange as follows:

> *This did the Tenney Committee put into words what the federal government had already put into action: Italian-Americans had to prove their loyalty. The way to do that was to forget – forget what they knew, forget who they were. To become American, that is, to be trusted as loyal Americans in the crisis at hand, a kind of cultural amnesia was required.*[52]

If you were not a citizen of the United States, your loyalty was divided. Again, we see the binary thinking of Americans; there are Americans (specifically citizens of the United States – Mexicans and Canadians don't count) and everyone else. Everyone else was suspect.

As the prospect of war became more imminent, the United States government grew increasingly concerned about the Italian population. Remember, Italians accounted for the largest single ethnic group to have immigrated to the United States in the 20th century. Finally, the Alien Registration Act was passed and signed by President Roosevelt in June of 1941.

The legislation resulted in 600,000 resident Italian-Americans being required to carry identification cards with their photo. Stamped across this card were the words "enemy alien."

---

[52] DiStasi, Lawrence, (Ed), *Una Storia Segreta: The Secret History of Italian American Evacuation and Internment During World War II*, Heyday Books, 2001, pg. XVII

Think of that.

You were required to carry identification that singled you out as an enemy simply because you were Italian. Of course, you might argue these people should have become citizens but, prior to the war, there was no real compelling reason to do so. While at the same time, many who were uneducated or illiterate did not want to expose themselves to possible humiliation for no apparent reason. One 1911 study found that Italians were the least likely of all immigrant groups to become citizens. In 1920 New York, only 31% of Italian men and 27% of Italian women had become citizens.

Beyond simple registration, there were arrests. Fifteen hundred Italian-Americans were arrested for simply being Italian. Of these, 257 Italian-Americans were thought of as being such a threat to the United States they were held in internment camps for the duration of the war. These arrests included men such as Filippo Fordelone, a radio broadcaster in Los Angeles who was interned at Fort Missoula, Montana. Ezio Pinza, a renowned opera star, who was arrested obtained his freedom only through the intervention of Mayor La Guardia. During Pinza's second hearing, which was arranged by the mayor, it was revealed how his arrest was based on an unsubstantiated accusation by an unreliable witness. You can't help but wonder how many others were in similar situations. How many others had their lives overturned by unreliable witnesses, but did not have the friendship of people in high places?

When we say someone was arrested, you might envision two policemen leading a suspect away in handcuffs in the light of day, helping him into the back seat of a patrol car whereupon he is taken to the nearby police station to undergo due process. This was not the case with these arrests. Filippo Molinari's description of his arrest after the attack on Pearl Harbor is representative of what happened to many of us.

> I was the first one arrested in San Jose the night of the attack on Pearl Harbor. At 11 P.M. three policemen came to the front door and two at the back. They told me that, by order of President Roosevelt, I must go with them. They didn't even give me time to go to my room and put on my shoes. I was wearing slippers. They took me to prison... and finally to

Missoula, Montana, on the train, over the snow, still with slippers on my feet, the temperature at seventeen below and no coat or heavy clothes.[53]

Some have argued that these arrests were only upon those who were non-citizens, as if that somehow made it acceptable, but this is incorrect. The Department of Justice notes, "raids were made on scores of persons of Italian descent, most but not all of them aliens." The document goes on to state, "persons were not told of the specific reason for the raid, only that their arrest was by order of President Roosevelt."[54]

As I have said, I believe the United States is exceptional, but the internment of Italian-Americans during the war was an example of when we did not live up to our principles. To me, this is reminiscent of Aleksandr Solzhenitsyn's *The Gulag Archipelago*. Police come to the door in the dark of night. No time to change, no time to prepare for a long journey. You need to come with us, and come now. There is no time. No time. Where? Not your concern. Let's go. Then, when the sun does come up the next day, you are gone. Neighbors, friends, and co-workers find there is a hole where you once were. At the end of the journey, you are someplace far from home in the snow.

This happened to 1,500 of us.

The number of Italian-Americans interned during the war is small in comparison to those of Japanese heritage. The number of Japanese interned only increases the severity of what was done to them; it does not lessen what was done to the Italians. The role racism played in this difference is interesting. One group argued Italians and Germans were a worse threat than the Japanese. The Japanese, because of differences in appearance, stood out and could not as easily infiltrate honest and hardworking American society like the Germans and the Italians. Another group argued the Japanese *all look alike* so we can't tell which ones were *the good ones*.

Part of the government's problem with the internment of Italian-Americans is there were simply too many of us. When the War

---

[53] DiStasi, Lawrence, (Ed), *Una Storia Segreta: The Secret History of Italian American Evacuation and Internment During World War II*, Heyday Books, 2001, pg. XVII

[54] U.S. Department of Justice, *A Review of the Restrictions on Persons of Italian Ancestry During World War II*, 2001, pg. 5

Department hinted that all Italian-Americans and German-Americans might be relocated, they were quickly told to forget about it. As it was, the number of relocated Japanese had already overwhelmed the army's resources. More importantly, to remove Italian-Americans from general society would have huge economic repercussions. It was estimated nearly fifteen million people would be adversely affected if Italians were taken out of the economy. Removing such a hardworking group from the labor force would have a significant negative impact on war production as well. Don't forget Rosie the Riveter, the iconic image of a woman worker who supported the war effort, was Italian. Who would have built all those nice shiny bombers if Rosie was in Fort Missoula, Montana freezing her *scungilli* off?

The number of Italian-Americans also saved many of us from the internment camps in another way: the ballot box. Italian-Americans, especially those in the cities of the east, were losing their loyalty to the Democratic Party. Roosevelt knew well how the optics of a mass internment of Italian-Americans could easily cost him the White House.

Men such as Albert Einstein, Thomas Mann, and Bruno Frank wrote to President Roosevelt pointing out many of the people they were talking about putting into camps had been in opposition to our enemies longer than many Americans, longer than Roosevelt himself. Although there were competing views within the War Department concerning the relocation of Italians and Germans, ultimately it was the Secretary of War, Henry Stimson, who recommended Italian-Americans not be interned. So, on Columbus Day 1942, Attorney General Biddle made it known Italians would no longer be considered enemy aliens.

The damage done to Italian-Americans was not simply limited to arrest or internment, it also included the destruction of their businesses. As described in the previous chapter, many Italians were drawn to the rich fishing grounds off the west coast which were untouched in comparison to those back in Italy. Italian fishermen were restricted on where and when they could fish. Also, being considered enemy aliens, they were prohibited from wharves and piers.

Worse yet, many of the fishing boats were requisitioned by the navy, which is a nice way of saying taken. Of course, they were told they would be given *fair* compensation, but what is fair? A sale in which either party can walk away establishes a *fair* price. When the government took these boats, they were the ones who determined what was fair. Beyond the actual price, what is a fisherman without his boat? When the government took these boats, they took the livelihood of these Italian-Americans.

Losing Italianità

The message we had to forget our *Italianità* was very clear. Posters to *"not speak the language of the enemy"* with caricatures of the Axis dictators appeared in Italian neighborhoods. Italian language schools began to disappear and parents did not encourage their children to speak Italian. "A powerful message was sent and received. Italian language and culture, and those who represented either or both, represented a danger to America . . . after the war, people were afraid to be too Italian. To this day, large numbers of Italian-Americans remain in an ethnic shadow. Most feel stigmatized without knowing why."[55] This, I believe, is at the heart of the lost *Italianità* of Italian-Americans.

Often when speaking with Italian-Americans of my generation, you will hear them say, "my parents did not want us to learn to speak Italian. They wanted us to only speak English." I am third generation Italian. My parents, who were born before the war spoke Italian, it was the only way they could communicate with their parents' generation, but more on that in a bit. It was Italian-American parents who were raising children born during or after WWII that did not want their children speaking Italian. What many of my generation don't understand is it was not done out of a sense of patriotism, but from a need to fit into the rest of society, a fear of being seen as *other*. This is not a lauded virtue. It is a loss. An entire generation of Italian-Americans is cut off from the literature, poetry, and music of our people. The very meat of our culture.

Looks Like We Made It

The good news, if you could call it that, is for all our efforts Italian-Americans have arrived. We are white, part of the club. Recently, I was at a social event where a person was discussing Latinos in a very unpleasant way. "Latins are this terrible thing. Latins are that terrible

---

[55] DiStasi, Lawrence, (Ed), *Una Storia Segreta: The Secret History of Italian American Evacuation and Internment During World War II*, Heyday Books, 2001, pg XVII

thing. Latins are ruining our country," she ranted. I pointed out I was Latin. "You aren't Latin," she responded, "you're Italian." This is a real frustration for me.

Today in the United States, *Latin* has become synonymous with *Hispanic*. It is not. A *Latin* is a person of a country whose language developed from Latin. Although Latin is thought of as Roman, it was first spoken in Latium, a region of central western Italy. We, Italians, are the *original* Latins.

When you discuss the past with Italian-Americans – the lynching, the prejudice, the internment – they shrug it off. Sometimes you will hear them say every group that comes to America goes through it. You experience prejudice and social injustice, but you work hard and you will eventually work your way up the ladder. Look at the Irish. They used to have signs "Irish need not apply" but today they are like everyone else.

This may be common wisdom but, however common it may be, there is nothing wise about it. The statement is wrong on two major points. First, the idea we climb *up* a mythical ladder to find acceptance in society, a predominately white society, is inherently racist. It places all others beneath those who are deemed as white. Telling them if they work hard and forget who they are, they can someday be seen as white or at least equal to whites. "To become white is to buy into a racist insurance fraud. The message is "Become likes us, and then you too can be better than those others who cannot become like us. We'll stop racism against your people, if you help keep it alive against others."[56]

This goes to the heart of the subject of this book. Italian-Americans have lost their *Italianità* and have adopted an invented tradition substantially different from true Italian culture. This is what drove the loss. The fear of what was done to us along with the desire for acceptance has caused us to forget who we are. As Fred Gardaphé noted in his essay *Invisible People*, "By becoming white, they have paid a price, and that price is the extinction of their culture. It is that near extinction of Italian-American culture that has enabled them to remain invisible."

The idea 'we all go through it' is incorrect on another level as well. There is always a reference made to the proverbial "Irish need not

---

[56] Connell, William J., & Gardaphé, Fred, (Eds), *Anti-Italianism, Essays on a Prejudice*, Palgrave Macmillan, 2010, pg. 2.

apply" sign in these discussions. Yet, I know of no mass lynchings of the Irish or Polish. I do not know when Swedish, French, or English immigrants were interned for simply being who they were. Absent World War II, I know of no bias against Germans to the extent suffered by Italians or Japanese. African-Americans have suffered greatly in the United States; they can't as easily hide their origins as some. Neither can the Japanese hide their identity. For as we were told during World War II, they all look alike so you can't tell the good ones from the bad.

Our Invented Tradition

There is an interesting meme being passed around social media these days by conservative Italian-Americans. It shows a number of immigrant children, presumably Italian immigrant children. The caption reads "Legal Italian Immigrants did not wave Italian flags coming into America. They did not riot and try to stop the legal election process. They did not try to make America speak Italian. They learned English." Let's deconstruct this a bit.

First, Italian-Americans in the past and today quite proudly wave Italian flags. Many wear them on their clothing or have bumper stickers on their cars. Typically, Italian-Americans wave American flags as well. Really the point of the statement is that Italians did not put their *Italianità* before America, so let's address this point. Prior to World War II, Italian-Americans waved Italian flags in defiance of the government of the United States. When Italy invaded Ethiopia, Italians rallied to support Italy. As I mentioned earlier, many found ways around the copper embargo. At that same time, a rally was held in New York City, where many Italian-Americans waved Italian flags to show their support for Italy and disagreement with the government's policies.

The second error in this meme is the claim they did not riot. We discussed the activism of the Italian-Americans during the American Labor Movement. What they did during the *Crusade for Bread and Roses* was one example of the activism of many Italian-Americans. It may be technically true Italians did not try to stop a legal election, but it is also true some supported the violent overthrow of the government.

They, however, saved the best bromide for last. "They did not try to make America speak Italian. They learned English." I never had a conversation with either of my grandmothers. When they were alive, I didn't speak Italian and they didn't speak English. Pretty much every Italian I knew of that generation spoke Italian exclusively. According to the 1911 Dillingham Commission, only 23% of Italian men and 5% of Italian women spoke English.

In itself, this one meme is not significant. It is, however, indicative of the invented tradition of Italian-Americans. In today's politically correct America, ethnic stereotypes are met with an outcry across social networks and mass media, except when those stereotypes are Italian. Quite the opposite has occurred within the Italian-American community. Today, Italian-Americans embrace the stereotypes of Italians, stereotypes which previous generations have worked to dispel. More than embrace them, they have integrated these caricatures into their invented tradition along with the myths that Italian immigrants were all flag-waving uber-patriots.

We weren't.

Some of us were even terrorists.

In the next chapter, we will discuss Italian stereotypes and how they have been integrated into Italian-Americans' invented tradition.

Chapter 5: What is an Italian?

Hath Not an Italian-American Eyes

I am an Italian-American. Hath not an Italian-American eyes? Hath not an Italian-American hands, organs, dimensions, senses, affections, passions? Fed with the same food, hurt with the same weapons, subject to the same diseases, healed by the same means, warmed and cooled by the same winter and summer as an American is? If you prick us, do we not bleed? If you tickle us, do we not laugh? If you poison us, do we not die? And if you wrong us, shall we not revenge?

I have modified the words of Shakespeare's Shylock to ask about Italian-Americans what Shylock had asked about Jews. At the time Shakespeare wrote this, Jews were seen as *other*. They were different, not even human in the minds of some. For much of our history in the United States, Italian-Americans were also seen as *other*, in the sense we were something less, not even human in the minds of some.

Although today we are accepted, Italian-Americans are still seen as sometimes quirky, sometimes lustful, and sometimes even murderous. Italian stereotypes reinforce these images; whether through food labels, commercials, television shows, or movies. As I have written earlier, if you were to make some of the same types of ethnic jokes of the Jews as are made of the Italians, you would be labeled an anti-Semite. In movies, if you portrayed African-Americans with the same hackneyed images as the well-worn images of Italians, you would be a racist. With Italians, however, it's OK. Why is that?

There is an old adage: *within every lie, there is a truth and within every truth, there is a lie.* A good lie, one that is the most believable, is one that contains a bit of truth. That little seasoning of truth makes the lie much tastier, much more believable. This is part of both the pervasiveness and the acceptability of Italian stereotypes. There seems to be enough truth mixed in to give these caricatures resonance.

Rather than rejecting these images, Italian-Americans seem to have done the exact opposite. We have embraced them. We have reinforced these stereotypes through our *invented tradition*. As noted in Chapter 1, *The Awakening*, the space created in not knowing our true culture and history has been filled with what others have told us. So, in our daily lives, we act in ways that support the image rest of America has of Italians.

This creates a cycle that feeds on itself, which over time amplifies the stereotype. In essence, the image becomes the reality.

Part of this reality is we don't balk at stereotypes. Of course, there are a few organizations and various Italian-Americans who object. And they are right. We shouldn't laugh at these things. Italian-Americans, however, typically respond to these objections along the lines of, "What the hell is wrong with you? It's just a God damn joke, grow up for Christ's sake." For the most part, we kind of roll with it. Many of us, myself included at times, play up to the expectation. If you call us obnoxious and loud, we respond with a hearty *vaffanculo* (go f--- yourself). If you accuse us of being mobbed up, we respond, "You're a funny guy. Real comedian. You better be careful when you start your car, mister comedian."

At the end of the day, a lot of Italian-Americans think it is funny too. After all, who would you rather be, the virile Sonny Corleone or Puccini? If your boss gives you a hard time at the staff meeting because your report is not done on time, and when you are alone with your peers, what would you rather do: offer some Machiavellian quip or grab your crotch and say, "I got your report for you, right here."

So, let's look at some of these stereotypes.

Italian Stereotypes

There are two continua of Italian-American characters, a continuum for men and another for women. In this chapter, we will deal with the stereotypes of the Italian male that ranges from the apish to the Mafioso. The apish caricatures are presented as nearly subhuman laborers; seen most frequently in the early 20th century when Southern Italians were thought of as a race *in-between* Europeans and Africans. At the other extreme is the Mafioso who, through his scheming, can make politicians dance "like puppets on a string," as said in *The Godfather* where the Mafioso reached its apogee with Don Corleone.

Notice, as we move along this continuum, how the stereotypes become darker, more of a threat. As we shall see in our discussion, the apish Italian is a beast of burden, something that can be controlled. The momma's boy is just that, a child in an adult's body. As we move closer to the Mafioso, however, we begin to see Italians as a threat. The Guido, for example, is a sexual predator and the Mafioso is a criminal mastermind.

An important point about these continua is that they are meant to demonstrate a range of images. A particular character will not necessarily be a discreet point on this scale, but a combination of characteristics represented on it. For example, an Italian male may be seen as both a Mafioso and a momma's boy, think of the Tommy DeVito (Joe Pesci) character in *Goodfellas*. Tommy is both a merciless killer and a loving son.

An Italian Joke

As I said above, most Italian-Americans get a kick out of many of the jokes. Over the years, I have counted on a steady supply of emails from my brother poking fun at Italians. One of his most recent was, *when you have one Italian you have an organ grinder; when you have two you have an argument; when you have three you have a barbershop, and when you have four or more you have organized crime.* Admittedly, it is not one of his best, but this one captures a number of the many images of Italian-Americans, from the organ grinder to organized crime.

Today, the organ grinder is not as common a stereotype as it once was but, in its time, it was an iconic image of Italian-Americans. So, let me tell you a story about an organ grinder:

There was once a man who hated Italians. One day, as he was walking down the street with an acquaintance he vented his spleen of his dislike for Italians.

"Those Dagos are filthy people. If a WOP isn't in the mob, you can bet money that one of his paesanos are. I tell you those garlic eaters can't be trusted," the man ranted as they walked.

As luck would have it, when they turned a corner, there was an Italian organ grinder with his monkey. The mustachioed barrel-chested man sang out in Italian as he ground out a tune on the mechanical organ. The innocent chimp held its dented and tarnished tin cup up to the man.

The man looked down. His face grew red and the veins stood out in his neck. The acquaintance was sure that the man was about to kick that cute little monkey.

"Ooo – Ooo," the monkey begged with wide, trusting eyes, quite unaware that the man was ready to do him harm.

Then, suddenly, the man's countenance softened. Reaching into his pocket he pulled out a shiny new quarter and tossed it into the cup.

The man stormed off.

"Wait a minute," his acquaintance said catching up with him. "I thought you hated Italians. Now, I see you giving one money!!"

With his shoulder sagging, the man looked at his friend. "Yeah, but even Italians are cute when they're little."

Pa-dump-pum!

If you laughed at this joke you are not a terrible person. You probably don't foster some latent hatred of Italians. The joke is funny. Yet, despite its humor, in addition to the ethnic slurs, the joke touches on a number of Italian stereotypes which are what makes the joke *work*.

A joke requires some connection with the audience for it to be funny, some hook to which they can grasp. A good joke leverages something which is already out in society at large. The organ grinder and his monkey are cultural icons to which people can relate, whether they are accurate or not. Equally important to the joke is the image of Italians as hairy and ape-like. If the joke had been about someone who was Swedish or Irish it wouldn't have been funny. Swedes and the Irish are not associated with organ grinders or seen as apish.

The Monkey

There are two stereotypes in this joke. The first is the monkey while the second is the organ grinder himself. The monkey is the furthest to the left on the scale of Italian male stereotypes. The ape-like image goes back to when Italians first began to immigrate to the United States, as shown in the cartoon below. Note the simian-like features; the muzzled face, bowed arms and slouched back. The following image is taken from *Life Magazine* (1911).

A WOP
A pound of spaghett' and a red-a bandan'
A stilet' and a corduroy suit;
Add garlic wat make for him stronga da mus'
And a talent for black-a da boot!

It is a comical image, cute in a way. Looking at this cartoon, one could easily imagine the shoeshine hopping around like a chimp, arms swinging, excitedly dancing in rhythm to the shining of the shoe. Remember the period in which this cartoon was published; it was a time when Italians were seen as the *in-between* race, closely related to African-Americans. The ape reference is all part of that racism, associating Italians with Africa and Africans.

The poem beneath the image reads:

A pound of spaghett' and a red-a bandan'
A stilet' and a corduroy suit;
Add garlic wat make for him stronga da mus'
And a talent for black-a da boot!

This, of course, lists what much of America saw as the hallmarks of Italianità: spaghetti and garlic as well as a stiletto, implying criminal activity. The concluding line, however, is key – *and a talent for back-a da boot*. Again, Italians are dismissed as brutes, fit only for manual labor. Dress him up in a corduroy suit and red bandana, feed him some garlic and spaghetti, and he will be ready to do the work appropriate for him – shining the shoes of a proper white person.

You might claim I am making *much ado about nothing*, but let's understand the demeaning position of the shoeshine. In biblical times, as well as many parts of the world today, feet and shoes are seen as unclean. When Jesus washed the feet of his disciples, he was lowering himself. The act of humility was not only about performing a service, but he was touching the feet of his disciples. We see this multiple times in the scriptures. The woman who washes the feet of Jesus with her hair or when John the Baptist said he was not worthy to lace Christ's sandals.

All these acts were a symbol of humility because they involved touching the feet, an unclean part of the body.

This is still the attitude in many parts of the world today. When a shoe was thrown at President Bush, in Iraq in 2008, the thrower intended the President more humiliation than physical harm. The idea being the shoe was an unclean thing. In some cultures, it is seen as impolite to even sit with your legs crossed so that others can see the bottom of your shoes.

Even in the United States today, the shoeshine is used as a demeaning image. During the 2008 Presidential campaign, racists distributed a Photoshopped image of then-candidate Obama polishing the shoes of Sarah Palin. Added to the racist element of portraying a Harvard graduate as a shoeshine, is the image of Obama kneeling at the feet of Sarah Palin. In the cartoon above, we see this same racism applied to Italians.

So where is the truth in this lie? The image of the Italian as the laborer, the unskilled worker, of course, has its origin in when Italians first came to the United States. If you recall from Chapter 2, *To Your Scattered Bodies Go,* a large percentage of Italians were *Birds of Passage,* laborers who were in the United States to build up some savings and then return to Italy. They were simply visiting. They were not interested in starting a business or buying a farm. If the rest of America saw us as physical laborers, it is because we were.

The Italian immigrants' attitude towards education, as described in the previous chapter, did not help break the laborer stereotype either. While the children of Jewish immigrants advanced themselves, second-generation Italian-Americans continued in the blue-collar professions of their parents. Although approximately two-thirds of Italian-Americans are white-collar professionals today, we need to do better. According to at least one study, Italian-Americans have the third highest dropout rate in New York City high schools.[57]

---

[57] Milione, Vincenzo, Rosa, Ciro, & Pelizzoli, Itala, *Italian American Youth and Educational Achievement levels: How are we doing?* https://qcpages.qc.cuny.edu/calandra/sites/calandra.i-italy.org/files/files/Youth%20and%20Educational%20Achievement.pdf

The Organ Grinder

Lacking education, Italians who came to the United States did whatever they could to get by. This included various forms of panhandling which brings us back to the organ grinder. Although Generation X and Millennials may not be familiar with the organ grinder, he is one of the quintessential Italian characters.

Now, I am not certain if the inventor of the mechanical organ, the organ grinder's *instrument,* should be given credit or blame, but he was not an Italian. The mechanical organ came from northern Europe. You didn't actually play a mechanical organ as you would a normal instrument, you more or less operated it. On its side was a crank which the operator, the organ grinder, would turn in order to produce something similar to music. The turning motion is the grinding, as in the turning of a crank to grind coffee beans. There was no musical talent involved in being an organ grinder, a fact which was frequently made obvious by many of the operators' lack of rhythm in the turning of the handle. They would grind away oblivious to the actual result.

The merging of the mechanical organ with Italians was more a coincidence of history. The organ grinder was a street performer common to Europe and the United States from the late 1800's to the early 1900's, the same era as the Italian diaspora. When unskilled immigrants came to the States, one way to earn money was to lug a mechanical organ around giving street performances for whatever change passers-by would toss their way.

Today, the organ grinder may seem to have been innocent enough, a humorous image of times past. In the early twentieth century, however, they were seen as vagabonds, nothing more than extortionists and criminals. In the eyes of the public, they were, at best, witnesses to crime who would gladly accept payment for their silence. At worst, they were intimately involved in the commission of the act. Their knowledge of the neighborhoods was valuable information that could be used to plan villainy, such as when people would come and go, as well as the most vulnerable locations. During the actual crime, they could be lookouts, warning their co-conspirators if the police were nearby.

For these reasons, Mayor Fiorello La Guardia banned mechanical organs in New York City in 1936. Although some claim the mayor's love of music and disdain for the noise created by the mechanical organ played a role in the ban, I suspect it has more to do with a childhood experience. In his autobiography, he wrote, "I must have been about 10 when a street organ-grinder with a monkey blew into town. He, and particularly the monkey, attracted a great deal of attention. I can still hear the cries of the kids: 'A dago with a monkey! Hey, Fiorello, you're a dago too. Where's your monkey?' It hurt. And what made it worse, along came Dad, and he started to chatter Neapolitan with the organ-grinder... He promptly invited him to our house for a macaroni dinner. The kids taunted me for a long time after that. I couldn't understand it. What difference was there between us? Some of their families hadn't been in the country any longer than mine."[58]

If we look at some of the early images of the organ grinder, we can see how they set the stage for some of the modern-day images of Italians. We can see what typical Americans thought in the sheet music cover for the song *Organ Grinder's Swing*. The organ grinder is portrayed with a beat-up hat and large bushy mustache. He holds his monkey on a leash as it swings from the words of the title.

In 1933, shortly before LaGuardia's ban, Looney Tunes released the cartoon *The Organ Grinder* in which life in *Little Italy* is shown through the eyes of an organ grinder and his monkey. It is rich with all the stereotypes of the time. The organ grinder is fat with a thick mustache and wearing a beat-up hat. He speaks with an Italian accent replacing "the" with "da." At one point, he exclaims "What's a matta you?!" The monkey is named Tony, thus implying he too is Italian. The neighborhood also reflects the Italian stereotypes of the day. There is the fruit vendor with his pushcart, the stores with meat and cheeses hanging from the rafters, and between the buildings clotheslines sag with drying laundry.

One of the interesting aspects of Looney Tunes cartoons is their target audience was much broader than simply children. These cartoons were shown before the main feature, or between films in a double showing. To keep the adults in the audience engaged, they would add small *gags* for them. Of course, the children, who were not intended to necessarily understand the *gags*, would still assimilate the cartoon's message into their way of thinking.

One such *gag* in the above-mentioned *The Organ Grinder* is a reference to Harpo Marx, one of the Marx Brothers. As the monkey creates mischief in the neighborhood, he goes into a used clothing store where, taking a

---

[58] Perlmutter, Philip, *Legacy of Hate: A Short History of Ethnic, Religious and Racial Prejudice in America*, Routledge, 1999, pg. 231

wig and ragged hat from a mannequin, places it on his head and *mugs* for the camera with an obvious reference to Harpo. He then starts to play a harp, the instrument for which Harpo was known.

Although they were Jewish and not Italian, the Marx Brothers exploited Italian stereotypes. Leonard 'Chico' Marx speaking with a heavy faux-Italian accent had all the trappings of an Italian organ grinder save the mustache. He wore shabby clothes and had the funny hat associated with the Italian organ grinder.

He also had his brother, Adolph 'Harpo' Marx. I am hesitant in casting Harpo as the monkey to Chico's organ grinder. Such a characterization would diminish the lovable character Adolph Marx created with Harpo. Also, it would fail to recognize his great comedic and musical talents. However…

Harpo is silent while consistently performing all manner of mischievous and illogical behaviors. Often, Chico's role was to keep Harpo on a leash, at least figuratively. For example, in the film *Duck Soup* (1933), there is a scene in which Harpo is leering menacingly at a woman and starts to follow her out of a room. Chico, with a word, brings Harpo back into line. In the film *The Big Store* (1941), they have a piano duet. When Harpo starts to get carried away, a stern look from Chico quickly gets him under control. The relationship between Chico and Harpo seems to parallel the relationship between an organ grinder and his monkey.

Son of the Organ Grinder

Although I did not include the organ grinder on the continuum of Italian stereotypes, he is the predecessor of the *pizzaman* which is the second character on our continuum. As the image of the organ grinder declined in popularity, the pizzaman began to take his place. This is the mustachioed large man with a big grin on his face you see on the cover of pizza boxes and the menus of Italian restaurants.

The pizzaman and the organ grinder are of the same class of Italian males, harmless and happy. The implication, of course, is these are men without depth. From their girth, we can see they are ruled by their passions as much as the other stereotypes further along our continuum of Italian males. In this case, however, their passion is food. *A pound of spaghett', Add garlic wat make for him stronga da mus'*, and they are happy in their innocence.

In 1955, Disney released *Lady and the Tramp* with the classic pizzaman happily singing to a couple of dogs in an alley. By this time, the iconic image of a grinning Italian chef had been firmly established. After World War I, Americans began to notice Italian food, venturing into their local *Little Italies* to experience what to them were exotic Mediterranean flavors.

In that era, the 1920's, Ettore Boiardi took advantage of this trend, growing the popularity of his restaurant into a line of canned Italian meals. Soon, housewives would walk down the aisles of their grocery stores with the image of Chef Boyardee smiling at them from the shelves; the picture was complete with the full mustachioed face under a white hat and, in many cases, a nice big plate of *da spaghett'!* In combining this image with the popularity of Italian food, we can see the basis for the pizzaman stereotype.

The Momma's Boys

The Marx Brothers, organ grinders, and even Looney Tune cartoons are part of a time when Italian and Italian-American images were primarily outside the home. Then came television, and the outside world invaded the intimacy of family. In the case of Italian-Americans, beginning in the 1950's, the new media of television did, and still does, more than use Italian-American stock characters as entertainment; it helped solidify society's attitudes towards Italian-Americans. A society that *included* Italian-Americans and the attitudes they had towards themselves.

While it may seem obvious to say 1950's television was a totally different experience to what television is today, you have no idea of the extent of this difference if you have not experienced the joys of rabbit ears and VHF/UHF. The mere mention of this era brings back a flood of memories.

The television was a veritable cornucopia of adventures beyond my little pedestrian city. Experiences spilled out of that horn into my imagination taking me to places beyond my grasp. In my mind's eye, I can look down on myself in our den, cross-legged and glassy-eyed, engulfed in a non-existent reality. Saturday mornings in the early to mid-1960's was idle time for me which I put to good use, watching reruns of old television shows. While Bill Gates was learning to write software, I used my time in pursuit of such intellectual activities as determining if Lassie would get Timmy out of the well; if anyone other than Wilbur would hear Mr. Ed speak; and if Ricky, for the love of God, would let Lucy into that damn show. Half-hour, by half-hour, by half-hour, Saturday morning would creep in this petty pace from channel to channel to the last credit of recorded viewing.[59]

In addition to being shown how the rest of America lived, television also taught me, along with other Italian-Americans, what it meant to be Italian or at least what the television industry thought was Italian. The next Italian characters we will discuss are from this era, the *golden age of television*, moving us to the right on our scale of male Italian stereotypes to the *momma's boy*.

When television invaded the family home, one of those to first disembark the landing craft onto the shores of American living rooms was the little Italian immigrant, Luigi. As was common in the early 50's, CBS took the radio show *Life with Luigi* to television in 1952. It told the story of Luigi Bosco an Italian immigrant who settled in Chicago.

Each episode began with Luigi writing a letter to his *momma mia,*[60] which was the mechanism to introduce the plot for that particular evening. Usually, there was a conflict between Luigi and Pasquale, his landlord, who was trying to con Luigi into marrying his daughter Rosa. The landlord, Pasquale, was a stereotype himself. He was literally a *pizzaman*, a mustachioed rotund man who ran an Italian restaurant.

In several ways, they created in the character of Luigi Bosco a child, the consummate momma's boy. First, there was his devotion to his mother. He was obviously a loving son, certainly more than most men of his time. In each episode, he was there, faithfully writing to his loving *momma mia*, keeping her informed as to what was happening in his life. His love for her was almost palpable.

Second, he was innocent, virginal. Although this was the sexually repressed 1950's, there were ways to introduce romantic interests. Luigi,

---

[59] Tomorrow, and Tomorrow, and Tomorrow / Creeps in this petty pace from day to day / to the last syllable of recorded time, *Macbeth*, Act 5, Scene 5

[60] The salutation of Luigi's letters, "Dear *Momma Mia*," was itself a stereotype. *Momma mia* means *my mother* or *mother of mine*. It is typically an expression of surprise. No one starts a letter, Italian or otherwise, to their mother with *"Dear mother of mine."* More appropriately, Luigi would have started with *Cara Momma*, meaning *Dear Mother*, but Italians are supposed to run around all the time saying *Momma Mia!* So, that is how Luigi addresses his letter.

however, had none. As I had noted above, many of the episodes were about Luigi avoiding any romantic involvement with his landlord's daughter. Of course, the daughter was unattractive to ensure Luigi's lack of interest in her would not raise any suspicion. While there was a certain comedic value in the situation, there was nothing to prevent Luigi, other than being cast as an innocent, to have a love interest.

Finally, every momma's boy needs a momma from whom he seeks guidance. In addition to dealing with the machinations of his landlord, Luigi attended a citizenship class taught by a younger, wiser, and more responsible, Amarighan woman, Miss Spaulding. Although Luigi was older and ran his own business, he looked to this woman for direction, almost as a child would look to his mother. In one episode, Luigi was falsely accused of some offense and was about to be denied citizenship. Fortunately, Miss Spaulding was there to look out for Luigi, to protect him when he could not protect himself.

I've Been a Baaad Boy

Another Saturday morning favorite was *The Abbott and Costello Show* which ran from 1952 to 1954. This duo started off in burlesque, but then advanced to movies and eventually television. Bud Abbott was the straight man; he was the adult in the relationship. From the name, we can see he was not Italian. Lou Costello, the Italian, was the child, the momma's boy sans momma. Lou's character had the mannerisms of a boy, speaking and gesturing as a child. Typically, he would refer to himself as a boy. His catchphrase was "I've been a b-a-a-a-d boy", extending out the vowel. Frequently, Lou would have childlike spats with Stinky, played by Joe Besser (an adult). Stinky was not an adult who appeared childlike, similar to Costello's character, but was meant to be an actual child complete with the garb of Little Lord Fauntleroy.

Let's look at the context in which Lou Costello's man/child lived. The smart people in the show, the characters you might want to emulate, were the nice average Amarighan. They weren't ethnic in any regard. Whether it was Joe the cop, Sid Fields, or Hillary Brooke, they were all nice *normal* people, well-groomed and well-mannered. The entertainment industry, at the time, would have liked us to perceive these nice white characters as typical Americans.

The Italians on the show, on the other hand, were, for the most part, the source of the humor. They were the ones who made the audience laugh. In order to get this laugh, they drew on the images popular in the overall consciousness of the audience. In addition to the momma's boy character, they had their own version of the *organ grinder*, Mr. Bacciagalupe, a character who possessed all the features of the stereotype from the funny hat to the thick bushy mustache. To make the character complete, Mr. Bacciagalupe spoke in a thick Italian accent, frequently referring to Lou Costello with his Sicilian name, Luigi.

The character was played by Joe Kirk, whose actual name was Ignazio Curcuruto and Lou Costello's brother-in-law in real life. The stage name speaks volumes about American attitudes. To have changed a great name like Ignazio Curcuruto to something as banal as Joe Kirk only speaks to the insipidness of American television. It needs to be understood even though Mr. Bacciagalupe was based on an Italian stereotype, he was no less loved by Italian-Americans. Often, he mumbled in Sicilian and the Italians in the audience, who were the only ones who knew what he was saying, loved it. His little asides became an inside joke between him and Lou Costello, often causing Costello to laugh, breaking character.

Mr. Bacciagalupe would take on a variety of professions from one episode to the next: fruit vendor, grocer, baker, peanut vendor, cook, music store salesman, and barber. Either the guy couldn't hold a job or he was the most industrious man in all of New York. In either case, Mr. Bacciagalupe was exceptionally versatile. What you didn't see, however, was Mr. Bacciagalupe play a white-collar professional. In my recollection, he was never a lawyer or a doctor. After all, he was Italian.

There is an important point to make about the last name of Ignazio's character, *Bacciagalupe*. It is a common Italian last name meaning *kiss of the wolf*. In Italy, when you call someone Bacciagalupe, you are saying they are lucky; he or she has been kissed by the wolf. Although in modern times, wolves are seen as a nuisance at best, and a threat at worst, in Roman times they were seen in a more positive light. For half of February, Romans would celebrate the *Lupercalia* which was the wolf festival meant to purify the city and avert evil. Italian-Americans, however, use the name to mean dummy, but not in a mean way. Say, for example, a wife sends her husband to the store to get milk. When he returns with a bag full of groceries but no milk, she might respond by saying, "You're such a *Bacciagalupe*." At other times, you may see it used as a generic last name, as I have done throughout this book. It is somewhat equivalent to *Smith* in English. This is very convenient to tell a story about someone without identifying them, especially when that story is less than complimentary.

Everybody Loves Momma's Boy

In returning to the momma's boy stereotype, we can see this is another stock Italian character still used by television. *Everybody Loves Raymond* which ran on CBS from 1996 to 2005 focused on the life of Ray Romano who married a non-Italian girl, then moved back into his old neighborhood across from his parents. *Life with Luigi*'s momma mia was across the ocean whilst Ray Romano's mother was across the street, bringing the mother-son relationship center stage.

Most episodes of the series focused on this relationship. It was a relationship in which his mother, Marie, happily cooked and cleaned for him, competing with the Amarighan wife. She was totally dedicated to her son; Raymond was her baby boy upon whom she lavished praise for the smallest accomplishments and defended any flaws fiercely, even against other family members. The wife simply could not measure up to the mother.

The writers for *Everybody Loves Raymond* clearly understood this dynamic and played off it. At one point in the series, Raymond and his wife undergo marriage counseling which ultimately leads to a conversation with his entire family. In the scene in which they discuss their marital issues, Raymond's mother sits between him and his wife on the family sofa. As the argument comes to its climax, Raymond admits that what he wants from his wife is to be taken care of, to have someone who pampers him, doing the cooking and cleaning. His wife, Debra, responds by saying what he wants is not a wife, but a mother. Angrily, Raymond responds that is exactly what he wants, not at first realizing what he is saying. Once the words are out, everyone in the room realizes the implications of what he had said. His mother sits there, a subtle yet victorious smile on her face. The concluding scene of that particular episode is Raymond sitting at the breakfast table next to a life-size cardboard image of his mother in a wedding dress.

Guarda La Luna

The movie *Nine* captures the Italian mother/son relationship well. Daniel Day-Lewis plays the fictional movie director, Guido Cantini. At one point, in a kind of vision/flashback, his deceased mother, played by Sophia Loren, sings to him *Guarda La Luna* (Look at the Moon). In the song, in addition to telling him she will always love him and he will always be hers, she asks him if he thinks if anyone will love him as she does. That's it right there. To an Italian male, there is no other woman in life who will love him like his mother.

At the end of the movie, Guido is shown directing a scene on a large soundstage. Behind him there is scaffolding. As he directs the scene, each of the women in his life takes her place on the scaffold. The last to take her place at the center of the scaffolding is his mother, Sophia Loren. She enters holding the hand of a boy, Guido's nine-year-old self.

Concerning how much truth is in these stereotypes, the TLC series *Momma's Boys of the Bronx* captures what is going on in many Italian-American homes across the country. The *reality TV* series focused on the lives of five adult Italian-American men who still lived with their mothers. The mothers took complete care of their sons, cooking their meals, shopping for them, and doing their laundry even to the point of ironing their underwear. One son proudly proclaimed his mother did everything to take care of him so he saw no need to get married. In this aspect of our culture, Italians and Italian-Americans have much in common.

Mammoni

Italy had its own version of the TLC show, *Mammoni - Chi vuole sposare mio figlio?* (Momma's Boy's: Who Wants to Marry My Son?) Men continuing to live at home is so common in Italy they have their own word for it; *mammoni*, which roughly translates to *momma's boys*. While two-thirds of all Italian young adults continue to live at home with their mothers, this trend is more common among Italian men than women.

This is not a recent development in Italy. The very term *mammoni* was first introduced by Corrado Alvaro in his book *Il nostro tempo e la speranza* (In Our Time and Hope) which was published in 1952. At the time, Alvaro credited the phenomenon with the conditions in Italy at the end of World War II. The economy was in a shambles and the Italian army did not employ young men as they once had. Naturally, being Italian, these young men would return to the safe harbor of their mother's homes.

Today, the conditions that lead to this prolonged childhood seem only to have intensified. The life-enriching benefits of a family are diminished by the demands of providing for that family in an economy such as Italy's which has limited opportunity. At the same time, staying at home means momma is there to take care of you. She cooks, does your laundry, and even packs you a lunch to take to work. It's like when you were in the fourth grade, but now you don't have a bedtime. Why would anyone want to leave such a pampered environment?

At the same time, women are no more in a hurry to marry than men. As more opportunities open up outside the home, Italian women need not turn to the traditional role of wife and mother to find fulfillment. They are able to have careers of their own without the burden of having both a day job and a night job of caring for children and a dependent male. When working women in Italy, as like many working women around the world, return home, they have to perform the traditional work of wife and mother. Why burden yourself?

The situation is a serious problem for Italy's economy. With a birth rate of approximately 1.4, Italy has one of the lowest birth rates in the western world. It is projected that by 2050, there will be 14 million fewer Italians. Consider the impact this has on the overall economy. While other economies are expanding, Italy is faced with contracting demand. Fewer people getting married means fewer homes reducing demand for new construction. It also leads to dwindling demand for all those things that go into maintaining a home such as appliances, furniture, and electronics.

The Greaser

The *mammoni* of American television, from Luigi Bosco to Ray Romano, basically were all lovable characters. Although they were stereotypes, there was no meanness about them. Sure, they were silly. Yes, they were out of the mainstream, but they were people with good hearts and good intentions. Yet, there was a darker view of the Italian male, the *Guido*, the next stereotypical Italian on our scale. The Guido depicts Italian males as sexual predators, violent, and narcissistic. To understand the Guido, we need to understand his lineage. Both culturally and literally, the Guido is the son of the *Greaser*.

Greasers, disaffected blue-collar youth, were best known in the 1940's and 1950's. From the music to which they listened, to the way in which they dressed, to the attitude they portrayed, the Greaser subculture began in the United States and spread around the world. Working class Italian-Americans were a significantly large subset of the Greaser culture. Being a Greaser did not mean you were Italian-American, but if you were young, working class, and Italian-American in the 1950's, you were probably a Greaser.

The music of the Greaser was doo-wop, which began in black America shortly after World War II. The original doo-wop, however, was too real, too black for the palate of respectable Americans. So, corporate America, never missing an opportunity to profit from an emerging market, cleaned up doo-wop and used Italian-American performers. Since they were an *in-between race*, they were perfect to fill this role. Seen as part white and part black, Italians could bring the sense of *otherness* while still being somewhat familiar to white America. The Capris, Dion and the Belmonts, and – the Jersey Boys themselves – The Four Seasons, were all Italian-American. Doo-wop became the music of the Greaser and the Greaser became the image of the young Italian-American male.

The uniform of the Greaser was the black leather jacket, straight-legged jeans, and hair greased back into a DA (Duck's Ass). The legend is the DA was created in Philadelphia by Joe Cirello, an Italian of course. The heavily greased hair was piled high on top with the sides swept back forming a furrow down the center. Technically what made the Greaser a Greaser was his hairstyle which was the DA. The Greaser was also closely associated with cars and car repair.

At about this time, the automobile became central to American living; drive-in movies, drive-thru's, and cruising on a Saturday night. To participate in American culture in the 1950's, you needed a car. Still very much a working-class group, we Italian-Americans did not have parents who could buy us new cars. New cars? Most of our parents couldn't afford to buy us *any* kind of car, much less a new one.

Although the movie *Grease* is set in California, it captured the essence of the Greaser. As in the movie, the car was the vehicle (pun intended) by which we did more than participate in society; it was the way we established our identity. We wanted to attract girls, be considered cool, and to assert our masculinity. So, we needed more than a car, we needed a symbol of our prowess. Our necessity to be mobile became the mother of invention in terms of our mechanical skills. We learned, as they did in the movie, how to turn old wrecks into *Greased Lightning* hot rods. Powerful cars that, as John Travolta said in movie, will make the 'chicks cream.' Our parents saw this as a good thing. We were learning a skill that would support us later in life.

Greasers were all tough guys, always ready for a fight which was in their mind the measure of a man. Beer was the drink of choice, not wine. Of course, the women matched them. It was an era of big hair and lots of makeup. If they weren't chewing gum, they were smoking cigarettes.

The lives of the Greasers all took the same basic trajectory: drop out of high school, get a job, get married, and live paycheck to paycheck. If you played your cards right, you could get yourself a nice little tract house in a decent part of town.

When I think of Greasers, I think of one guy in the old neighborhood; if you will forgive the alliteration, we will call him Billy Bacciagalupe. Although this was the 1960's, a decade behind the peak period of Greasers, Billy was it… blue-collar and a pack of cigarettes rolled into the sleeve of his white tee shirt. If there wasn't a wrench of some sort in his hand, there was a beer. Billy was always ready for a fight and frequently in trouble with the law. On more than one occasion, he was brought home in the back of a cop car. He had the hands of a mechanic, and probably still does, where the grease is worked into every crack and crevice of the skin. In the entire time we were growing up on Lansing Street, there was always an old wreck or two in his driveway. I can't remember seeing any of them moving under their own power.

Aaay!!

For the rest of America, those who did not know Billy Bacciagalupe, the personification of a Greaser was Marlon Brando or James Dean, who was too cool for school. This, however, changed on January the 15th, 1974, with the airing of the first episode of *Happy Days* when we were all introduced to Arthur Fonzarelli, Duh Fonz. Like Harpo & Chico before him, Duh Fonz, an Italian character, was played by someone Jewish, Henry Winkler.

It is interesting to watch the arc of development for this character. When the series began, he was a blue-collar, high-school dropout mechanic who lived alone in an apartment. Although Duh Fonz was cleaned up for television, the image was of an oversexed male who could summon women with the snap of his fingers. There was always the threat of violence. A threat so great, and a prowess so renowned, he never actually had to resort to fighting, he simply needed to threaten it.

As I describe this character, I am struck by how little there is of anything positive about being Italian. Fonzi had the Italian name, and the negative characteristics of an Italian-American, but he wasn't at all Italian. I can't recall anything he did as part of his character that was particularly Italian. He didn't speak Italian. I can't recall him demonstrating any interest in Italian food or any recognition of his Italian heritage. So, what are we to gather from this? Why did the show's creator, Garry Marshall, an Italian-American himself, not bring out those other aspects of being Italian? Was Fonzi another stock character picked from the zeitgeist?

As the show and the character evolved, Fonzi integrated into the nice Amarighan Cunningham family. Eventually, he became a high school teacher with a family. Along with his ethnicity, he is cleansed of his roughness, making him a good Amarighan. Thank God the Cunninghams took him in, eh?

What was done to Duh Fonz has been done to many Italian-Americans on television: Peter Falk as the detective Columbo, Daniel J. Travanti as Captain Frank Furillo in *Hill Street Blues*, and Bonnie Franklin as Ann Romano in *One Day at a Time*. They are all positive images of Italian-Americans, but there is one problem. All the ethnicity has been sucked out of them. I can think of no instance when Columbo or Ann Romano demonstrated any Italian characteristics. As far as Captain Furillo is concerned, his girlfriend called him *pizzaman*, but that was about it. There is one common feature of these positive Italian-American characters – they aren't Italian. They are Amarighans with Italian names. The assimilation has become complete; they have been submerged into a milky homogeneity of bland whiteness. They are now respectable and acceptable.

The Guido

As we said earlier, the Guido evolved from the Greaser. This evolution was precipitated by three main catalysts. The first was cultural. In the sixties, everything blew up. It was the decade known for the toppling of societal mores, the most significant of which were the rules that governed sexual behavior. Where traditional values discouraged sex before marriage, the 1960's was the era of free love. The *pill* gave women greater control of their reproductive life resulting in greater sexual freedom. Men didn't need to get married for a *nice girl* to sleep with them. At the same time, many women did not see a husband and family as necessary to define their worth. As a result, marriage was delayed.

As the drive to get married at a young age decreased, so too did children's desire to leave home. The Guido became the ultimate momma's boy. Once they graduated from high school, or dropped out, they continued living with mom & dad. Mom did the cooking and cleaning while dad took care of the bothersome stuff like mortgages and utility bills. Many still worked in blue-collar jobs, as their parents had, but they did not have the previous generation's financial demands of supporting a family or even themselves. This gave them a greater disposable income as well as the time to enjoy it.

The second change was a blight unleashed on American culture that could have destroyed all of western civilization. Yes, you know what I am talking about ... *Disco*. The mere thought of the Bee Gees, the Hustle, and white polyester suites causes my hands to tremble in fear of what could have been. Alright, my hyperbole here may be demonstrating a personal bias, but disco was a major factor in the evolution of the Greaser to the Guido.

The disco was the arena in which the Guido competed for the admiration of his peers as well as sexual partners. It was a stage upon which the Guido would strut to display his faux affluence. Simple straight-legged jeans and a white tee shirt was no longer acceptable attire. Neither were calloused, grease-stained hands. So, Guido donned his designer suit, coiffed his hair, and draped himself in gold chains to give the appearance he was a person of means.

The Guido's self-absorption extended beyond the disco and Saturday night. Guidos everywhere lived in gyms, bodybuilding to get a chiseled defined look. It became a way of life, an avocation. Italian males now plucked their eyebrows, manicured their fingernails, and tanned their backsides. It is a real irony how Italian men now shave, wax, and laser hair from their bodies to appear more *cut*, when the hairy-chested male was once a symbol of Italian virility.

As mentioned with the Greaser, the Guido is always ready for a fight. The Guido has inherited a *ba fungul* attitude that can erupt into violence with the merest slight. This attitude permeates the Guido psyche. It is seen as a virtue, a symbol of strength.

The third catalyst is a fiction, a fiction Italian-Americans accepted as a truth, incorporating it into their *invented tradition*. The Guido was birthed with the movie *Saturday Night Fever* which was based on a *New York* magazine article, *The Tribal Rites of the New Saturday Night*. According to the article, what we saw in the film was a portrayal of how young Italian-Americans lived. The only trouble was it was all one big con job.

The author, Nik Cohn, openly said, "My story was a fraud," but the damage was done long before this admission. The film itself, however, created a wave of Tony Manero, the main Guido of the film, imitators. Young Italian-American men, empowered by the factors described earlier, began to live the Guido life. They all wanted to be John Travolta with the white suit and girls lusting after them. It was an image of

Italian-Americans which was a complete fabrication but made real by the behavior of those who believed this was the way to behave if you were Italian. Again, an Italian-American *invented tradition* that became a reality.

Jersey Shore

With the Guido, Italians began to be portrayed as crass, loud-mouthed, obnoxious characters. The image of the annoying, objectionable Italian-American reached its height in 2009 with the *reality* television series *Jersey Shore*. The series followed eight *Jerseyites* who, with the help of MTV, set up house in Seaside Heights, New Jersey. The house was decorated with supposed icons of Italian culture: posters of Al Pacino, Italian Flags, and a map of New Jersey tinted with three broad stripes of green, white, and red.

The series which ran from 2009 to 2012 was controversial from its beginning with its liberal use of *Guido* in its promotion of the show. The series was presented as, "eight of the hottest, tannest, craziest Guidos," while another promised the series "exposes one of the tri-state[61] area's most misunderstood species... the Guido. Yes, they really do exist! Our Guidos and Guidettes... ...." Italian-Americans are a species? There is doubt of the existence of such a species, as if we are Big Foot or the Loch Ness monster?

Jersey Shore portrayed Italian-Americans in the worst possible light. At one point, Brad Ferro, a gym teacher from North Queens Community High School, was arrested for punching Snooki, a 21-year-old girl who was a character on the show. On another occasion, Snooki herself spent a night in the drunk tank, having been arrested for public intoxication. In yet another incident, Ronald Ortiz-Magro was arrested for aggravated assault. He claimed the person he assaulted was being disrespectful to Snooki, the same character arrested for public intoxication.

It was unfortunate someone thought *Jersey Shore* was a good idea. It was even more unfortunate the series was popular. It was most unfortunate it was seen not only in the United States, but around the world as

---

[61] Tri-state is a term used across the United States, but is best known in relation to the metropolitan New York area. Tri-state in this instance refers to New York, New Jersey, and Connecticut.

representative of Italian-Americans. UNICO[62] took issue with the series and its portrayal of Italian-Americans. They rightfully saw it as "… a direct, deliberate and disgraceful attack on Italian-Americans."[63] UNICO was not alone. The National Italian-American Foundation (NAIF), the Order of the Sons of Italy in America, and Italian Aware joined in condemnation of the show.

One of the show's detractors who deserves special attention is Governor Chris Christie, the former Governor of New Jersey. Having a Sicilian mother, one would expect he would object to how Italians were portrayed. Sadly, his chief criticism seemed to be not the portrayal of Italians, but the cast was imported from New York and portrayed as being from New Jersey. Christie's problem with the show was that it, "takes a bunch of New Yorkers and drops them at the Jersey Shore and tries to sell them as the real New Jersey."[64] The case can be made as Governor of the state his chief concern should have been with how the state of New Jersey was portrayed!

The irony, however, is the behavior in the show, that many Italian-Americans found so objectionable, was the exact behavior of Chris Christie's brand. The thing for which the governor is best known is his *in your face style* of politics. The expression, *in your face*, is another way of saying boorish, abrasive, and offensive. He has called members of the media 'idiots' and berated a law student when speaking at a university. He fulfills the stereotype of the crass Italian-American; in so doing he has garnered a good deal of attention from the press. This furthers the negative Italian-American image.

Italian-Americans are seen not only by many in the United States as vulgar and common, we are also seen as that by our cousins back home in Italy. The *Jersey Shore* series is a particularly sore point. During part of the final season of the show, the cast relocated to Italy. I had the

---

[62] UNICO National is the largest Italian-American service organization in the United States. Established in Waterbury, Connecticut, in 1922, its mission is to "engage in charitable works, support higher education, and perform patriotic deeds." The name of the organization is the Italian word for "unique."

[63] *More Reality Crap Saves MTV*, 2010, https://bozell.com/more-reality-crap-saves-mtv/

[64] UNICO is Italian for unique. The word stands for Unity, Neighborliness, Integrity, Charity, Opportunity.

unfortunate experience of being in Italy at the time and their escapades frequently made the news. Italian friends would look at me expecting some kind of explanation. "I don't know," I would say with a shrug of my shoulders, "I am disgusted by it too."

Mafioso

The final Italian Stereotype to explore is the *Mafioso*. We will explore the Mafia, in more detail, in a later chapter of this book. In this chapter, however, I would like to discuss how Italian-Americans are seen by many as being *mobbed up;* i.e. part of the Mafia.

There are two basic categories of Mafia stereotypes. The first, which is modeled after the characters in *The Godfather*, is the image of the noble criminal. They are bound by a code of honor and respect. They are typically portrayed as men who are Machiavellian intellectuals. Their criminal intrigues are strategic chess-like maneuvers.

The other type is more akin to the Mafiosi you would see in the movie *Goodfellas* or the television series *The Sopranos*. With these mobsters, the code of honor is not quite there. They will turn on anyone; lifelong friends or family members. It is all about profit, making money. In *The Sopranos*, even the main character's own mother is willing to turn on him. This second type is closer to the reality. There is no romance or code of honor with the Mafia. It is an organization that deserves none of the admiration given to it by some Italian-Americans. Again, this is something we will discuss, in much more detail, later.

Perhaps one of the better movies concerning Italian-Americans and organized crime is *A Bronx Tale*. The movie contrasts a hardworking blue-collar Italian-American bus driver, Lorenzo Anello, and a local mobster, Sonny LoSpecchio. The movie shows the two men through the eyes of Lorenzo's son.

While both act as father figures to the boy, painting Sonny the Mafioso in a more favorable light than I believe he deserves, it is the father who is shown to have the real strength of character. Most importantly, the movie demonstrates that there are many Italian-Americans who are resentful of the mob and any association with it. They may not have a lot, but what they do have they came by honestly.

Bella Figura

The image of Italians, however, is the polar opposite of the mobbed-up, Italian-American Guido. As far back as the Elizabethan era, Italians have been seen to be at the forefront of fashion and grace. In *Richard II*, Shakespeare's Duke of York says, "Report of fashions in proud Italy, / whose manners still our tardy apish nation / Limps after in base imitation." Neither was Italy's leadership in the world limited to superficial fashion. Even Milton realized that to be truly educated he had to travel to Italy. He explained that Italy, "was the seat of civilization and hospitable domicile of every species of erudition."[65] These images, however, are derived from the north, not the *Mezzogiorno* where most Italian-Americans originate.

The Italian sense of style is something which is an essential attribute of their psyche; it is in their DNA. Italians refer to it as the *bella figura*, the beautiful image. It is the idea that you are conscious of the image you present to the world; you are mindful of how others see you. At first blush, you might think it simply means proper etiquette, but it is much more than correct manners. *Bella figura* is the art of living gracefully. When thinking of Italian art we think of Michelangelo's David or The Fountain of Four Rivers, or the Mona Lisa. Despite the greatness Italy has achieved in these areas, "our greatest art [*is*] the art of living."[66]

Bella figura takes into consideration not only how you appear to others, but how you treat others. The full weight of *bella figura* is not easy to communicate. In Chapter 1, *The Awakening*, I described my initial encounter with *bella figura*. When on our first night in Italy we were told by the concierge restaurants did not serve dinner to guests until after the staff had eaten. It simply wasn't proper for hungry people to serve food.

In Chapter 2, *Italy What a Concept*, I discussed Mazzini's view that Italy wasn't about individualism, but rather a community working together. Mazzini's view was shaped by the Italian sense of *bella figura*. Steven Pinker in his book *The Better Angels of Our Nature* examines how etiquette has brought about a more civilized society. He references the work of Norbert Elias who proposed that through manners Europeans took the feelings of others into consideration when acting. In this way, a sense of

---

[65] Barzini, Luigi, *The Italians*, Simon & Schuster, 1964, pg. 27

[66] Hales, Dianne, *La Bella Lingua: My Love Affair with Italian, the World's Most Enchanting Language*, Broadway Books, 2009, pg. 141

empathy was developed in western culture which, in turn, led to a more civil society.

Bella figura is, in effect, the national practice of empathy; stepping outside of yourself to look at your own behavior through the eyes of the society in which you live. Kurt Vonnegut once wrote, "We are what we pretend to be, so we must be careful about what we pretend to be." Even if you were to argue *bella figura* is an affectation put on by Italians, it is what they have become.

The evidence for this is the Italian demonstration of a genuine concern for others. If you watch, you will see this concern play out in hundreds of small ways throughout Italy. For example, my wife and I were having breakfast in a piazza in Bergamo. As we sat there sipping our cappuccinos, I noticed how many people were out walking their dogs, a lot of Italians have dogs. I also noticed the common mess that comes from dogs was not so common in Italy. Italians are conscious about cleaning up after their pets. In the United States, I have noticed this problem not only in parks, but on my front lawn, sidewalks, shopping centers, and any number of public places where dogs are allowed; including, somewhat surprisingly, airports.

The concern Italians show for others also plays large in how the nation sees social issues. During the early days of the Obama administration while visiting Italy a friend of mine could not understand the debate going on in the United States. "I don't get it; how could you not want everyone to get medical help when they needed it?" The idea that healthcare would be denied simply because of money was unfathomable. It was obvious to Italians that healthcare was a right.

Living graciously is more than outward facing, considering how we treat others. Living graciously also takes into consideration how you treat yourself. Invariably, when discussing the Italian lifestyle, there is an admiration on the part of some Americans. They will say to me, "They sure know how to live over there. Why don't we live like that?" After all, the idea of long lunches and eating good fresh food has a real appeal. The food. The wine. The more relaxed pace of life. Why would you want to live any other way? Why not live like that in the United States? The answer is simple: we can't. We cannot replicate a few select elements of their way of life because *all* aspects of the Italian way of life work together.

In the United States, life is about individualism, something which was seen, by Alexis de Tocqueville, as contrary to an egalitarian society. Not only do we not have the supportive social safety nets that can be found in Italy, Americans value wealth and social status too highly. If you were to take a two-hour lunch on a regular basis, there would be people back at the office working through lunch to get your job. Eventually, not only would they have advanced, but you would find yourself unemployed (and without healthcare).

I have painted an idyllic image of Italy. I understand not all Italians are as polite and concerned about others as I seem to be describing them. As in the United States, there is a certain percentage of the Italian population that demonstrates less than socially acceptable manners; who do not necessarily live up to the cultural standard. I also understand not all Italians are able to lead the relaxed lifestyle I have described.

Italy itself is changing. Global competition pits Italy against other countries whose cultures do not place the *quality* of a person's life as high a priority. We can see, however, the stereotype of Italian life has some substantive basis in fact. As Italy changes, as a result of our more connected world, the reality of *bella figura* may fade.

Italian Style

From my perspective, if there is any one thing that is the embodiment of Italian style, one iconic image, it is the Italian Suit. How it became this symbol was by no means an accident. In her essay, *The Double Life of the Italian Suit*[67] Courtney Ritter describes how in marketing the Italian Suit the ITC (Italian Trade Commission) did more than market a thing, a product. They created an identity associated with the suit. The identity of the Italian suit is more than an indication of financial success; it is a success with style and panache.

In marketing goods to the American public, the ITC disassociated themselves with Italian-Americans, going directly to the more general population of the United States. You did not go to Little Italy to buy an Armani suit. These suits were to be had in the more upscale, fashionable districts. This was insightful marketing. The *Made in Italy* label meant style, class, and sophistication. The images of Little Italy were the opposite. Little Italy was loud, blue-collar, crass.

---

[67] Cinotto, Simone, (Ed), *Making Italian America: Consumer Culture and the Production of Ethnic Identities (Critical Studies in Italian America)*, Fordham University Press, 2014, pg. 195

Referring to the movie *Nine*, once again, we see how Kate Hudson captures the essence of the Italian suit when speaking to the main character of the film, Guido Contini. "Style, that is what I love about your movies," she says to him. "You care as much about the suit as the man wearing it. It's the Italian man in you. Pays for the drinks… Undresses you with his eyes." She then goes on to sing her big number in the movie with the line, "I feel my body chill / Gives me a special thrill."

Now think of Kate Hudson. Now think of giving Kate Hudson *a special thrill*. It is not the Italian suit, but the Italian man who has been sold to America. And if you dress like us, you too will have that effect on women. Who would not want that?

Menefreghismo

Now compare the Italian way of living to how I have described the Guido. Where the Italian is concerned with the correct way of doing things, the Guido doesn't *give a shit*, to use their terminology. The Italians I have encountered are deferential and courteous. The Guido stares others in the face, challenging them with a "what the f--- you lookin at" defiance. A way of describing this is *menefreghismo*, which means an uncaring attitude. In Italy, *menefreghismo* is not considered a virtue as it is within some circles of the Italian-American community.

Again, part of the difference between these two images is a matter of region. The north has always been more industrialized and close to the rest of Europe. In the south, people weren't necessarily concerned with many of the niceties of the social graces. When we came to America, we continued this attitude. Appearing stylish, or carrying yourself in a certain way, did not necessarily mean a great deal after working a twelve-hour day in a sweatshop.

These differences, however, do not account for the bulk of this behavior. The image of the Italian-American, both male and female, is one of unyielding strength. The Italian-American *menefreghismo* is something which has been adopted, and only a relatively short time ago, to reflect this strength. This is not, however, the behavior of most Italian-Americans. When I was young I laughed at people whose parents would wash their mouth out with soap for using inappropriate language. My parent's punishments were enacted much more quickly and severely. You learned quickly what accepted vocabulary was. In the early 1970's one woman with whom I am unfortunately acquainted, returned from college for a visit. Every word out of her mouth was "F--- this" and "F--- that." Most people in the family thought less of her for such behavior.

In Every Lie

As I said at the beginning of this chapter, *within every lie, there is a truth and within every truth, there is a lie.* As I consider the stereotypes we have discussed above, as well as the truths upon which they are based, I think of something Frank Sinatra said,

> *You know what radio show I hated the most? It was called "Life with Luigi", With J. Carrol Naish – there's a good Italian name for you – and it was all about Italians who spoke like-a dis, and worried about ladies who squeeze-a da tomatoes on-a da fruit stand. The terrible thing was, it made me laugh. Because it did have some truth to it. We all knew guys like that growing up. But then I would hate myself for laughing at the goddamned thing.* '68

I think Sinatra answers the question I asked at the beginning of this chapter. Namely, why are Italian stereotypes OK? Sinatra points out, above, that stereotypes endure, and are propagated in our culture, because they have resonance with people; they have an element of reality. Part of the reality, as we have shown with characters such as the Guido, is how we ourselves act.

The introduction to *Life with Luigi* said that the producers were seeking to symbolize the American spirit of tolerance and goodwill by celebrating the diversity of newly-arrived immigrants to the United States. They did this with the most broadly painted stereotypes of the era. The other immigrants on the show, those in Luigi's citizenship class (Germans and Norwegians) spoke with expected accents. They demonstrated the behaviors and personality traits Americans required of German and Norwegian immigrants. Italians were not the only ones on the show who were caricatures. In a time that was unencumbered by political correctness, when *Life with Luigi* played with ethnic stereotypes, even members of those ethnic groups laughed.

So, what is the conclusion we are to draw from all this? Is there something wrong with Ray Romano or The Marx Brothers? Were Lou

---

[68] Hamill, Pete, *Why Sinatra Matters,* Little, Brown and Company, 1998, pg. 48-49

Costello and Ignazio Curcuruto doing harm to their cultural heritage? Was I wrong to repeat the organ grinder joke?

I don't think so.

Here is the conclusion I draw from all this. Like Sinatra said, it's okay to laugh. It's even okay to watch *The Godfather*, it is a great film. Even Mario Cuomo, who refused to see the film for four decades, finally admitted the artistry of it was great. We need to understand these stereotypes are a fiction with a tenuous grasp of reality. It is most important we understand what it means to be Italian, that we have a true understanding of *Italianità*. We need to replace our *invented tradition* with the reality of Italian and Italian-American culture which we will continue to do across the remaining chapters of this book.

Before proceeding, however, did you hear the one about the old Italian guy who won the lottery?

Chapter 6: Italian Steel

Italian Steel

A brief lesson in metallurgy: yield strength is the amount of stress required to permanently deform a material. Tensile strength, another attribute of material, is the amount of force something can withstand before it weakens and breaks. Italian steel is very interesting in that it has both the greatest yield and tensile strength of anything I have ever seen. In my life, I have seen Italian steel keep its true nature, regardless of the amount of stress placed upon it. It does not break.

What is Italian steel? Italian steel is Anita Garibaldi who fought shoulder to shoulder with her husband for the freedom of the Italian people. During the Ragamuffin War in Brazil, while nearing the end of her pregnancy, she was captured in the Battle of Curitibanos, but escaped on horseback. Even after the French shot the horse out from under her, heavy with child, she continued on foot. For four days, she survived without provisions until reunited with her husband. Ultimately, she gave birth to a son, Menotti, who grew up to be a freedom fighter like his mother.

She died as she had lived, fighting for Italy. In 1849, pregnant again, she defended Rome against the French with her husband, Giuseppe. During the retreat, she died from malaria in her husband's arms with the final words, "remember the children."

Although Brazilian of Portuguese ascent, she is the adopted daughter of Italy who has become a symbol of Italian unification. Many interpret her final word to remind Giuseppe of not only their own children, but all the children of Italy, making her the mother of a united country. When, in 1929, the Vatican unofficially requested the removal of Giuseppe Garibaldi's statue from the top of the *Gianicolo*, Mussolini responded by adding a statue of Anita to the top of the hill. A three-day celebration commemorated the monument's installation.

Italian steel is Maria Roda, a labor activist whose passion for social justice was born in the silk mills of Como, Italy. Immigrating to the United States in 1893, her charisma and beauty drew overwhelming crowds despite the fact she spoke only Italian. Maria was fearless in the face of authority. She challenged men to change their view of women saying, "undo the old concept that we women must always be humiliated" and "women also have a heart and a brain; a soul that must be free." About men, she said, "they spend their lives at work, in the café or tavern, with little curiosity about the moral education of their wives and children. They never offer a newspaper to their wives, never invite them to attend the lectures, and never care to interest them in the social question... You believe that a woman, who takes care of the entire home and the children, is not concerned with education, that she cannot find the time in her long day, to dedicate herself to her emancipation."[69] Maria was at the forefront of the fight for workers' and women's rights in both Italy and the United States.

Italian steel is Clorinda Menguzzato, the *Lioness of the Italian Resistance*, who fought the Nazis. Captured, tortured, raped, and set upon by wild dogs, Clorinda remained defiant in the face of death. She told her tormentors, SS officer Karl Julius Hegenbart and his assistants, "When I can no longer bear your torture, I'll sever my tongue with my teeth so as not to speak." Finally, after her refusal to break down, they took her out and shot her. They then threw her body over a cliff where it landed in the branches of the trees below. A local priest recovered her remains and buried her with honors in her village.

These women have carried within them the flame of *Italianità*, the essence of Italy, as have many other Italian and Italian-American women. Minerva, the goddess of wisdom and war, is the patron of poetry, medicine, and music. She is roughly to Italy what Uncle Sam is to the United States. Where in the States you would see the white-bearded man in red and white striped pants, in Italy you see Minerva. As you travel through the country, you see her image on schools and official seals, and her likeness in statues and as part of monuments. As we shall see in this chapter, she seems to be the template of Italian women; although wise, she is fierce in defense of those she loves.

At one point in the movie *The Godfather*, one of Michael Corleone's bodyguards tells him, "In Sicily, women are more dangerous than shotguns." Although Sicilians consider themselves Sicilian and not Italian, I believe this description holds true of all Italian women. While Anita Garibaldi, Maria Roda, and Clorinda Menguzzato are famous examples, I believe all Italian women are Italian steel. They are more

---

[69] Guglielmo, Jennifer, *Living the Revolution: Italian Women's Resistance and Radicalism in New York City, 1880-1945 (Gender and American Culture)*, The University of North Carolina Press, 2012, pg. 156

dangerous than shotguns. At first glance, this may seem like I am supporting yet another stereotype of Italians, however, the history of Italian women proves the statement's truth. Contrary to other stereotypes we have seen in the media, from round little old women dressed in black to buxom Mediterranean beauties, I can think of no single group as resilient and strong as Italian women. Throughout the years, they have suffered a great deal, yet they have persevered.

I will address female stereotypes in this chapter, but there is a dimension to Italian women that must first be addressed. Women are the center of the Italian home and family. As such, I would like to first discuss the relationship between Italian women and Italian domestic life.

Domestic Violence

To many men, women were a means to an end, not an end in and of themselves. They were a means to heighten and satisfy sexual desire. They were the means to have sons; daughters were nice, but every man wanted a son to *carry on his name*. Women provided all manner of domestic services, such as cooking, cleaning, and mending clothes. If you were a farmer, they would work in the field beside you. The attitude was "women are the earth that is to be discovered, entered, named, inseminated and, above all, owned."[70] In the minds of men, women basically were just another possession, like a sow or plow horse.

Since women were a man's possession, men felt it was their every right to beat them. It was said, "God gave the man the right to control the woman when he made him stronger."[71] The extent to which society condoned this behavior included beatings as public spectacles, taking place in the local *piazza*. In one instance of a public beating in northern Italy in the late 1800's, a man broke his wife's arm. After the doctor set the arm, the husband paid him for setting two arms. He announced to

[70] Guglielmo, Jennifer, *Living the Revolution: Italian Women's Resistance and Radicalism in New York City, 1880-1945 (Gender and American Culture)*, The University of North Carolina Press, 2012, pg. 51

[71] Guglielmo, Jennifer, *Living the Revolution: Italian Women's Resistance and Radicalism in New York City, 1880-1945 (Gender and American Culture)*, The University of North Carolina Press, 2012, pg. 25

those nearby he was paying in advance for the next time she spoke back.[72]

We should not think domestic violence is a thing of the past. Violence towards women is a serious problem in both the Italian and the Italian-American community. As recently as 1981, Italian law encouraged leniency for men who murdered women to preserve *family honor*.[73] Studies estimate that one in seven women throughout Italy are the victims of violence while in some regions this figure goes to one in five.[74] Although statistics related specifically to the Italian-American community are not available, one in three women in the United States have been the victim of domestic violence, while one in five women have suffered severe abuse. In the United States, domestic violence is most often associated with income, education, substance abuse, and the cohabitation of unmarried partners. Most of these crimes, both in Italy and the United States, go unreported. This, of course, means the frequency of such abuse is probably higher than what gets reported.

Although things have changed in many ways, at times I fear violence against women is as accepted today as in the past. For example, the promotional trailer for the debut season of *Jersey Shore*, shows a male character punching one of the female characters, Snooki, squarely in the face. If this is part of our entertainment, what is acceptable in private?

Italians are attempting to address this issue. On Valentine's Day in 2013, the comedian Luciana Littizzetto addressed this issue during the Sanremo song festival. At the festival, she said:

> *In Italy, a man kills a woman – a partner, daughter, lover, sister or "ex" – on average once every two or three days, and probably at home because the family isn't always and necessarily that magical place in which all is love. He kills her because he considers her his property, because he cannot*

---

[72] Guglielmo, Jennifer, *Living the Revolution: Italian Women's Resistance and Radicalism in New York City, 1880-1945 (Gender and American Culture)*, The University of North Carolina Press, 2012, pg. 24

[73] https://www.washingtonpost.com/world/europe/scarred-survivors-inspire-italy-to-combat-violence-on-women/2017/03/08/40d65720-03df-11e7-9d14-9724d48f5666_story.html?utm_term=.a15381fc0558

[74] http://www.lastampa.it/2015/11/25/esteri/lastampa-in-english/the-hardship-of-women-trying-to-escape-domestic-violence-in-italy-yuSvHTsBudNuk9ViNWKy9O/pagina.html

imagine that a woman might belong to herself, to be free to live as she
wants and even fall in love with another man. And we women, because we
are ingenious, often mistake all sorts of things for love. But love has damn
all to do with violence and blows... A man who beats us up does not love
us. Let us get that into our heads. Let us save it onto our hard disks...
A man who beats us up is a shit. Always. And we must understand that
straightaway, at the first slap, because then the second will come along,
and then a third and a fourth. Love creates happiness and swells the
heart. It does not break ribs and it does not leave bruises on the face.[75]

I am troubled by the term *domestic violence*. It is a nice clean antiseptic
term for something that is none of those things. What we are really
talking about is wife beating, something which is more common in the
Italian-American community than I like to admit. Years ago, I had
become friends with a divorced woman from my hometown. While
married, her husband would beat her on a regular basis. One sunny
Saturday morning, he lost his temper and took out after her. Hoping
that making the abuse public would cause it to stop, she ran out to the
front yard. Although all the neighbors were out mowing their lawns and
washing their cars, he followed her to continue the beating. No one
came to her assistance. They stood and watched. Eventually, she
divorced him, but the neighborhood in which she lived turned against
her. He was a nice guy, in their minds; she had no reason to dump him.

People who have never witnessed such beatings do not understand.
They do not know what it is like for a child to witness the beating of his
mother or sister. You go to your room, or some other corner of the
house, where you hope you will be out of harm's way. But you can still
hear it. There is no hiding from the sound: the cursing, the splintering of
wood, the crashing of dishes, and their cries for the hitting to stop.
Then there are the days afterward which are nearly as bad as the actual
beatings. You lightly walk on a veneer of tranquility, knowing a wrong
word or look will start it all over again. Then there is the meaningless
repentance of the abuser, his words of remorse carry as much weight as
the air used to say them. Feelings are tender and raw. While he is at
work, there will be peace in the home. For a time, for a brief time, there
will be some rest. Then, when he returns, the joy-dampening fear
returns with him. You know it will happen again. You know there will
be some night when you will wake up to the shouting of profanities.

---

[75] Hooper, John, *The Italians*, Penguin Books, 2015, pg. 151

That is what those nice little antiseptic words *domestic violence* mean: a beaten woman and terrorized children.

This is what a father passes to his son in some Italian families. At first, it may be a shock to learn many men who beat their wives witnessed their mothers being beaten by their fathers. You would think that to live that hell would cause them to not replicate the behavior. Unfortunately, men learn how to treat women from their fathers. Violence is an inheritance, passed from father to son, although it is not genetic. What the sons did not realize was that violence alienates women, in most cases women they sincerely loved. Many an Italian woman thought of men as vile. Many had no control over their own sexuality, forced to have sex regardless of desire. The wife-beaters, when refused by their wives, never seemed to understand that physical abuse and public humiliation turned any desire to revulsion.

The Resistance

Just as Italian sons learn from their fathers, so too do Italian daughters learn from their mothers. Women have their own subculture which dates back to life in Italy. Although women often worked in the fields, there were also times when they attended to domestic chores in communal areas such as the *piazza*. Mothers would teach their daughters the arts of spinning, weaving, or doing needlework. As they worked, older women would also share stories. Many of these stories focused on how women could undermine the dominance of men, or highlight the strength of women to stand against male suppression.

In most Italian-American households, the big event of the year was Christmas Eve dinner; what we called *The Feast of Seven Fishes*. After the main course, there is a brief rest before dessert. During this pause in the festivities, my father would hold court, telling stories of the old days with the other men. At the same time, the women would clear the table, going off to the kitchen to tidy things up a bit and make a pot of coffee. As the men sat around the table, I would hear laughter coming from the kitchen. A lot of laughter. I am sure I am not the first man to wonder what was so funny, harboring a fear it might be about us, the men. One year, I wandered in just to check out what was going on. Quickly and unceremoniously they repelled my invasion with a chorus of, "get the hell out of here, we're working." As I retreated to the safety of the other men, I heard them laughing even more heartily than before my attempted incursion.

Italian women learned from their mothers and taught their daughters how to deal with men. They advised girls, *pigghiari cu bonu* – play the fool and act submissive in order to get what you want.[76] This dynamic between husband and wife seems to permeate the very texture of Italian-American family life. To me, many Italian-American marriages seem to be a contest of wills where each party is vying for ultimate authority. Men, through sheer strength, attempt to dominate.

Yet, despite the brutality of men, women get their way, typically through subterfuge. They are like the resistance during the war. In the face of the totalitarian regime of men, they work behind the scenes undermining male rule to the extent where many become the true source of power in the family.

I have witnessed a variety of methods women have used to get their way. My paternal grandfather was a Pentecostal Christian in the early 20th century. Since part of his belief was that motion pictures were evil, he forbade my grandmother from going to the movies. Of course, she simply told my grandfather she was visiting the sick as she left the house on a circuitous route to the theater. The other women bore witness to my grandmother's visitations if anyone asked questions. This was a common practice. Women would tell their husbands they were meeting with friends to play cards, then they would gather at someone's house before going off for a night of dancing. They would all be each other's alibis.

There is an expression, "Men are like the government in Rome, all pomp; the wife is like the Mafia, all power."[77] Beyond subterfuge, women really controlled family life. When the father came home from working in the fields, the day to day household trivialities were not his concern. He simply did not bother himself with who did what to whom, or the many banalities of domesticity. This left it to the women.

They watched what happened in the village and often defined reputations. The village gossip determined if you were seen as a good or

[76] Guglielmo, Jennifer, *Living the Revolution: Italian Women's Resistance and Radicalism in New York City, 1880-1945 (Gender and American Culture)*, The University of North Carolina Press, 2012, pg. 26

[77] Gabaccia, Donna R., *From Sicily to Elizabeth Street: Housing and Social Change Among Italian Immigrants, 1880-1930 (Suny Series in American Social History)*, State University of New York Press, 1984

bad person. Women arranged the marriages and assisted at the births. In a thousand different ways, women controlled daily activities which meant they controlled the daily operations of the family. This included finances. Women typically managed the family's daily financial transactions giving them greater control of wealth than women in the rest of Europe. They also had greater control of their dowry, passing it on directly to their children when they died which also was not common in Europe.

Famiglia

If you ask most Italian-Americans what they love about being Italian, one of the first things they will list is *la famiglia*, the family, which is the center of Italian and Italian-American life. In turn, women are the center of the family. Image a group of concentric circles. The innermost circle is your mother (well, you and your mother). Next is the family, then the extended family, and finally your *paisani* – Italians from the same region or village, typically close friends. The trust of Italians and Italian-Americans fade the further you move from the center. A mother was the only person on whom you could rely, as my dear sainted Sicilian mother often reminded me, "You never trust anyone other than your mother." If you were outside of these circles, you were definitely up to no good.

I have never attended a high school reunion as a result of this suspicion of strangers. I had moved from my hometown many years ago. When my school finally did have a reunion they attempted to contact me via my sister Judy, my second mother. Now, my sister Judy is as protective of me as every good Sicilian mother is of her son. So, when they tried to get information from her on where I might be, she didn't know anything, at least that is what she told them. My understanding is the conversation went something like:

"Hi, I am trying to reach Bill Giovinazzo. He went to Notre Dame High School" – strange voice over the phone.

"Who?" – my sister.

"Bill Giovinazzo, he went to Notre Dame. I am trying to reach him."

"Who are you?"

"I am Joe Bacciagalupe. I went to school with your brother."

"I don't know you."

"Well, I am trying to reach your brother."

"I can't help you."

"But you're his sister, aren't you?"

"Yeah."

"Don't you speak with him? Can you tell me how to reach him?"

"I haven't talked to him in years. Who the hell ever talks to him?! I don't know you. Goodbye."

I wish I could capture, in text, my dear sister's sing-song way of saying goodbye. She is saying *goodbye*, but it sure sounds like *vaffanculo*.

My sister told me about the conversation when I called her on the phone which I do regularly. Of course, she would not admit to a stranger she even knew if I was alive. That was my big sister, my second mom, protecting me just like she did when I was kid.

Edward Banfield, a Harvard sociologist, described the closeness of Italian families as *amoral familism*. In the late 1950's, he studied parts of Southern Italy including the village of Montegrano (a fictional place to protect the identity of the town of Chiaromonte). In his book *The Moral Basis of a Backward Society*, a title to which I take particular exception, he makes the point "[i]t is not too much to say that most people of Montegrano have no morality except, perhaps, that which requires service to the family."[78] To Banfield, the familism of Italians was amoral since it put loyalty to family above the rest of society.

While Banfield is still cited to this day, even within Italy, his work has been discredited. You see, when Banfield described the *backward people* of Southern Italy as having an *amoral familism* he missed the point. Fortunately, Filippo Sabetti of McGill University in Canada went back to where Banfield did his study 50 years prior. "The real problem with Banfield's work, suggests Sabetti, is that he never considered whether the villagers could have been '*moral familists*', trapped inside an

---

[78] Laurino, Maria, *Were You Always an Italian? Ancestors and Other Icons of Italian America*, W.W. Norton & Company, 2000, pg. 39

exclusionary system and working as best they could to help their families survive the paradox of southern Italy's pastoral yet infertile land."[79]

Where Banfield saw poverty as the result of the bunker mentality of southern Italian families, the suspicion and distrust of non-family was really the result and not the cause of poverty. As you consider what has already been said of Italian history, it is of little wonder Italian culture is one of distrust of outsiders, especially the government. In such a climate, it was only natural for the disenfranchised working poor to develop networks of trust which relied on family and personal relationships.

Italian folk wisdom tells us a fish with his mouth shut never gets caught. The less you speak, the less that can be used against you. The Italian-American distrust of anyone outside the family is bred into us from the beginning. In many American homes, it is common for kids to have *sleepovers* where a playmate or neighborhood kid spends the night. This was not something we did growing up. Having someone outside of the family snooping around wasn't a good idea. Other Italian-Americans tell stories of how friends were asked to leave when family dinners began. The parents did not want the outsiders to learn about the inner workings of the family.

While this bunker mentality kept outsiders at a distance, it also served to advance the family. Nathan Glazer, yet another sociologist, explained in the book *Beyond the Melting Pot* that *self*-advancement is a contemporary American value, while Italians still value *family* advancement.[80] This is absolutely the case. In my own family, the attitude was that we were all links in a chain, as one link is raised so is the entire chain. There was no feeling of sibling rivalry in my family; when my brother was the first to get a college degree, we felt it was the entire family's achievement. I once explained this to an Amarighan who was shocked by the attitude. She thought it put too much pressure on a child. To me, this simply seemed to be common sense. When one of us does better, we all do better.

---

[79] Laurino, Maria, *Were You Always an Italian? Ancestors and Other Icons of Italian America*, W.W. Norton & Company, 2000, pg. 45

[80] Laurino, Maria, *Were You Always an Italian? Ancestors and Other Icons of Italian America*, W.W. Norton & Company, 2000, pg. 39

The Extended Family

Keep in mind how, as siblings married, they formed new family units. They moved from the inner circle out to the extended family. As they moved out, the bonds weakened. It is really not uncommon to see two groups within a family go decades without speaking to one another. I experienced this first hand.

From a time before I can remember, my father and my Uncle Crash[81] did not speak. I never knew what was at the heart of the schism, nor do I want to know now. If my uncle happened to be in Tony's Sweetshop (see chapter 1) at the same time as my father, the two would sit at opposite ends of the counter, not speaking. As a result, I grew up without the big extended Italian-American family. There were no grand family dinners, or picnics, or reunions. For most of my life, I didn't even know who my cousins were. Some even went to the same school as I did, but I didn't know they were family.

Years later, when my father's health declined to the point where it was apparent he did not have long to live, my Uncle Crash initiated a reconciliation between them, renewing their relationship. I was able to get to know my uncle and his family. I realized what I had missed. The Italian sense of family has a real substantive value to it.

I should also make note that while these divisions are common, they are not necessary. My other uncles, Tony and Patrick, as well as my Aunt Josephine, Uncle Pat's wife, were wise. They were like the Switzerland of my family. They stayed out of the feud. They demonstrated that while family feuds may be common, they are by no means necessary.

Divisions, like the one in my father's family, were more common amongst Italians than Italian-Americans. The strong extended family was something that happened once we arrived in the United States and was not something we brought with us, at least those of us who came from the south. Most people were somehow related in the small villages of the south, a cousin in one way or another. It was natural that divisions would grow.

Once here, Italian immigrants quickly realized the importance of the support network the web of the extended family provided. Although I

---

[81] Crash was his nickname; his given name was Ralph.

had missed out on this experience, my father and his siblings did not. The fame of my paternal grandfather's Sunday dinners far outlived him.

My grandfather was a chicken farmer in New York Mills, New York. Each Sunday, my grandfather would butcher several chickens for Sunday dinner to which most of the people from his church were invited. If my father is to be believed these bacchanalian feasts bankrupted the man. As I grew older, I became cynical of many of my father's stories, especially this one. When I was entering college, however, I met a man who recognized my name and introduced himself as a member of my grandfather's church. Without prompting, he began to tell me stories of my grandparents. He told me of the Sunday dinners where long tables were piled high with food that was freely shared with the other members of the church.

The Enemy of the *Contadini*

Beyond the government, distrust extended to the social classes and institutions that supported the government. In Gerhard Lenski's *Power and Privilege: A Theory of Social Stratification*, the merchant class along with retainers and priests supported the governing class in the suppression of the lower classes: the *contadini*. The wealthy, the aristocracy, priests, and corporations all had one intent: to leech off the work of honest working men and women.

One Sicilian woman I knew, often told me when you go into a working man's home you never touch anything that does not belong to you, no matter what it is. They worked for what they have. If you go into a rich man's home, however, you take whatever you can get into your pockets. Those bastards stole for what they got and it is okay to steal from them. As the Italian proverb reminds the worker: *the poor feed the rich* and *the peasant sows while the owner reaps*.

To Southern Italians, it was moral to steal from the rich, as they stole what they had from the workers. This attitude, which came over on the boats with the Italian immigrants, has stayed with many. My first job out of high school was in retail. It was at one of these jobs that I learned of one retired Sicilian woman who pulled off the greatest grand larceny I have ever heard of. It is known back in the hometown as *The Great Coupon Caper*.

You see, back in the days before checkout scanners and the interconnectivity of supply chains, things were very different. When manufacturers put their coupons in magazines, they had no real way to associate a particular purchase and a coupon. Today, with scanners and integrated data exchanges, the sharing of this information is virtually instantaneous. Now, there was this one very smart, very devious, Sicilian woman who in her youth had worked in retail. She knew the coupon to the retailer is as good as paper money since they are reimbursed by the manufacturer.

So, one day she went to a manager for whom she had worked in the past to make a deal. She told him that, after retirement, she and her husband read a lot of magazines which meant they ended up with a lot of coupons for which she had no use. After all, how many coupons for 15 cents off a roll of toilet paper does an old retired couple need? So, she had a proposition for her old boss. If she brought in, say 20 dollars' worth of toilet paper coupons, he would give her in return ten dollars' worth of other products. Maybe she could get five dollars' worth of hamburger and a couple of dollars' worth of eggs or bread. The manager, seeing a way to make his store more profitable, readily agreed. That was one end of the pipeline.

Now, this woman was very resourceful; she knew stores took magazines off the shelves each month and sent them to the local paper recycling plant. So, she had a proposition for the guys who ran the recycling facility. She told them she ran a small preschool, which she didn't, and her kids liked to cut out pictures from the magazines to make collages. So, she wanted to borrow for a few days some of the magazines that were to be recycled. You know, for the kids. The few scraps of paper they cut out of the magazine wouldn't be noticeable. Besides, she would make it worth their while. The people with whom she spoke were relatively low-level guys who really didn't care, so they agreed.

She started off small: 40 or 50 dollars a week to test the system. Things went well. Then she doubled it, handing the store manager a 100 to 150 dollars' worth of coupons a week. When she finally reached full production, she was turning in roughly a couple of thousand dollars, per week, in coupons and getting half back in various groceries. This meant there was more than a thousand dollars a week in pure profit for the store manager, albeit illicit profit. The guys at the recycling center got a bottle of scotch each week and an envelope with 50 bucks. Everyone was happy. Well, almost everyone. I think one of the guys at the recycling center developed a drinking problem.

This actually went on for several years until the store's parent company went bankrupt. The manager moved to Arizona and the entire operation shut down. The Sicilian woman was never caught. I don't think there was even a suspicion anything was going on. Everyone was happy, no problem.

There is no moral quandary here, at least in the mind of the woman. The corporations, because they stole to get what they got, had no legitimate claim to their wealth. This, of course, meant it was moral to steal from them. This thinking was the result of centuries of oppression. Corporations and the wealthy are all part of the same system that oppressed the workers. She was simply doing what Southern Italian women have done for centuries: protecting her family.

Vedove Bianche

This is the character of Italian women, protectors of the family. It is interesting how the Italian diaspora brought this trait out in Italian women, both in Italy and the United States. As we have discussed in previous chapters, there were many Italian men referred to as *Birds of Passage,* men who intended to come to the United States for a short period of time, build up some savings, and return home. This left many wives back home as the de facto heads of household. In turn, those areas of Italy where the women were most politically active were those that had the highest level of *birds of passage*. These Italian women, with husbands who worked in the United States, were referred to as *vedove bianche* (widows in white), and were a powerful force in bringing about political change in Italy.

The *piazza* was the focal point for Italy's various towns and cities. It was where people gathered, whether it was to find work or sell goods, which is exactly why women took their protests there. Primarily, women focused their wrath on the state. In these instances, however, the women did not limit themselves to the simple subversion they had practiced in their homes. Their resistance was overt, standing up to those in power through civil disobedience such as tax revolts and the occupation of government-owned land, to the outright destruction of private property as well as municipal offices.

Although many of these women had taken charge when men had temporarily immigrated to the United States, it would be a mistake to simply characterize them as filling a space left by men. As you read the history of the activism of Italian women, you see they are not mere stand-ins for men, but at the forefront of the movement – the prow of the proverbial ship. In many instances, women fought shoulder to shoulder with men just as Anita Garibaldi had.

During the resistance to the government in Southern Italy, there were bands of peasants labeled as brigands. Among them was Maria Pastora, *the Goddess of the Peasant War*. A folk hero to the locals, she was thought of "as a 'beautiful peasant woman who lived with her lover in the wooded mountains, fighting and robbing at his side, clad like a man, and always on horseback'…she was never captured. The last news of her was that 'she was seen in Pisticci, swathed in black; then she disappeared on horseback into the woods and was never heard of again.'"[82] I see women such as her as the bulwark of the *contadini*, standing against the aristocracy, the state, and the church.

The diaspora brought these women to America. In order to wrest a livable income from their new home, Italian women worked in the garment industry to supplement their husbands' incomes. They challenged the traditional role of women. They also challenged the image of women in terms of social activism. Just as they were at the forefront in fighting for their families in Italy, they were also leaders in the United States. In previous chapters, we discussed how Italians were a force in the labor movement. You will recall how many of those protests, such the Bread and Roses Strike in Lawrence, Massachusetts, in 1912, were led by women. They did not know, or perhaps they did not care, as women, they were not supposed to challenge authority; they did.

The women's movement in Italy was different to those in England and the United States. These were not nice upper-class feminists fighting for the right to vote, as important as that may be. To quote one source, "Some described their activism with the word *femminismo* (feminism), but more often they used *emancipazione*, because this distinguished their activism from bourgeois feminism and signified their commitment to freedom from oppression in all forms. Some did not call themselves feminists, but their actions directly challenged gender conventions and patriarchal power relations."[83] Although Italian women's right to vote was not fully recognized until 1945, their concerns had a much broader scope. They were fighting for the well-being of their families.

---

[82] Levi, Carlo, *Christ Stopped at Eboli*, Farrar, Straus, and Giroux, 2006, pg. 138-40

[83] Guglielmo, Jennifer, *Living the Revolution: Italian Women's Resistance and Radicalism in New York City, 1880-1945 (Gender and American Culture)*, The University of North Carolina Press, 2012, pg. 141

Woman's Work

In terms of supporting the family, Italian women, when they arrived in the United States, were not shy about working. Having a means through which women could contribute to the family income was important. Most of the Italian men were construction workers. Although they were the majority of unskilled workers, or perhaps because of it, Italians typically earned less than their non-Italian counterparts, even less than African-Americans. The average Italian worker earned about $300 a year while it took about $800 a year to support a family. Italian women made up the difference.

In 1905, 45% of Italian-born women were wage earners. This was twice the number for all other American women. In 1925, this rose to an incredible 85% of Italian women, both first and second generation.[84] While quite a few Italian women did *piecework* at home, the majority worked in factories. One of the many things that differentiated the Italian-American from their American counterparts was that there was no shame in women contributing to the family income.

The work ethic on the part of Italian-American women is something that came from Italy and which is a shared value to this day. In the Italy our *contadini* grandparents left, there was little distinction as to what was *woman's work* and what was not, all work was *woman's work* in Italy; it is just that some work was not *man's work.*

Italian women were responsible for the laundry, food preparation, and mending clothes, which were the tasks traditionally thought of as *woman's work* in other cultures. For Italian women, *woman's work* was actually secondary to tasks such as assisting in the fields or tending to the animals. In the winter, when there was not a great deal of work for the men to do, the women still did not rest. This was the time they turned their attention to the work that needed to be done in the home itself.

When these strong Italian women came to the United States, they raised Italian-American women who were equally strong, equally willing to work. This had an effect on Italian-American culture. In a previous chapter, I discussed how the *campanilismo* of Italy waned as Italians from

---

[84] Bevilacqua, Piero, Emigrazione transoceanica e mutamenti dell'alimetazione calabrese tra Ottocento e novecento, *Quaderni Strici*, 47, no. 2, 1981, pg. 520-555

different regions began to work and live together. Part of this cultural shift involved women working together as well. Women from Apulia developed friendships with women from Basilicata or women from Calabria with women from Abruzzo.

At the same time, as the second generation of Italian-American women began to learn how American women lived, they began to see a different freer way of living. They began to question the old ways their parents had insisted upon. They were making their own money and not necessarily beholden to a man for survival. As women began to feel a greater sense of economic freedom, they began to exercise the autonomy this gave them. Daughters would challenge their fathers, saying that since they were earning their own living they didn't have to follow their fathers' rules. While such a lack of respect would have been unthinkable back in Italy, the older generation knew that in some ways they were right. The economic freedom these women were experiencing gave them the ability to reject being imprisoned by old-world male dominated ways.

Italian Women Stereotypes

Amarighans did not quite know what to make of Italian women. Therefore, they simply bucketed them into stereotypes that fitted with their conception of who Italians were. Just as there is a continuum of Italian male stereotypes, which I discussed in the previous chapter, there is another for women. While I have presented the stereotypes as a continuum, it has really been thought of, in the past, as a binary choice. A woman was either a pure mother-like figure or a whore, i.e. the Madonna/*Puttana* complex. The complex – where men see women as either saintly mothers or prostitutes – was explored by Freud who said of men with this complex, "where such men love they have no desire and where they desire they cannot love."

An excellent example of this is in the movie *Analyze This* in which the mob boss, Paul Vitti (Robert De Niro), undergoes therapy with Dr. Ben Sobel (Billy Crystal). During the film the two have the following exchange:

Dr. Ben Sobel: What happened with your wife last night?

Boss Paul Vitti: I wasn't with my wife, I was with my girlfriend.

Dr. Ben Sobel: Are you having marriage problems?

Boss Paul Vitti: No.

Dr. Ben Sobel: Then why do you have a girlfriend?

Boss Paul Vitti: What, are you gonna start moralizing on me?

Dr. Ben Sobel: No, I'm not, I'm just trying to understand, why do you have a girlfriend?

Boss Paul Vitti: I do things with her I can't do with my wife.

Dr. Ben Sobel: Why can't you do them with your wife?

Boss Paul Vitti: Hey, that's the mouth she kisses my kids goodnight with! What are you, crazy?

In the mind of Paul Vitti, since his wife is the mother of his children, she could not possibly do things only a *puttana* would do. While, as I have noted above, this has typically been thought of as a binary choice, in the case of Italian female stereotypes, I see there are variations on each of these choices. Whereas previously discussed male stereotypes seem to be dependent on a tendency towards violence, the degree to which a woman shifts along the continuum of female stereotypes is dependent on not only their sexuality, but their sexual awareness and criminality.

A Good Woman is a Chaste Woman

The disconnect between motherhood and sexuality is ironic. Despite the Italian veneration of motherhood, there seems to be a real distaste for the reality of becoming a mother. Although I have not done a scientific study on the population of Italy, it is highly unlikely all, or even a majority of, Italians were the result of a virgin birth.

Even the anticipation of motherhood seems to be couched in niceties. Although, today, people use the word pregnant without a second thought, there was a time in the United States when you could not use the word on television. Italy seems to be stuck in this period. Women who are pregnant are referred to as being in *dolce attesa* (sweet expectation). The closer women are to giving birth, the less they are seen in public to the point where they make few public appearances in the last trimester.

In Italian folklore, a good woman was a chaste woman. There is, for example, Saint Agatha of Catania who was tortured including the removal of her breasts for having refused the advances of a Roman senator. There is also Saint Rosalia who fled an arranged marriage, choosing instead to live in the hills outside of Palermo.

Santa Lucia, a woman who plays an important role in the *Divine Comedy*, was willing to sacrifice her eyes rather than her virginity. There are multiple versions of her story, but the main points remain the same. There was a suitor who was overwhelmed with her beauty, especially her eyes. One story claims her mother, not knowing Lucia had taken a vow of chastity, betrothed her to a nobleman. Another version claims it was a powerful Roman official who had lustful designs on the maiden. He was equally captivated by her beautiful eyes. In either case, the pursuer was unwilling to take no for an answer. Lucia, rather than succumbing to his advances, presented him with her eyes on a platter. She has since become the patron saint for those with eye problems.

As I noted above, the relationships between women and men were contentious in the *Mezzogiorno* with women forming a subculture separate from men. Community matriarchs shared the stories of these saints with girls and young women. In these stories, men are the base aggressors seeking to rob the women of their virtue. This is not only reflective of the antagonistic nature of male/female relationships in Southern-Italy, it helped maintain that division. It also assisted in preserving the virginity of young girls.

The Blessed Mother

Any discussion of female purity ultimately leads to the Madonna, the Blessed Mother. In the same way that the mother is the center of the Italian family, the Madonna, Mary, is the center of the Italian spiritual family. When we pray the *Hail Mary*, we pray, "Holy Mary, mother of God." Take that in for a moment. In the prayer, Mary is not just the mother of the incarnation, but she is *the Mother of God*. This is a title given to her by the Council of Ephesus in 431 C.E. There are even factions within the Catholic Church, today, that claim she is divine. This emphasis on a feminine deity has a sense of attempting to balance masculinity and femininity in the spiritual realm which seems lacking in traditional Christianity.

The Madonna in the Madonna/*Puttana* dichotomy is Mary; she is the ultimate pure woman. While other female saints had to rise above their sexuality to establish their purity, Mary, in exceeding the piety of all other saints, had to rise above human sexuality proportionally. Mary, the actual Madonna, is the purest of the pure, so pure that – despite motherhood – she was proclaimed to have been a *perpetual virgin*. The Catholic Church maintains that before, during, and after the birth of Christ, Mary maintained her virginal integrity. The birth of Christ was just as miraculous as his conception. According to the church throughout her life, she remained celibate and bore no other children. The Catholic image of the perfect woman is one who has not been debased by sex.

Even Mary's conception was out of the norm. The Immaculate Conception is often confused with the virgin birth. Jesus was the product of the *virgin birth*. The Immaculate Conception, however, is the conception of Mary. The 51st Psalm says, "In sin did my mother conceive me." The accepted interpretation of this verse is that, at the moment of conception, we are sinful. This is the basis for the belief in *original sin* which is the sin all humanity has inherited from Adam, the first man. This is not the case with Mary, however; she is unique in that she came into this world without sin. In being the ultimate mother, *the mother of God*, and the mother of us all, she is so pure that not only does she maintain her virginity while being a mother, her very nature from the moment of conception is sinless.

God's Garden

There are many different manifestations of the Blessed Virgin Mary: Our Lady of Lourdes, Our Lady of Sorrows, Our Lady of Fatima, and even the Madonna of the Long Neck. As you travel through the United States, however, the Madonna you will find most often is Our Lady of Mount Carmel.

Mount Carmel, 20 miles from Nazareth, was the site of the first church dedicated to Mary. Carmel comes from the Hebrew *Karm el* meaning God's Garden. Mary is, in a sense, God's garden – the place where he planted his seed, whose fruit is the Lord Jesus. Recall, the angel Gabriel's greeting quoted in the *Hail Mary*, "Blessed is the fruit of thy womb Jesus." There is a significance here that often escapes the modern reader. In antiquity, they had no idea of genetics or an understanding of how conception worked. In their minds, when a man *planted his seed*, as the expression goes, he was literally planting a seed in the same sense that a farmer would plant seeds for his crop. Women were just fertile ground from which the seed sprung forth.

Mount Carmel is of particular importance to Italian immigrants. Again, the vast majority of Italian immigrants came from the *Mezzogiorno*. The majority of these immigrants left for the United States through the port of Naples. Overlooking the Bay of Naples is the Basilica Santuario Del Carmine Maggiore, The Basilica of Our Lady of Mount Carmel.

You could imagine the fear felt by these immigrants who were leaving for the United States, knowing that they would most likely never again see Italy or the families they were leaving behind. Would they survive the journey? How were they to feed themselves and their children in a place where they did not speak the language? Like many of us, they bargained with God. Going through his mother, the Our Lady of Mount Carmel version, they promised to honor her when they reached their destination. They would bring her with them and spread word of her throughout the world.

Wherever they settled, the Italian immigrants built churches to honor the Madonna whose help they implored. In Frankfort, New York, when they wouldn't let us worship in the Sanctuary of Saints Peter and Paul, we built the Church of Our Lady of Mount Carmel. In New York City, the Irish had their Saint Patrick's Cathedral, so we built the Church of Our Lady of Mount Carmel in East Harlem. In Newark, New Jersey, when the Catholic hierarchy wanted to name their church Saint Joseph's we named it Our Lady of Mount Carmel. We were good to our word.

Equally important is that the Italian community has continued to keep its word to Our Lady of Mount Carmel. Each of these parishes hold festivals in her honor. Although the congregations of some of these parishes have dwindled over the years, the feasts are still enormously popular. The feast held by the Harlem parish, for example, attracts Italian-Americans from all over the country. It is a celebration of not only Mary of Mount Carmel, but of Italian-American culture.

Mater Dolorosa

Another incarnation of Mary is the *Mater Dolorosa*. To understand a *Mater Dolorosa*, look at the statue of her in the Church of the Holy Cross in Salamanca, Spain. It shows Mary's heart pierced with seven swords. The swords represent the Seven Sorrows of Mary. These sorrows spanned the life of Christ, from the Prophecy of Simeon when Christ was a child, through to his burial after the crucifixion.

In the previous chapter, we discussed the *mammoni*, momma's boys. The *Mater Dolorosa* is the other half of that relationship. We also discussed, from the son's perspective, how the CBS television show *Everybody Loves Raymond* captured the Italian-American mother/son relationship. Here I would like to focus on the mother, Marie. Marie is a *Mater Dolorosa*, the mother of sorrows. Of course, her very name emphasizes the symbolism. Raymond's mother could never have been named Rosalie or

Annette. The sorrows of Raymond's Marie span her son's life, just as the sorrows of Mary spanned the life of Christ.

Marie gladly puts her son's desires before her own, making sure he is well aware of those sacrifices. She is motivated by wanting to serve her son. Yet, she also knows that reminding him of her sorrows enables her to manipulate him. So, while there is a sincere love, it is also tinged with an element of control. This stereotype of the *Mater Dolorosa* continues the image of Southern Italian women peddled by the Northern Italian anthropologists who saw Southern Italians as having a passion for tumult and drama.

Gina

As we move along the continuum, the next stereotype we have is the *Gina*. As a pre-teen, Gina was what we call a *tomboy*. She is the girl in the neighborhood who plays baseball, climbs trees, and rides a skateboard. In the cartoon *Dennis the Menace*, Dennis has a friend Gina Gillotti who is the iconic Gina. Compare her to Dennis' nemesis, Margaret Wade, who is all girl. Margret wears a skirt and her hair is in ringlets. Gina wears pants and her hair is straight. Where Margaret is continually carrying a doll, Gina has a baseball bat or glove.

As the Gina matures (the stereotype not the cartoon character), her tomboy attitude gives way to a more feminine side, although she never really becomes what some would call a *girly-girl*. Gina is the girl in the sundress leaning on a Vespa eating a gelato. She has long, straight, dark hair over one shoulder. While the *Gina* is attractive, her sexuality is understated. She is the Italian version of *the girl next door*, with sparkling eyes and a clear smile.

If you want to see the Gina in action, refer to the Fiat 2012 Super Bowl commercial. In the ad, a slightly less than average guy is walking down the street minding his own business carrying a latte. He is a little shorter than average and a bit disheveled. As he is walking, he notices a beautiful Italian woman in a sundress, bent over adjusting the strap of her shoe.

She catches him staring at her a bit too long. Immediately, she launches into a stream of Italian, the translation of which is, "What are you looking at!? Uh! What are you looking at!?" [SLAP!] "Are you undressing me with your eyes?"

Holding this poor sap by his tie, her voice softens and she is inches from him. "Poor guy... you can't help it? Is your heart beating?" She leans in and whispers in his ear, "Is your head spinning? Do you feel lost thinking that I could be yours forever?"

His jaw goes slack. She takes her finger and scoops a bit of the foam from his latte. As she brings it to his lips, a bit drops off into the cleavage exposed by her low-cut dress. His knees are weak. He can't believe this beautiful woman is speaking to him this way. She is so close, just about to kiss him. He closes his eyes and …

Bombshell

As we move further along the continuum, we encounter the *bombshell*. Where the Gina is innocent, the *bombshell* is not. When I think of the *bombshell*, I think of the expression: Italian girls, God's way of tapping us on the shoulder and saying "I exist."

The *bombshell* is the olive-skinned, buxom, Italian woman. She is Claudia Cardinale in the movie *The Leopard*, Sophia Loren in *Man of La Mancha*, or Monica Bellucci in *Malèna*. Italian *bombshells* are the personification of fecundity. There is a rich earthiness about them. Their sexuality is more than just sensual, although it is certainly so. It is fertility. The Italian *bombshell* takes your breath away and weakens your knees. No matter what the size of the man, the *bombshell* can easily take him down.

The Guidette

The *bombshell* gives way to the *Guidette*. I have discussed the *Guidette* in the previous chapter and her relationship to the *Guido*. Unlike the *bombshell*, though, the *Guidette*'s attitude is tinged with a hardness and, like the *Guido*, an unspoken threat of violence.

You will recall, in the previous chapter, I discussed how the characters on *Jersey Shore* exhibited violence throughout the show. Violence, however, was not just a characteristic of the male members of the cast. In one incident, for example, Samantha Giancola, also known as Sammi, punches her boyfriend in the face. *Guidettes* are as tasteless, violent, and over-sexualized as their male counterparts. They are acting out a fictional culture to replace their lost sense of *Italianità*.

The Puttana

The final stereotype of Italian women is the *puttana*, the whore. We need to realize, as we examine this particular stereotype, there is a nuanced difference between the *puttana* as seen in the United States and the *puttana* as seen in Italy. In the United States, the definition of a whore is a woman who has sex for money. Some use the term to mean a woman who is promiscuous. In either case, the term focuses on a woman's sexual behavior. In Italy, however, the branding of a Southern Italian woman as a *puttana* had an additional dimension.

As described earlier, the north saw Southern Italians as a barbarous rebellious people. This was especially the case with Southern Italian women who were far from submissive. In the minds of the northern establishment, women's resistance to northern authority was proof enough of a criminal nature. It comes as no surprise, therefore, that they should combine these stereotypes into the *puttana*, a woman with both licentious and criminal tendencies. Their supposed sexual wantonness was merely just another facet of their moral deficiency.

To give credibility to their belief, a *lesser than* people filled the south; they leaned on the work of positivist anthropologists who provided (what they claimed) were objective facts proving southern Italians were racially inferior. Remember, in this era, racism was thought to have a scientific basis. Part of the attack on Southern Italians focused on Southern Italian women. The anthropologists argued it was part of the nature of Southern Italian women to be criminals. Sexual deviancy was simply inherent in their biology. They portrayed these women as savages who had no control of their sexual appetites.

I cannot help but feel that this thinking is a matter of fantasy on the part of these northern men. Men often have this delusion that women are burning with desire for them; behind demure smiles are unseen smoldering fires of lust. As you read the writing of these Northern Italian *scientists*, you can see their imagination run away with them.

During the Italian diaspora, the British travel writer Norman Douglas thanked God for the absence of men in San Giovanni, Calabria, because it enabled him to approach women as his "chief objects of interest." These "attractive and mirthful *creatures*," he noted "had too little coyness about what was natural."[85] Carlo Levi, in his classic memoir *Christ Stopped at Eboli*, wrote, "Behind their veils the women were like wild beasts. They thought of nothing but love-making, in the most natural way in the world, and they spoke of it with a license and simplicity of language that was astonishing. When you went by them on the street their black eyes stared at you, with a slanting downward glance as if to measure your virility, and behind your back you could hear them pass whispered judgments on your hidden charms."[86]

Unfortunately for these men, Southern Italian women probably had very little interest in their *hidden charms*. Many of them were just struggling to feed their children while their husbands were away. The risk of having another mouth to feed was not worth some dalliance. Also, one needs to remember there was a high price for promiscuous women to pay. As noted earlier in this chapter, women were a source of power. In small villages there were no secrets; if a woman was sexually indiscriminate, it would quickly become a subject of gossip, spreading through the community. These were honor-based cultures where, sometimes, all you had was the respect for your name. Fear of shame in front of the entire village, most of whom were a relative of some sort, was enough to dampen any wild behavior.

If you were to look at the statistics for this period, there is nothing to indicate Southern Italian women, once freed from the dominance of their men by the diaspora, suddenly became *Italian Girls Gone Wild!* There was no increase in the birth rates for children born outside of marriage. Considering the state of birth control at the time, if Southern Italian women were truly seething with sexual desire, we would expect to see it reflected in these birth rates.

The thought of Douglas and Levi walking around Southern Italy, thinking of themselves eyed like the last *cannoli* in the *pasticceria,* is actually quite comical. As they strutted about the town thinking they were cutting quite the image for these poor peasant girls, the poor peasant girls were thinking something quite the opposite. I am quite certain Carlo Levi heard whispers after passing them on the street, but I

---

[85] Guglielmo, Jennifer, *Living the Revolution: Italian Women's Resistance and Radicalism in New York City, 1880-1945 (Gender and American Culture)*, The University of North Carolina Press, 2012, pg. 42

[86] Levi, Carlo, *Christ Stopped at Eboli*, Farrar, Straus, and Giroux, 2006, pg. 101-102

would make a substantial wager what they were saying wasn't what he was imagining.

There is an interesting difference here in how Italian women and Italian-American women were seen. What drove much of the speculation on the sexuality of southern Italian women was their intractable character. In Italy, it was assumed that a woman with a liberated spirit was also liberated from their sexual morals. This was not the case in the United States, however. Why? We have seen how Italian women who immigrated to the United States were politically active. They led major labor strikes as well as being integral to socialist and anarchist organizations. Yet, they were not seen as sexually deviant.

In the United States, women's suffrage was a movement that exceeded ethnicity. In the United States, it wasn't just Italian women who were challenging norms, but all women, women from the accepted social classes as well as women from various immigrant groups. As a result, the link between criminality and social activism was not established.

The Mob Wife

The final stereotype I would like to discuss is the *mob wife*. It is difficult to place this stereotype on the continuum. A woman can be a mob wife and still be any of the above-mentioned stereotypes.

In the old-school Mafia movies, such as *The Godfather*, the mob wife was either a Madonna or a whore. Talia Shire's character, Connie Corleone, provides a good case study of the stereotypes around Italian-American women. In the first film of the trilogy, she starts out as the blushing bride (*a Gina?*) whose character quickly becomes a *Mater Dolorosa*, brutalized by her husband. At the end of the first movie, she is an innocent who is suffering the loss of her spouse, even though he is the source of pain. In the second film, she is sleeping around and not taking responsibility for her children. Although she is sexually indiscriminate, she is not criminal. She is not involved in the machinations of the family *business*.

It is not until we reach the final film that we see her not only become the matriarch of the family, but become just as Machiavellian as her brother. Note, however, these are distinct periods in her life; when she is promiscuous she is not criminal. The wanton stage of her life gives way to the felonious. This change in Connie Corleone, I believe, represents more of a change in the times in which the screenwriters lived, as opposed to an evolution in Italian-American women. As society evolved and greater equality between the sexes developed, Italian-American women became equally criminal with Italian-American men. *Hurrah for equality!*

As Mafia movies evolved into a less romanticized view of organized crime, we see an evolution in the role of women as well. We see other fictional Italian-American women become participants in crime, e.g. *The Soprano's* Carmela Soprano. Although Carmela was not involved in the day to day activities of her husband's business, she knew enough. In one episode, for example, her husband Tony needed to make a quick get-away. As they packed, Carmela knew the hiding places of the emergency guns and cash.

In the many of the fictional accounts of the Mafia, the wives lead glamorous lives. They have nice homes, jewelry, and fancy clothes. In the film *Goodfellas,* wives are taken to the best restaurants and have front row seats at the best nightclubs. As the saying goes, don't believe what you see in the movies. This is especially the case for the lives of Mafia wives.

In a January 22nd 2018 *New Yorker* article, *Blood and Justice,* Alex Perry describes the lives of Mafia wives, specifically the lives of 'Ndrangheta (see chapter 10). In the article, he explains how women were mere possessions of the family. He outlines how, returning to the habits of royalty hundreds of years ago, fathers would use their daughters as a way to secure alliances. "Women who did not uphold exacting codes of respect were beaten, often in the street. Wives who were unfaithful, even to the memory of a husband dead for fifteen years, were killed, typically by their closest male relatives, and their bodies were often burned or dissolved in acid to be sure of erasing the family shame."[87] Not quite so glamorous, is it?

Italian Women

Looking back over the history of Italy, I see various women, both of myth and reality, that represent not only their time, but *Italianità.* If you go back to Imperial Rome, you have Livia who was a partner to Caesar Augustus in ruling the empire, often without him realizing. There is no better-known Renaissance woman, Italian or otherwise, than Dante's Beatrice. Without Beatrice there would have been no *Divine Comedy.* We

---

[87] Perry, Alex, Blood and Justice, *The New Yorker,* January 22, 2018

can go through the list: Trota, the world's first gynecologist; Artemisia Gentileschi, a Baroque painter who focused on the female experience; and Dorotea Bucca, one of the first scientists to open the field to women.

Of the Italian women of our time, Sophia Loren is one who I greatly admire. She rose from a life of poverty in a small town outside Napoli to become the first actor to receive an Academy Award for a foreign language film. Beyond her acting and great beauty, Sophia Loren has carried herself with great elegance and dignity. Despite her international fame, when interviewed, she seems to possess a gracious humility. In her films, she has portrayed so many of the types of Italian women I have described in this chapter that you cannot help but think of her as an iconic Italian woman.

When I think of Italian and Italian-American women, I also think of those of whom history will take little notice. Of course, being a *mammoni*, I also think of my mother. I am reminded of how hard she worked and the great pains she experienced in life. I cannot help but think of my Aunt Josephine whose hearty laughter is forever seared in my memory. I think of my sister, Judy, who, like my mother, worked hard and raised a family. I think of one childhood playmate who now has grown sons; how she cooks the traditional Sunday and holiday meals for them as her mother did.

I think of the Italian girls I knew as a boy whose arc of life I have witnessed. I have seen them grow from a *Gina* to mothers, and ultimately grandmothers. I see how they carry the flame of *Italianità*, passing it on to their children and grandchildren. And I think how blessed I am to have come from a culture with such strong, loving women.

Chapter 7: At the Table, No One Grows Old

The Lutefisk Garden?

I have a father-in-law who is of Swedish ancestry. For many years now, he has gotten a kick out of teasing me, in a good-natured way, about my Italian heritage. Quite frequently when we invite him to dinner he will respond in an exaggerated Amarighan version of an Italian accent, "Are we gonna eata da Pole-lent-TA and da Pasta SHOOT?!"

"Gordon," I respond, "here's a conversation that has never happened...

- You hungry?

- Yeah, sure. You wanna go grab some dinner?

- OK, what do you feel like?

- Man, I could really go for some Swedish food right now."

Whenever I tell this to anyone, they typically respond with, "There are lots of good Swedish dishes." When I ask for examples, the universal answer is *meatballs*. On occasion, they might add lutefisk, but that dish does not meet the criteria of good, plus it is more Norwegian than Swedish. For those of you who are unfamiliar with lutefisk, it is dried whitefish soaked in cold water for two weeks. Lye is then added for another two days of soaking. Now, as appetizing as this may sound, keep in mind the process also has the added benefit of reducing the protein content of the fish by more than 50%. I think we can see why there are no popular Swedish-themed restaurant chains across the United States. Have you ever eaten at a *Lutefisk Garden?*

Italian food, on the other hand, has become engrained in not only American eating habits but in many countries around the world. John Mariani, an Esquire magazine food correspondent, titled his history of Italian cooking *How Italian Food Conquered the World*. And, it has.

On a recent trip to Europe, my son and I decided to spend a few days in Paris before continuing on to Venice. Being his first visit to the City of Lights, I wanted him to experience real French food. Unfortunately, it seemed all the restaurants within walking distance of our hotel were

Italian. In all my travels, whether it be Atlanta or Australia, Tulsa or Tokyo, San Jose or Singapore, I have found Italian restaurants.

Many have suggested Italian food has had a greater impact on other countries than the whole of Italian culture. Alberto Capatti and Massimo Montanari, in their book *Italian Cuisine* remind us, "What is the glory of Dante compared to spaghetti? … pastas have entered many American homes where the name of Dante is never pronounced."[88]

Why is Italian Food So Good?

There is a pragmatic reason for the success of Italian food. In examining Italian history, we have seen the poverty of the *contadini* where the *abbondanza* of the Italian table was more myth than reality. As a result, for centuries, the ingenuity of the Italian people has focused on transforming everyday, inexpensive ingredients into meals that were both appetizing and nourishing. I know of no traditional Italian meal requiring saffron which, as of this writing, is selling for $5,000 a pound. Most ingredients to an Italian meal can be grown right in your own backyard, which they were for many of us.

In addition to the cost, is the simplicity. Italian food is easy to make. Try to make Hollandaise sauce. Go ahead, I dare you. If you are not comfortable in the kitchen, the first attempt will surely be a failure. While some Italian dishes may be more challenging than others, a simple pasta with tomato sauce is relatively quick and easy. It is not necessary to study the culinary arts. My Amarighan wife mastered *stromboli* after a conversation on the phone with my sister.

When we consider these features of Italian food, is it any wonder that it is so popular? Corporate America's restaurants and food processing companies can turn out Italian meals quickly and at a low cost. Consumers, who are equally price conscious, get a delicious but inexpensive healthy meal.

---

[88] Capatti, Alberto, Montanari, Massimo, & O'Healy, Aine (Translator), *Italian Cuisine: A Cultural History (Arts and Traditions of the Table: Perspectives on Culinary History)*, Columbia University Press, 2003, pg. XX

Life is Food

There are many reasons for the popularity of Italian food; chief among them being food is at the heart of Italian culture. Ursula Ferrigno, the renowned chef and author, wrote, "To learn about Italian food is to understand Italian people – their respect for food and the role that it has played in their history. For to Italians, food represents more than satisfying hunger: it is the focal point of their lives and their traditions … Italian food encapsulates history, tradition, and folklore, plus an acute and unique awareness of nature and seasonality."[89]

Italians do not simply eat to live. The consumption of food goes beyond providing the body with nutrients. Neither would I say we live to eat. Food, the sharing and eating of food, the time spent with friends and family at the table, is life itself. So, much of our existence is focused on food.

A Familia Communion

To Italians, food is a domestic sacrament, a family communion. Speaking within the context of Roman Catholicism, which is the dominant religion of Italians, receiving communion is the consumption of the actual flesh and blood of the Lord Jesus Christ. When we receive communion, we take Christ into our bodies; it is metabolized, making us not only of one flesh with Christ, but with all other Catholics who have consumed that same flesh.

When I was an altar boy at Saint Agnes church during communion, the choir would sing, "We are one in the spirit. We are one in the Lord." This was especially the case with the domestic communion served at the family dinner table. My parents' love provided and prepared the food. They then shared this food with the family. The same meat and bread I took in making my flesh was the same meat and bread taken in by my siblings, family members, and guests which made theirs. We were one flesh.

This is the Italian family meal.

---

[89] Ferrigno, Ursula, *Truly Italian: Quick & Simple Vegetarian Cooking*, Mitchell Beazley, 1999, pg. 5

Not only did the substance of the food become the substance of our bodies, but the familial love that was a part of the meal also became part of who we were. When I ate my mother's *escarole*,[90] what made it so good was the love with which she made it. I understand this could easily be dismissed as sentimental tripe, but the care in the preparation and presentation of the food was an expression of love. It is a caring which those who consume the food, experience in a tangible way. When something is made with love, special attention is paid to selecting the ingredients. Love is translated into making sure everything is fresh and of high quality.

I could see the love in my mother's eyes when she made one of our favorite meals. My family and I lived on the second floor of a house with three apartments. I can remember how, on more than one occasion, when opening the door to the stairway that led to our apartment, the smell of my mother's stuffed artichokes would hit me. Like a runner leaping from the blocks, I would take flight up those stairs. Rushing to the stove, I would lift the lid off the pot; I savored the fragrance as the steam rose, bathing my face. Although she did not especially crave artichokes the way I did, there was a smile on my mother's face, as she watched me eat. Looking back, I realize the pleasure she had was in knowing how happy her efforts made me.

I remember a friend once remarked how, when my mother served something, it looked like a picture out of a magazine. The care with which my mother presented the food was equal to the care she took when making it. It was all part of the experience. Her antipasto salad was served in individual bowls each with the ingredients specifically arranged the same way, all topped with an anchovy cross. When the pasta was served the sausage link was to the side on the upper right-hand corner of the plate.

Food as an expression of love is not an Italian-American thing, but is shared by Italians around the world. I believe it is something inherent in our DNA. An Italian friend, who attended college in the Los Angeles area, returned to Italy upon graduation. She thought the majority of the food in the United States was terrible; manufactured, preprocessed, artificial slop. Even the Italian-American food was not to her liking. She, like most Italians, think Italian-Americans use too much garlic; a fault to which I must confess. Upon returning to Italy, her aunties celebrated

---

[90] Some people refer to this as "Italian Wedding Soup."

166

her return by, as she phrased it, stuffing her with all of her favorite meals for her first few weeks at home.

While it may seem that I am waxing poetic in my description of the family meal, it is something of which Italians are conscious. Many years ago, when I had first started on my career, I worked for a second generation Sicilian. I was the only other Sicilian, or at least partial Sicilian, who worked in the office. I recall once, during a business meeting, how my colleague had learned another person in the company had undercut him in an unethical way. After his initial shock, he looked over at me with a pained look on his face. I happened to have been sitting next to him. "How could that guy do this to me?" he said in a hushed voice only I could hear. "He's been to my home. He's eaten at my table." To an Italian, there is something especially heinous about a man who could one day eat your bread and, another day, stab you in the back.

When a Meal is Just Food

Growing up, I thought everyone cooked the way my mother did. I realized, when I started working my first job that, even in the kitchen, there was great diversity among Italian-Americans. The holidays were approaching and I had mentioned to some co-workers during lunch how I was looking forward to my mother's lasagna. As we were discussing it, one woman mentioned she didn't have time for all that work. She said she made *lazy man's lasagna* which she described as throwing everything into a pot at once. She was an older Italian who lived alone which is no surprise with an attitude like that.

I knew of one Amarighan who, an hour before dinner, would thaw a couple of frozen chicken breasts in the microwave. She would then dump a bottle of ooze that was labeled marinade onto the flavorless lumps of meat and throw the entire thing in the oven for 30 minutes at 350 degrees. In parallel, she would boil the life out of some vegetables she pulled from the freezer. She called the mess, dinner.

Italian Men in the Kitchen

While these examples refer to various women I have known, this should not be interpreted as some sexist rant that Italian womanhood is best expressed in the kitchen. The love of preparing food, for Italians at least, is not bound by gender. My father was as at home in the kitchen as my mother. He, however, used his skills as a weapon.

I hated going to mass on Sunday morning. Rather than forcing me out of bed, my father would make what he called *The Giovinazzo Special*. He would cook potatoes, sausage, and whatever cold cuts he happened to find in the refrigerator's meat drawer in one big skillet. At the last minute, before serving, he would mix in a half dozen eggs. On those mornings, when I awoke to that wonderful aroma, we both knew the game; he would lure me out of bed with breakfast. Then, once I had eaten, there was no reason for me not to go to mass.

I promised myself, as I dozed in bed, that I would not fall for it, not this day. Then the delicious smell would wander into my room, seductively curling about me, tickling my nose, luring me to give into my desire. I would resist. I would roll over in bed, turning my face to the wall. No, I would not get up. I heard the table being set, the sound of the dishes, the clink of the knives and forks being put in place. I pulled the covers over my head. I tried not to think about it. Then I began to weigh the alternatives; was mass worse than missing my dad's Sunday breakfast? Before I knew it, I was sitting at the table. I had eaten my fill and breakfast was over. Yet again, I had given into gastronomic lust. Then as my father got up from the table, he would simply command, "Get dressed and go to mass."

Sunday Dinner

Sundays were a special day for Italians. When we first came to the United States, we worked six days a week in factories, on construction sites, and in textile mills; six long, hard days. Sunday was a precious day when we could relax with our families and enjoy one another's company. The entire extended family would come together for Sunday dinner.

Mothers, sisters, aunts, and grandmothers would spend the morning preparing the banquet. A long table would be set up with the father at the head; he was master of the feast. The rest of the family gathered around. Then they ate.

What made those meals so important – what was critical about them – was not the wonderful food, but the conversation, the stories that were told. After the meal, over an espresso and some pastry, the diners would reminisce about the old days. This was the preservation of *Italianità*, passing it from one generation to the next.

Although not a conscious objective, these meals enabled the family to remain united as well as retain our sense of *Italianità*. No one thought, "Well, if I want to maintain my ethnicity, I'd better have a bowl of pasta fazool with Uncle Tony." We ate with Uncle Tony, as well as our grandparents, and our aunts, and our cousins, and our cousin's wives, because there was a joy to being with family.

If the Italian meal is domestic communion, Sundays were familial holy days of obligation. Although you were expected to attend, the expectation was based on the belief a person who appreciated their family would be willing to set aside time to be with them. In those days, you didn't pass on the family meal for a football game or a day skiing. There was no television blaring in the background.

The Sunday family dinner, for the Italian immigrant, was the point at which the past and the future converged. It was, at one and the same time, a meal in which the past was remembered and the promise of life in America was celebrated. It enabled the children and grandchildren of those who came here, to hear first-hand the stories of the old country, to understand the world left behind. In Italy, the *contadini* were hungrily scratching out an existence on tired land. The stories of those times were told around the table; a table which held an abundance of food. It was an abundance that gave the once impoverished people hope for tomorrow. It was an abundance that gave testimony to the hope of life in America.

This is the meaning of the Italian expression *a tavola non s'invecchia* (at the table no one grows old). There is an important point concerning the translation. The word used in this expression for table is feminine, *tavola*, as opposed to the masculine, *tavolo*. In Italian, when you speak of a table as a piece of furniture you use the masculine form of the word; e.g. *il tavolo della cucina* – the kitchen table; or *il tavolo da biliardo* – the pool table. When you are referring to the place where the family shares a meal, as in the expression above, you use the feminine. It is something much more than a piece of furniture; it is the place where people come together in communion.

At the table, *tavola*, we do not age. For it is at the table where all the people who were part of our past are brought back to life. At the table, my father told us of the grandfather I had never met. At the table, my mother told us of how she was abandoned as an infant by her mother, as well as the love she had for her father. At the table, my siblings told stories of their own childhood and the mischief they created. At my table, my children hear these same stories as well as some of my own.

For a time, all those generations are brought back together in one place, *la tavola*. My father and mother are young again, my brothers are teenagers, and my sister is a young Italian beauty.

As important as these stories were in providing us with a knowledge of the previous generations, it was also in these stories that we defined our morality, our ethics. We did not need to hear a list of rules; we were given case studies of the previous generations. When my father talked about how he had almost no education, which resulted in a life of physical labor, we came to understand the nobility of manual labor and the value of an education. When my mother told us of her father's devotion to her, we understood the importance of a loving relationship between a father and daughter. No one needed to tell us to treat our daughters well. We knew from the examples we were given.

Each week, I see on social media friends from my hometown who post their plans for the Sunday dinner ritual, complete with a description of the menu. One friend, Denise, in particular, discusses the care she has taken in the preparation of the meal. She proclaims with pride, "The sauce is simmering, the meatballs are frying, and my sons are on their way." I am more than a little envious of her and her family. I am familiar with the bouquet of aromas that must emanate from her kitchen, the sons arriving and kissing their mother on the cheek as they pass through, then joining their father to watch the game while waiting for dinner to be served. This simple observance of the Sunday dinner ritual quietly preserves Italian culture in a concrete way.

Italian and Italian-American Eating Habits

In the transformation from Italian to Italian-American, both what and how we eat has evolved. While many Italian-Americans try to preserve some traditions, many more are quickly becoming Amarighan. Perhaps the meal we have most in common with Italians is breakfast, although there are some significant differences. In Italy, breakfast is frequently a quick meal. When eaten at home, it is simply some bread or roll with a little jam or butter. Often breakfast is purchased at the local bar on the way to work or school. People will have a café latte with a *biscotto* or light pastry such as a *cornetto* or *sfogliatelle*.

We should note the difference here between a bar in the United States and a bar in Italy. The two could not be more different. When you go to a bar in the United States you are going there to drink. While there may be food available, the attraction to most American bars is alcohol. Many of the corner neighborhood bars on the east coast are windowless stuffy places. In Italy, a bar is a place where you can grab a quick bite to eat. They are airy and full of natural light. In the morning, there are various types of pastry and as you move on to the afternoon they will start to put out their lunchtime foods, such as *panini*. So, when you hear of an Italian stopping at a bar on the way to work, they may not necessarily have a drinking problem. They are simply hungry.

Today in the States, breakfast is also a quick affair. If we eat at home, we will have some manufactured cereal where the salt, sugar, and fat are hidden to salve our dietary conscience. Alternatives for the health food enthusiasts include granola bars covered in chocolate and gummy bears or custards labeled as yogurt. If we do grab breakfast on the way to work, it is typically a sausage & egg or bacon & egg breakfast sandwich accompanied by greasy hash browns. Note that I do not mean to denigrate the American breakfast; I love greasy hash browns! While Italians may grab a light snack midway through the morning, an American who is particularly lucky will arrive at the office to find that some kind soul had brought in donuts; deep fried, icing coated, sprinkle-bearing donuts. To quote Homer, Mmmmm… donuts.

As I noted in chapter 1, Italians seem to have the proper respect for meals, taking the time to enjoy not only the food, but the company of others. It is commonly reported that Italy basically shuts down for lunch. Based on my own experience, I see this as a bit of an exaggeration, but only a bit. In comparison to the United States, though, Italy is pretty much closed from 1:00 to 3:00 in the afternoon.

For those of us living in the States, we need to keep turning the wheels of industry, we haven't the time to enjoy a meal. In every office with which I am familiar, there is always a significant number of people who don't stop working for lunch; they simply eat at their desk, if they eat at all. There is no time for slackers. Those who do take a break at lunchtime typically limit it to an hour or less. Many companies, especially those who employ unskilled workers, limit lunch to the scant 30 minutes required by law.

Where the Italian-American will wolf down a lite lunch at his or her desk and go home to a heavy dinner, an Italian eats a heavier lunch and a lite meal in the evening. This is not to say they quickly dismiss the evening meal. A traditional Italian evening incorporates a number of activities in which family, friends, and neighbors interact with one another. For example; you might start your evening with a *passeggiata*, an evening stroll which I discussed previously. You might end up at a *piazza* where you and some friends enjoy an *aperitivo* which is a small drink such as a *spritz* or *prosecco*. Later in the evening, you have a small meal of *panino* or salad. Some people save the evening walk and gathering in the *piazza* until after their meal, having an *espresso* or scoop of *gelato* when there.

Dinner with Italian friends is a long affair. We eat. We talk. We tell stories. There isn't a rush to complete what is the best part of the day. Even in Italian restaurants, there is no rush. In the United States, a table at a restaurant is a fixed cost that needs to be amortized across many diners. *Get'em in. Move'em out. We have people waiting for the table.* The more people we could move through, the higher the profit margin on that table.

When you have a meal in an Italian restaurant, it is understood enjoying the meal means more than the food; it is also the company of the people with whom you are eating. Some of the most golden moments I have spent in Italy are those that were spent after a meal with a bit of *espresso* or finishing off the last drops of wine. It would have been a tragedy to have missed those experiences because an impatient server rushed us out of the restaurant.

Italian and Italian-American dinners are quite different. As I mentioned above, an Italian-American dinner is usually the largest meal of the day, but it is as rushed as any other. Many families have so packed their schedules that between the children's extracurricular activities and the parents working late, there is no time to gather as a family. I have witnessed, on more than one occasion, a neighbor pulling away, sandwich in hand, taking the daughter to a rehearsal for a school play as the other parent pulls into the driveway with a grease-stained sack from a fast food joint.

In the United States, we have to keep moving forward, even at the expense of family time. Our child has to be the greatest athlete or get accepted into the best schools. We have emails to answer and conference calls with offshore to join. There is no sense that at the end of the day, that hour you have with your family is your reward for having worked that day. Hour?! What am I saying? Even when families eat together, they gulp their food in a rush with the television playing in the background. Who has time to sit at the table? We have to study, or get online, or see the most recent happenings in whatever reality show has captured the attention of the great unwashed masses.

Again, I understand I am painting an idyllic image of Italy that is not necessarily true for many. One friend in Sorrento who carves beautiful cameos, is in his shop until late in the evening six days a week. He, like many Italians, especially those serving tourists, does not have the luxury to close up shop for lunch or early in the evening. Also, in order to compete in the global economy, the traditional way of life in Italy is giving way to a more aggressive business-focused existence. What I have discussed here, however, is the more traditional way of life that has been prevalent throughout the country for many years.

The Structure of an Italian Meal

If you speak with someone who has recently returned from Italy, they will undoubtedly tell you about how Italians eat many courses during a meal – implying they eat substantially more food at a sitting. This is partially correct. Although the number of courses is greater in Italy than in the United States, the volume of food over the entire meal is not significantly different. Usually, in the States, there are three, or at most four courses, to a meal: a soup or salad, an entrée, and then dessert. At times, people will start with an appetizer prior to the salad. At other times, they may have an appetizer in place of the salad.

A full formal Italian meal, will be served in the following order:

Aperitivo As I mentioned above, an *aperitivo* is a lite drink such as *spritz* or *prosecco*. Often *finger food* is served with the drinks such as puff pastry or toast spears topped with some sort of spread.

Antipasto This is one of the many terms frequently misunderstood in the United States. In the States, an *antipasto* is a specific type of salad. In Italy, antipasto is an appetizer such as *bruschetta, crostino, tramezzino,* or *charcuterie.*

Primo The primo course, the first course, is usually a carbohydrate of some sort such as a pasta, polenta, or risotto.

Secondo This is the protein portion of the meal, be it a meat or fish of some sort. In the United States, we usually consider this to be the central focus of the meal. If you were to ask someone what they had for dinner or lunch, they would typically say something like chicken, steak, or fish. The rest are merely supporting cast members. In Italy, what is considered the center of the meal is dependent on the region. In some parts of Italy, the *primo* is considered to be the main part of the meal, while others consider it to be *secondo*.

We should also understand both the *primo* and *secondo* servings are smaller than in the States. A *primo* serving of pasta in Italy, for example, is perhaps a quarter to half the size of a pasta serving in the United States, depending on the restaurant.

Insalata One of the many customs in which Italian culinary genius shines is in eating salad *after* the main course. Tolkien once used the phrase, "filling in the corners" when describing what is eaten after a main course. It is especially appropriate when it comes to salad. While salads are wonderful, they are rarely the star of the show. Rather than diminish your appetite for *primo* or *secondo*, the salad is saved for later in the meal to *fill in the corners*.

Fruit & Cheese The fruit and cheese portion of the meal is one of the customs Italian-Americans have forgotten, and which they should have remembered. First, the combination of the two is delicious. More importantly, this is the portion of the meal when the conversation is the real star. The dishes have been cleared away and a warm contentment starts to spread as the wine works its way through your veins. This is when the great philosophical conundrums of life are pondered, and the problems of the world are resolved.

Dessert (*Dolce*) Dessert seems to be a universal custom. Italians, like most other cultures, will top off a meal with a bit of something sweet, hence the name *dolce* which is Italian for sweet.

Espresso Again, as in many cultures, the meal is topped off with coffee. Italian coffee at the end of the meal is an *espresso*.

Digestivo This concludes the meal, although depending on the region, the *digestivo* is served either before or with the coffee. As the name implies, a *digestivo* is intended to aid in the digestion of the meal. In the south of Italy, especially in the Amalfi region, even the simplest of meals is topped off with a *limoncello*.

The Feast of Seven Fishes

When discussing formal meals, the most important meal of the year, at least in my home, was Christmas Eve, *The Feast of Seven Fishes*. The house would be lit, both inside and out, with colored lights. In the center of the front room, an aluminum Christmas tree reigned over a court of various-sized meticulously wrapped packages. Yes, our Christmas tree was aluminum; it was an Italian-American thing in the 1960's. Rather than pine needles there were stiff tiny strips of metal that sparkled as a spotlight with a color wheel changed from red, to green, to yellow, and to blue. Across from the tree was a large archway leading to the dining room. Every year, my mother would add to the dining room table with additional folding tables to accommodate all the guests.

Oh the anticipation!! It wasn't merely the excitement of a child the night before Christmas; it was also my mother's Christmas Eve dinner. Each year, it was a feast beyond belief. We did not start until late in the evening, or at least late for Amarighans, and go well into the night. Whole nuts, figs, and various fruit such as oranges, tangerines, pears, and pomegranates would be in bowls on a buffet next to the table. Although I would snack on these, I would be careful not to overindulge before the real feast began.

As the name implies, *The Feast of Seven Fishes* is composed of at least seven different types of fish. Seven is seen as both good luck and holy. Some say the seven fish symbolize the seven sacraments of the church. Others maintain seven is the number mentioned most often in the Bible which in some way gives it a spiritual significance. Still others refer to the seven days of creation. No one knows why seven was selected; it simply happens to be one of those numbers that appears repeatedly in both religion and folk traditions.

It is thought that Italians brought this tradition with them from Italy. As is the case with so much of Italian culture, Italy's regionalism makes it difficult to say anything is a tradition (or not) across the country. In Northern Italy, *The Feast of Seven Fishes* is not known. Some have attributed it to Southern Italians; however, I do not know of any Italians in the south who observe the tradition. *The Feast of Seven Fishes* may have evolved in the United States from Southern Italian immigrants who practiced a slightly different tradition. In Calabria, they will make sure they have 13 different types of fish on the table; 12 for the apostles and one for Jesus.

In many Italian homes, however, Christmas Eve dinner is usually a light meal prior to midnight mass, which is probably a good thing since you may have a difficult time staying awake through a mass at midnight after a heavy meal. The Catholic tradition is to fast before receiving communion which means any meal would have to be concluded well in advance. When I was a boy, we were not allowed to eat two hours prior to communion, which would mean the meal would have to conclude before 10:00 P.M. Today, the church is much more lenient, allowing people to eat and drink up to an hour before receiving communion.

Bella Figura of Food

As you can tell from what we have discussed to this point, the differences between Italian and Italian-American food is virtually a limitless subject. You could spend your life reading books, blogs, and magazines on this topic, especially when taking into account the various regional differences both in Italy and the United States. It is an impossible task to cover the differences between the two in a single chapter. Rather than focus on specifics, let's discuss the overall difference in attitudes towards food and then see how those attitudes affect actual eating practices.

Italian-Americans may have certain customs when it comes to food, but there are no hard and fast rules as demonstrated earlier with *lazy man's lasagna*. In Italy, however, there are strict culinary conventions. Underlying these restrictions are two important principles. The first of these is *bella figura*, living gracefully, as discussed in previous chapters. In Italian culture, there are things you do not do simply because they reflect poorly on you as a person. So, in Italy, lazily dumping all the ingredients of lasagna into one large pot would be a sign of living brutishly. It would be seen as lacking the civility of doing things properly.

To those who aren't Italian, and even some Italian-Americans, these diktats may seem, as the cliché says, capricious and arbitrary, but they are stringently followed. It is not at all surprising for a server to deny a request from a patron if it violates what is deemed proper. A few years back, I was having dinner with some friends in Vinci when, at the end of the meal, we were served some *biscotti* and a small glass of Vino Santo, an Italian dessert wine. The accepted practice is to dip the biscotti into the wine. One of our friends, however, requested a small glass of milk in place of the wine. Who hasn't dunked a cookie in milk, right? The server refused. It violated several important rules. Not only was it improper to dip the *biscotti* in anything other than the Vino Santo, the idea of milk at the end of dinner was especially unacceptable. This brings us to the second of our guiding principles.

Eating correctly is a matter of health. Italians understand that eating properly will lead to good health. Albeit, some of what they believe as healthy eating is contrary to what many Amarighans view as a proper diet. The Italian attitude toward milk is one example, and was referred to in Chapter 4, *What Shall We Do with the Dago*.

You will not find Italians drinking milk with a meal, or past midmorning, since it is believed to have ill health effects. Italians see milk as a meal in itself. To combine it with other foods hinders digestion. Also, it takes time to properly digest milk; drinking it late in the day means your stomach will have to work on it all night. The waiter who denied my friend milk for her *biscotti* saw himself as doing her a favor.

After generations of living in the United States, Italian-Americans happily drink milk like Amarighans. Parents, nuns, and gym teachers all encouraged us to drink milk. "Drink your milk! It is good for you." Even many Italian-American parents pushed it on their children because that is what they were told would build nice strong bones.

Jack LaLanne, the *Godfather of Fitness*, got it right when he said "I'd rather see you drink a glass of wine than a glass of milk." He felt the same as many Italian mothers who, ever conscious of the threat milk poses to digestion, do not give it to their children. Wine? Yes. Milk? No.

Slow Food

An important aspect of healthy eating is the use of only the freshest of ingredients. In every Italian city I have visited, there are open air markets where produce is sold fresh from the farm. I remember purchasing some mushrooms on the Lido, a small island on the Venetian lagoon. The vendor selected a few from a bin for me, the dirt still clinging to their stems. There were no prepacked, cellophane-wrapped perfectly-formed cartoon mushrooms. These were the real thing found nearby, not manufactured.

As a result of the Italian aversion to factory food, fast food chains have found Italy to be a difficult market. Typically, when McDonald's invades a country, they begin in the cities and work their way out into the countryside, smaller cities, and towns. This didn't work in Italy. Italians in the cities rejected preprocessed foods. Realizing their typical strategy was not effective in Italy, McDonald's started in the countryside and worked their way back into the cities.

When I chided some friends for eating at McDonalds, they defended themselves saying it was quick and inexpensive. As I wrote previously, Italy is attempting to compete in this new globalized world with some of its customs suffering as a result. Now, you can find McDonalds in most Italian cities. You can find them in Rome and even dangerously close to Venice's Saint Mark's Square. As of this writing, there is currently an effort to keep them out of Florence's Piazza del Duomo, the home of Santa Maria del Fiore.

The battle between Italians and fast food gave birth to a movement that has since spread across the world. In 1986, McDonald's attempted to open a franchise on Via dei Condotti near the base of the Spanish Steps in Rome. This was a sacrilege. The Spanish Steps is one of the great icons of the city of Rome. If you visit Rome without seeing the Spanish Steps, Colosseum, the Trevi Fountain, and Saint Peter's Basilica, you have not been to Rome. It was particularly objectionable to Italians that McDonald's would open a franchise, the antithesis of Italian culture, so close to one of the great icons of the Eternal City.

In response, Carlo Petrini, a journalist and political activist, led a protest against not only McDonald's but the industry it represented. He, along with members of Associazione Ricreativa e Culturale Italiana, stood silently in front of the fast food joint holding plates of fresh penne pasta. Anyone wishing to enter the McDonald's would have to pass through the gauntlet they had formed. While they were successful in their protest, a more important result was the launch of the worldwide Slow Food Movement.

The principles of Slow Food are based on the same principles of Italian food culture. It is the belief that you don't eat simply to live, but are meant to truly experience food and life more fully. The Slow Food movement believes in taking joy in the preparation and consumption of food as well as the communal aspects of sharing that food with friends and family. Part of that joy is the flavor and richness of fresh local seasonal foods. This is what Ursula Ferrigno, who I quoted at the beginning of this chapter, meant when she said, "Italian food encapsulates… an acute and unique awareness of nature and seasonality."[91]

Local Food

As you travel through Italy, you will find locally run restaurants, *pasticceria*, *gelateria*, and markets with food from local farms. It is the simple wisdom that your dinner should not have seen more of the world than you. The eggplant in Sorrento, the seafood in Apulia, the wine in Tuscany; each of these are locally grown, locally prepared, and locally consumed.

---

[91] Ferrigno, Ursula, *Truly Italian: Quick & Simple Vegetarian Cooking*, Mitchell Beazley, 1999, pg. 5

Italians are fond of their home gardens where they can grow their own produce, eating freshly picked tomatoes, peppers, zucchini, and a host of other fruits and vegetables. Previous generations of Italian-Americans continued this practice. As I mentioned, when I was a boy most Italian families had their own gardens. Tomatoes were made into homemade sauce while the older Italian men, usually someone's grandfather, would press grapes for their own wine.

Making your own wine is a tradition that has been kept alive within the Italian-American community, although it is not as popular as it once was. In Italy, however, the practice is as alive and well as ever. There is a virtually endless list of rules concerning the proper way to make wine, from the correct method of crushing the grapes to which phase of the moon is the best time of the month in which to start the process. While fermenting the wine in oak barrels is a common tradition, I have been to *agriturismi* where they keep the wine in large nearly spherical clear glass jugs with long stem necks. The necks are filled with olive oil which seals the wine.

An *agriturismo* (singular of *agriturismi*) is basically a cross between a bed & breakfast and a farm. They are another demonstration of the Italian love of fresh, unprocessed food. The beauty of staying at an *agriturismo* is the food. To be classified as an *agriturismo*, more than 80% of the food served must be grown on the farm itself. In addition, by their nature, *agriturismi* are small, family-run affairs. You are eating with Italians; the way Italians eat. My experience has shown me how running an *agriturismo* is a labor of love for the owners who are proud of their farms and what they produce.

Pizza

The iconic Italian food is pizza. Or is it?

Every once in a while, you will hear the myth that pizza is not Italian. That it was invented in the United States and found its way back to Italy. This is entirely incorrect. Pizza has been enjoyed by the people of the Italian peninsula for centuries, even as far back as the Etruscans and Greeks. The 16th century chef Bartolomeo Scappi, whose writings provide great insight into both the Papal court and the culinary habits of that era, first wrote of pizza. At the time it was more like a pie or open tart.

Although the pizza has evolved over the years, if the birth of the modern pizza could be attributed to any one place it would be Napoli.

The Neapolitan Don Raffaele Esposito is credited with inventing the pizza we have today. In 1889, Queen Margherita was touring with her husband, King Umberto I, the newly united Kingdom of Italy. In honor of Queen Margherita, Don Esposito constructed the first pizza, which he named *pizza Margherita*, with the national colors of red (tomatoes), white (mozzarella), and green (basil leaves).

In order for a pizza to be considered a true Neapolitan pizza, it must meet the standards of the AVPN (Associazione Verace Pizza Napoletana).[92] The standards for a Neapolitan pizza specify the type of flour used in the dough, how it is rolled out, and how it is baked. Neapolitan *pizze* have a thin crust in the center, approximately 0.16 inches, and a slightly thicker crust along the edge, anywhere from 0.39 to 0.79 inches. Pizza does not take long to cook; the entire baking process should take a couple of minutes. So, a thin crust is important. A true Neapolitan pizza is baked in a wood oven at nearly 900° F for a minute. The correct way to bake a pizza is to bake the dough slightly at first, pull it out of the oven, add the toppings, and then pop it back in for a bit.

Some of the most incredible *pizze* and *panini* I have had in my life were in the South of Italy. In addition to *pizza Margherita*, there is *pizza alla Napoletana* which is a pizza topped with tomato sauce made from Marzano tomatoes, dried oregano or fresh basil, and olive oil. If you add anchovies, you have a *pizza alla marinara*.

As we have seen throughout this book, there are regional differences in all aspects of Italian culture; this includes food and especially pizza. While we have strict standards when it comes to Neapolitan pizza, each region has its own version. Where a Neapolitan pizza is round and cooked in a wood oven, a Roman pizza is made in square sheets and cooked in an electric oven. There are many more types of *pizze* in Rome as well. A Neapolitan pizza is one of the three types that I described above. A Roman bianca pizza is covered with olive oil and cheese. You can also find toppings such as mushrooms or sausage.

One of the pleasures of wandering around Rome is to pass a pizzeria where all the different varieties offered by the shop are on display in the

---

[92] Yes, there is actually a standards board that determines what a true Neapolitan pizza is. As I said earlier, food is important to Italians. We don't mess around. *Vera* in Italian means true. The intent of the AVPN is to promote and protect what is a true Pizza Napoletana.

window. For a quick snack, you can order a slice which is cut using scissors, something you will see in many East Coast Italian-American homes.

Romans selling pizza by the square is actually similar to the way in which people eat pizza in New York. Rarely do you order a personal pan pizza. You get it by the slice. If you ask someone what they are doing for lunch, they may respond with, "Oh, I am just going to grab a *slice*." When a New Yorker says this, they do not mean they are going to get a slice of pie or cheese for lunch. A *slice* in New York means a slice of pizza. There is an American pizza chain whose catchphrase is "piece of pizza." While this may be a cute phrase for marketing purposes, it is incorrect. An individual serving of pizza cut from a larger pizza is a slice not a piece.

This brings us to a discussion on what Americans have done to pizza. Unfortunately, in the United States, corporations are leveraging the economies of scale in the food industry, forcing out the authentic mom & pop *pizzerie*. Of course, corporations need to add variety and novelty to their menus to attract and keep customers, so they develop a wide variety of pizza types. Today, in the United States, they offer such Frankenstein-like monsters as stuffed crust pizza, pretzel crust pizza, bacon cheeseburger pizza, BBQ chicken pizza, and *Cali*[93] chicken bacon ranch pizza. As good villagers, we should all get out our pitchforks and torches to raze to the ground the insidious laboratories within which these sins against nature have been created. Understand, I am speaking metaphorically. Please do not burn down your local Papa John's, regardless of how satisfying it may be.

Of all the various types of pizza eaten by Americans, and woefully even some Italian-Americans, the worst is the heinous Pineapple & Canadian Bacon Pizza. Simply stated, it is wrong; morally wrong. If you are Italian and you eat a pineapple & Canadian bacon pizza, by law I will be forced to hunt you down in order to remove all rights, privileges, and honors associated with being Italian. You will be required, again by law, to change you name to Brad Miller. If you are female, your name will be changed to Jan Lewis. The only Italian restaurant that will be allowed to

---

[93] As a public service, let me advise you that no Californian refers to California, or anything Californian, as *Cali*. You should avoid the use of this phrase.

serve you is the Olive Garden and you will be forever damned to eat canned spaghetti sauce.

Don't let this happen to you. Do not eat pineapple & Canadian bacon pizza. I trust we have said enough about that subject and we can move on. I do not intend to raise the issue again.

Another difference between American and Italian pizza is the size. In the United States, most people think nothing of ordering a large pizza with one half having one set of toppings and the other half another. This is strictly an American thing. When Italians go out for pizza, they typically have an individual pizza with the specific toppings for that person. They do not mix toppings half and half. Italians, for the most part, do not like to mix a large variety of foods together.

Concerning the types of toppings, official Neapolitan pizza has a limited number. In Rome and other parts of Italy, however, you can get pretty much any topping you want as long as you are reasonable. NO PINEAPPLE! Typically, you do not go beyond four types of topping on one pizza, so you won't be seeing many meat lovers' *pizze* in Italy. Again, this is in line with the Italian view that foods should be simple. If you have a pizza with eight or ten different types of meat, you can no longer distinguish the sausage from the pepperoni.

Speaking of pepperoni, if you like pepperoni on your pizza you need to proceed with caution. During my daughter's first trip to Italy, not being familiar with the language, she ordered a pepperoni pizza only to be served a pizza topped with cubanelle peppers. She has since learned she confused *pepperoni* with *peperoncino* which translates to pepper. She now asks for a pizza with *salame piccante*.

Another difference in terminology is *marinara*. In Italian, the word *mare* means sea. Something which is seafood-based is *marinara*. As seen earlier, a *pizza alla Napoletana* is transformed into a *pizza alla marinara* with the addition of anchovies.

In Sardinia, they have *pissaladière* which is basically an anchovy pizza. They also have toppings such as caramelized onions and olives. The *pissaladière* is claimed, by some, to be the first pizza. It is surprising to me how out of favor anchovies have become. Recently, I ordered a pizza with anchovies only to be told that they did not even have anchovies on the premises! They had pineapple though! What is wrong with these people that… OK, I said I was going to drop the pineapple thing. I won't bring it up again.

Pizza's Culinary Cousins

When it comes to pizza, Neapolitan style is my preference, but the Sicilians serve *sfincione* that deserves special consideration. It is as thick as *focaccia* bread, but comes with a variety of toppings not normally found on focaccia. Although some claim that the Chicago deep dish pizza is a descendent of *sfincione*, I believe that the *pizza al padellino* (pizza in a pan) from Torino is much closer to what my Chicago *paisani* serve. Whereas the *sfincione* are traditionally square, a *pizza al padellino* is round, like a Chicago-style deep dish. The dough of a *pizza al padellino* is put into a small well-oiled pan, approximately six or seven inches in diameter, and given time to rise. The oiling slightly fries the dough giving it a nice chewy kind of crust. Again, something I find when eating a Chicago-style pizza.

The proper descendent of the *sfincione* is the *tomato pie*. Like the *sfincione*, it is as thick as a focaccia, but is topped with a thick layer of tomato sauce. They are usually made in rectangles two feet long and a foot wide and cut into squares. On occasion, you will go with the deluxe version that has a cheese topping as well. The cheese topping for a tomato pie, however, is not mozzarella as is the case with most *pizze*, but parmesan or Romano cheese. This gives the pie a bit of a bite that goes especially well with the tomato sauce.

Tomato pie is a wonderful thing that was a staple of my youth. For 25 cents at lunch, I would get two slices of tomato pie, a *pasticciotto*, and a coke. Everything a growing boy needed to get through the day. I can't think of a party where the host would not have a box or two of tomato pie. Each box had two layers of pie separated by wax paper.

While we are discussing pie, we need to clarify another misconception. There is tomato pie and there is pizza. These are two separate and distinct foods. A pizza is not a pie. Regardless of what Dean Martin may have sung in *Amore*, the moon will never hit your eye like a *big pizza pie*. I suppose that the song is the origin of this term, but it is not correct, although it has been picked up by many Italian-Americans. The lyricist for *Amore* probably realized that the line "when the moon hits your eye like a big tomato pie" probably didn't have the same resonance with the rest of America.

In addition to tomato pie, pizza has some other culinary cousins. There is the *calzone*, of course, which is simply a pizza folded over. Less well known is the *Stromboli*, which should not be confused with the character from *Pinocchio*. Basically, you lay out your pizza then roll it into a loaf. In my youth, *stromboli* came in two varieties: sausage or spinach. Today, there are as many types of *stromboli* filling as there are pizza toppings. Both *calzone* and *stromboli* have the advantage of being easier to eat than a pizza.

How to Eat a Pizza

In terms of the proper etiquette in eating a pizza, in Italy you use a knife and fork. In Rome, the correct way of eating pizza is different. There, when eating a square, as described above, you are expected to eat it with your hands. In the United States, however, it is never acceptable to eat pizza with a knife and fork. It is a symbol of being a real Amarighan.

In 2014, New York City Mayor Bill de Blasio became the target of late night television ridicule for being seen eating a pizza with a knife and fork, and rightfully so. Although Donald Trump and Sarah Palin were seen doing the same thing, they could be tolerated. They are Amarighans who don't know any better. New Yorkers expected more from their mayor, however; especially one named de Blasio.

We should also note that there is a bit of an art to eating a triangular slice of pizza. You take the slice in your hand with the fingers beneath. Then, with your thumb, you make a slight fold in the slice. This will give the slice of pizza a bit more rigidity, preventing the tip from flopping over and spilling the toppings onto your lap.

In the opening to the film *Saturday Night Fever*, John Travolta eats two slices by folding one over the top of the other. A lot of bad things came out of that movie. While it has grown in popularity since the movie, prior to the film I had never seen, or even heard of, anyone eating pizza in that way. You end up with a kind of open-sided calzone, which could turn out to be a real mess.

Final thoughts on pizza. The worldly wise traveler will often report to those back home that pizza in Italy is different. The truthiness of this common wisdom, however, is based on where in Italy the traveler had been and where back home is. If you are from New York or Boston, you will feel right at home with Roman pizza. If you are from Chicago, Torino or Sicily will feel familiar.

Just as Italy has regional differences in the toppings, dough, shape and preparation of pizza, so does the United States. Frequently, the differences found in the United States result from which part of Italy the immigrants in the area came. As noted earlier, national chains are coming through many cities and towns wiping out the old mom & pop pizza places. Not only do they offer inauthentic varieties of pizza, they also eliminate many of the regional differences that Italian-Americans have developed across the country. It is up to Italian-Americans to hang on to the traditional *pizze* with which we have all been raised, or pretty soon even our children will be eating pizza with pineapple…

An American Success Story

The other hero in the Italian-American culinary pantheon is spaghetti and meatballs. This dish exemplifies how Italian food is both inexpensive and easy to make. You could easily feed a family of four with spaghetti and meatballs for under 20 dollars, especially if you have your own garden. If you make it frequently, you could really save money, leveraging economies of scale by buying the ingredients in bulk. In many Italian-American homes, Wednesday night was spaghetti night. When I was an adolescent, I remember many of my friends dreading going home for dinner on Wednesday night because they had grown tired of the dish.

Most kids did not have this problem. Spaghetti and meatballs is a staple of children's menus across the United States. Amarighans used to feed their kids stuff out of a can. They loved it, an entire meal in a can! The big name in canned Italian food was Chef Boyardee, previously mentioned in chapter 5, who offered *Beefaroni*, macaroni in a meat sauce. For kids, there was *Mini Bites* which came either in the shape of O's or the alphabet. In 1965, the Campbell Soup Company competed with Boyardee with the introduction of SpaghettiOs. Their round shape was supposed to make it easier for American kids to eat. Spaghetti was not really a challenge for Italian-American kids; we knew how to twirl pasta around a fork before we knew how to ride a bike.

The history of canned spaghetti could easily get lost in what it has become. Although today no self-respecting Italian-American would ever profane their kitchen with canned spaghetti, that is not how it began. In New York City in 1924, *Il Giardino d'Italia* (The Garden of Italy), was THE place to go for authentic Italian food. People frequently asked its chef, Ettore Boiardi, for jars of sauce to take home. Sensing an opportunity, Ettore branched out of the restaurant business with his brothers Mario and Paul to provide authentic Italian flavors to a wider range of consumers. They began to label their products with the phonetic spelling of their name "Boyardee."

Pretentious Pasta

When I was a kid, there was basically spaghetti and macaroni. Candidly, I don't remember many people using the term pasta. I cannot think of a time when I asked my mother what was for dinner and she would say *pasta*. It was either spaghetti or macaroni. Even today, when I use the term *pasta*, I feel more than a little pretentious. In the back of my mind, when I hear an Amarighan say *pasta*, I envision Silicon Valley hipsters with ridiculous looking beards and handlebar mustaches telling one another of their most recent adventures in eating. "Last night, we had the most wonderful seafood gumbo *pasta* with truffles and parmareggio cheese made from the milk of grass-fed free-range Peruvian Alpacas."

Now don't get me wrong, the correct term is, of course, *pasta* which in Italian means paste. You can see the word used in other parts of the Italian language. Pasta can also be used to refer to pastry or dough. When you make *pasta*, you roll out your dough, which is the paste stage, then cut it into the appropriately-sized strips to form the strands.

The process of making spaghetti was not always done in the most sanitary of conditions. If you recall from the description of little Italy in Chapter 3, *To Your Scattered Bodies Go*, spaghetti was often made in the front room of storefront apartments and hung in the open air to dry. These conditions were not much worse than those in Italy where pasta was dried in the open, subject to any debris or contaminants, such as dust, that happened to be in the air.

Now this may seem less than appetizing, but in the old days people were not all that concerned about hygiene. It was common, at one time, to eat spaghetti with your hands. Simply grab a bunch of the noodles with your hand, toss your head back, and let it all slide down your throat.

As uncivilized as eating spaghetti with your hands may sound to the modern reader, there is a practice that is far worse: using a knife and fork. Don't do this. It is slightly more acceptable to cut the spaghetti with the side of your fork, but only slightly. The proper way to eat spaghetti is to twirl it with your fork. Some people need the assistance of a spoon, but I find that rather awkward. It may take a little practice, after all you don't want a clump of spaghetti the size of a baseball on the end of your fork, but it really is not all that difficult. Simply grab a few strands of spaghetti with your fork and twirl until you have a nice little knot of spaghetti. It's easy, I have been doing it since I was four.

Before we go much further in our discussion of *pasta*, we need to deal with what is perhaps one of the most frustrating myths concerning

Italians and Italian food. Spaghetti was NOT brought back from China by Marco Polo. When I get into this debate with friends, I simply tell them how, in reality, Marco Polo introduced the Chinese to chopsticks, which sends them off on a completely different argument and they forget about spaghetti.

Pasta, in various forms, had been known throughout Europe long before Marco Polo. While it is true that it had also developed in Asia, the two regions developed *pasta* independently of one another. You could follow the history of *pasta* back to the Etruscans and Greeks. The Romans prepared a *pasta* noodle which was cut into broad strips similar to the lasagna noodles of today. *Pasta* continued to evolve over time until we see pasta, like the pasta we see today, begin to appear in the middle ages.

Dried *pasta*, the type of pasta with which most of us are familiar, is something that Italians inherited from North Africa. Developing independently of the *pasta* in Italy, North Africans developed dried pasta which was a handy food for desert caravans. Brought to Italy via Sicily with the Muslim invasion, by the 12th century, Palermo boasted of a prosperous *dried pasta* industry that exported their products across Europe and the Mediterranean.

Who the Hell is Alfredo?

Spaghetti evokes a very Amarighan image in my mind. I see, on a plate, a mound of *pasta* noodles topped with a large meatball. The noodles are infused with the red of the sauce while the slopes of the mound are dusted with parmesan cheese. This is an image created by the mind of someone who has been raised in the States.

You see, as Amarighans prepare to leave for Italy, their friends, with profound and sage-like tones, will warn them that they do not have spaghetti and meatballs in Italy. This is partially correct. You will not see what I described in the previous paragraph in Italian restaurants, except those that cater to the appetites of tourists. Spaghetti, being a carbohydrate is served as part of the *primo* course and the meat is served as part of the *secondo*. To mix the two, on the same dish, violates culinary rules.

An important aspect of Italian cooking is foods are not mixed. You do not mix your meat with your pasta, or your vegetables with your meat. Italians prefer to keep their flavors separate so that you can savor the deliciousness of each ingredient. Ann Reavis, in her book *Italian Food*

Rules, told her readers to imagine serving a fussy four-year-old; nothing on the plate should touch. So not only will you not see spaghetti and meatballs, but authentic Italian cooking also avoids mixing foods such as chicken in with pasta as well.

Italian-Americans have no problem with mixing chicken in with their pasta. My home town of Utica, New York, for example, has gained some notoriety, as of late, for being the birthplace of *Chicken Riggies*, also known as *Utica Riggies*. Violating every rule of Italian cuisine, *Utica Riggies* is rigatoni pasta mixed with chicken in a creamy tomato sauce. On occasion, peppers may be added.

I am surprised by how much I have learned about Italian food once I have left the safe confines of my Italian-American community in Upstate New York. I should quickly add, however, that most of what I have learned is wrong. For example, it wasn't until I moved to Southern California that I encountered *Fettuccine Alfredo*.

I don't believe I will ever forget the first time I heard the term. I was at a party when the stereotypical California blonde, upon hearing my last name, began to tell me of her love of Italian food. Her blue eyes sparkled as she went through her list of Italian dishes, but the conversation took a turn when she began to talk about Fettuccine Alfredo. An overt sensual tone took over her voice. She closed her eyes and, with a carnal yet subtle licking of her lips, she talked of how she would order Fettuccine Alfredo at a local restaurant, devouring it in what seemed to be a near orgasmic frenzy.

"Do you know how to make Fettuccine Alfredo?" she asked looking into my eyes, the tips of her fingers resting ever so lightly on my forearm. "I have never had homemade Fettuccine Alfredo, not by a reeeal Italian."

"YES! Yes, I make it all the time. My mother taught me how. It is an old family recipe, not like the stuff you get in restaurants." In the back of my mind, I was thinking, what the hell is Fettuccine Alfredo? "I tell you what, I will make some just for you. Just like my mother's, just come by my place on Friday." I was sure my mother or sister knew how to make it.

"Really? No, I couldn't put you to all that bother."

"No, no, please. It will be no bother at all. I would really enjoy making it for you."

The next morning, I was on the phone. "Ma? How do you make Fettuccine Alfredo?"

"What? Who the hell is Alfredo?" she asked.

My heart sank.

Fettuccine Alfredo is an American creation, actually it is an American bastardization of an Italian dish, *pasta bianco*. When I was a boy, we would frequently have *pasta bianco* which was simply *pasta* and some butter, with a little sprinkle of Parmesan cheese. My favorite was *pasta bianco* made with *pastina* which is the smallest type of pasta.

It is said that early in the 1900's, Mary Pickford and Douglas Fairbanks, while on their honeymoon in Rome, visited the restaurant of Alfredo di Lelio. At the time, he served *pasta bianco*, but named it after himself – Alfredo. Upon their return to the United States, the couple made the dish popular with their friends and it eventually spread throughout the country. As it spread, the recipe evolved with the inclusion of heavy cream. People have also gotten carried away by adding shrimp, green peas, or chicken. As I noted above, such combinations are more American than they are Italian. What started out as a simple dish has grown into a concoction that bears little resemblance to the original *pasta bianco*.

How to Serve Pasta

So, let's talk about the correct way to prepare pasta. First, you do not put oil in the water. All you need to add is a bit of salt. You then stir your pasta, making sure that it does not clump together. Simple, right?

This leads us to another myth. How to tell when the *pasta* is done. A character in the 1983 film *The Big Chill* tells his friends that the way to tell if spaghetti is done is to throw it against the wall. If it sticks, it is done. This is an incredibly dumb thing to do. First, it is unsanitary. If my mother came into her spotless kitchen to find me throwing spaghetti against her walls, I would get a smack in the back of the head. Second, if you have cooked your spaghetti so long that it is soft and gummy enough to stick against a wall, you have overcooked it.

Many Italian-Americans from my parent's generation overcooked their spaghetti, soft all the way through. Italians prefer their *pasta* to be *al dente*, meaning the pasta should have tiny crunch to it. Italian-Americans today seem to have rediscovered *al dente*. We have gotten back in synch with our Italian cousins.

Another mistake made by Amarighans is to rinse the pasta once it has been drained. Don't do this. There is no reason to do this and all you do is cool it down. It also interferes with the application of the sauce, which is our next important point.

You can always spot an Amarighan by when they apply the sauce. One of the worst insults you can make to a plate of pasta is to add the sauce once it is on the plate. Many times I have been served a plate of spaghetti with nearly white strands and a dollop of tomato sauce on top. This is wrong. Once the pasta has finished cooking, it is drained and then the sauce is added while the pasta is still in the pot. Frequently, the pasta finishes cooking in the sauce itself. This is important. When done properly, the sauce and the pasta adhere to one another.

Another mistake frequently made in the United States is having too much sauce for the amount of pasta. Recently, when a friend hosted a pasta bar, I knew there was going to be a problem when I saw bowls instead of plates. When the chef behind the bar handed me my bowl, the vermicelli swam in a red soup like eels in the Nile. It is pasta, not tomato soup with noodles. The definition of a sauce is something that adds moistness and flavor. Sauce should enhance the flavor of the pasta, not overwhelm it.

Sauce or Gravy?

This leads us to a debate that has been simmering within the Italian-American community. Is it sauce or gravy? I am not aware of any other ethnic group that debates the correct terminology for one of their main foods. Do Koreans debate the correct translation of kimchi? For most of my life I was not even aware there was something to be debated. We always called it sauce. As I walked down the aisle of the grocery store, I saw cans of sauce, not gravy. In restaurants, it was referred to as sauce.

I first became aware of the controversy while watching one of many Mafia movies that supposedly shed light on authentic Italian-American culture. Apparently, real Italians call it *gravy*. I guess, despite my ancestry, I am not a real Italian because I call it sauce. Shortly after that, people I had known all my life were using the term gravy. So, I began to wonder if this was something which was manufactured in Hollywood like Fettuccine Alfredo.

As I have researched this topic, what I have seen is the consistent use of the word sauce. The *Oxford Companion to Italian Food* does not even contain an entry for gravy, although many an Italian would hardly accept Oxford as the ultimate arbiter of all things Italian. My oldest book on Italian food, *The Art of Italian Cooking* by Maria Lo Pinto and Milo

Miloradovich, consistently uses the term sauce and has no entries for gravy.

When Italians speak of what they put on their pasta, they use the word *salsa* which is not to be confused with what is found in Mexican restaurants. *Salsa* is translated from Italian as sauce. The Italian word for gravy is *salsetta*. More importantly, gravy isn't a typical Italian type of food. Think of what gravy does. Made from the drippings of meat, it mixes the flavor of the meat with whatever you put it on, often drowning out the flavor of the original thing. At Christmas dinner, if you put gravy on your mashed potatoes the flavor of the potatoes is lost in the taste of the gravy. As noted earlier in this chapter, food in traditional Italian cooking stands on its own. You don't mix different foods into an indiscernible mash.

On the English side of the translation, a sauce is defined as a thick liquid used to add moistness and flavor. Gravy is defined as a sauce made from the juices of cooked meat. Some have speculated that sauce is used for *marinara*, meaning the Italian-American use of the term marinara is a tomato sauce without meat. Meat-based sauces, according to these sages, is referred to as gravy. This is a distinction that would make sense, but it is not something I have seen in common use.

I have disclosed that I have come to this debate with a bias towards the term sauce, but I do not see any justification for the use of the term gravy. It simply does not fit the English use of the word. Based on the research I have done on this issue, it seems to me that the use of the term gravy for tomato sauce is the result of a mistranslation on the part of Italian immigrants, primarily those who settled in either Boston or Philadelphia. I am perhaps in the minority of Italian-Americans who do not believe it to be a grave error. If my Italian friends from Philadelphia or Boston prefer to use the term gravy, while those from New York and Chicago use the term sauce, we simply need to remember this difference in terminology is an Italian-American phenomenon.

A final note on sauce, which came to Italian cuisine relatively late in the game. Prior to tomato sauce, Italians used *agresto* to add flavor. It is similar to pesto sauce but *agresto* uses grapes as its primary ingredient. Although not very popular today, during the Renaissance it was a product made by every farmer. Then came the tomato, the *pomodoro*, the golden apple.

Tomatoes came to Europe from the Americas in the 16th century. At first, many thought tomatoes were poisonous. It has been suggested tomatoes would draw lead out of pewter. The wealthy, who used pewter utensils and did not understand the poison came from the utensils, blamed the tomatoes. Communities, such as Italians, who ate with wooden implements did not have this issue.

Partly because of their poisonous reputation, tomatoes made their way into Italian cuisine slowly. Most popular in southern Italy, specifically Napoli, the tomato found its way back to America with Italian immigrants.

Another American Immigrant

As I mentioned, once I left the little Italian enclave of my hometown, I began to learn how Italians ate, or at least how Amarighans thought Italians ate. Although most of the things I was told by Amarighans were wrong, there were a couple of little gems that I picked up. One of these was *polenta*.

The first time I heard of *polenta*, I thought the person was referring to *pastina*. It wasn't until many years after leaving home, decades in fact, that I had *polenta* for the first time. It was in a little family Italian restaurant in Chicago that was a half-level down from the street. On a whim, I ordered the fried *polenta* with porcini mushrooms. It was wonderful! Oh *polenta*, where had you been all my life? Why hadn't my mother made this for me when I was a kid?

During the following visit with my sister, I happened to mention to her, in front of her husband who was born and raised in Italy, how much I loved *polenta*. My brother-in-law looked up at me with a sour look on his face, "Polenta! Blech!" He then downed a glass of wine to get the imaginary taste out of his mouth. He explained to me that this was a meal eaten primarily by the poor, which he was as a boy. "*Polenta* for breakfast! *Polenta* for lunch! *Polenta* for dinner! *Polenta! Polenta! Polenta!* Basta!" Its association with poverty is probably the reason my mother never made it.

Polenta, like the tomato, is an American immigrant that has found a home in Italian kitchens. When Columbus returned to Europe, he took corn with him. He also described how Native Americans would cook cornmeal with water to make what has become *polenta*. Corn, being easy to grow in Southern Italy, quickly became the food of the poor.

Despite its reputation, I still love it. In a couple of steps, you can have a delicious side dish appropriate for any meal. Step one, brown some garlic, tomato paste, and sausage in some olive oil. Step two, add chicken stock and cream bringing it to a boil. Step three, gradually whisk in the cornmeal, one part cornmeal to every three parts liquid. Once it is nice and thick, you can serve it as a side dish that is so much tastier than mashed potatoes or rice.

Fare la Scarpetta

With the correct balance between pasta and sauce, you should have a small amount of sauce left on the plate at the end. This is one of my favorite parts of a pasta dinner because you sop this up with a bit of bread. It is basically that part of the meal where you fill in all the corners. This is referred to by Italians as *fare la scarpetta* (to make the little shoe).

Years ago, when my nice Amarighan wife was still trying to recover from the cultural shock of living with an Italian-American, we stopped at a local restaurant for their buffet. After finishing my plate of pasta, I began *fare la scarpetta*. That was when I got the look. It is perhaps one of the most powerful weapons in my wife's arsenal. I didn't even have to look up to feel the laser beams piercing the top of my head. When I did raise my eyes, I met her condemning scowl with puppy-like innocence.

"I hope you don't plan on doing that once we have children," she said haughtily. I should quickly add here that my wife is not a *stick in the mud,* as the expression goes. This was still at the point in our marriage when she was attempting to turn me into a civilized human being.

"Do what?" I kind of knew what the problem was, but I was hoping feigned naiveté would get me out of this jam.

"Wipe your plate with your bread like that. It's embarrassing."

"It is? Since when?"

"People are looking at you. Stop it."

I looked around. "I really don't think anyone cares." I continued *fare la scarpetta.*

The words barely passed over my lips when the waitress walked over. "Excuse me, sir. Would you like another plate?" Great, just what I needed. Now the Amarighans were ganging up on me.

"No, thanks. I'm good." I continued eating happily… Well actually, not so happily. I now had two Amarighans giving me the stink eye.

"Well, sir," the waitress said in as nice a voice as she could muster, "when you go back to the buffet we will give you a clean plate." Then she added, in a conspiratorial whisper, "In fact, we kind of insist on it." Then she gave her nose a cute little wrinkle.

I looked up at her, exasperated, but still not relinquishing my plate. "I understand. Thank you. I would never in my wildest dreams think of taking my plate back to buffet, but I like what I am doing." I made little circular motions over my plate. "I like this. When I am ready to go back I promise you, on the soul of my sainted Sicilian mother, that I will get a clean plate. I just want to finish with this one first." I then attempted to give my Calabrese honker the same cute little wrinkle.

"OK," she said with her most polite white Amarighan smile. "But here is a clean plate for when you are ready to go back." From out of nowhere a clean plate appeared on the table.

I looked up at my wife who sat with a victorious grin on her face. Things would have been quite different if we had been in Italy. In Italy, my manners would have been impeccable.

Soaking up sauce with a piece of bread has been a lifetime habit, passed down from my elders. When I was a boy, my mother worked in a textile mill, but on Saturday morning, before she left to work her shift, she would start her sauce for Sunday dinner. Throughout the day, the sauce would simmer on the stove. Around noon, my father would give me a quarter to go down to the local mom & pop store, Mezzanenni's, on the corner to pick up a couple of loaves of bread; usually, he let me keep the change. When I got back, my father would ladle out a couple of bowls of sauce for our lunch. We would break off a hunk of bread, slather on a pad of butter, and then dip it in the sauce. One of the best lunches a man could ask for.

American restaurants don't quite get *fare la scarpetta*. Even when they do recognize the custom, they get the application of it wrong. Years ago my wife and I tried a new Italian restaurant that opened in our area. It was part of a national chain, so I didn't expect it to be authentic, authentic Italian, or even authentic Italian-American. But what the heck? It was a Saturday night and the place was right next to where we were going to see a movie.

After we sat down, a cute little blonde-haired, blue-eyed waitress came over with the bread. She then poured some olive oil onto a small plate in the center of the table and proudly announced "Italian Butter!"

"You have Italian butter?" I looked up at her confused.

"Yup, it's right there."

I leaned over and looked at what she poured into the plate. "You melted the butter?"

"No, that is olive oil."

"I thought you said you had Italian Butter?"

"We do, the olive oil. That is what Italians use for butter."

"Really?" I looked over at my wife. She rolled her eyes. She knew what was probably going to come next.

"You know I am Italian. Well half-Italian, my mother was Sicilian. We had butter at home. My mother used olive oil for salad and cooking, but we put butter on our bread." The poor girl looked confused. I think she was still trying to figure out why I was only half-Italian if my mother was Sicilian.

"Well, that is how they do it in Italy."

"Really, because I go to Italy a lot and I…"

"That's fine," my wife interrupted, having mercy on the poor girl. "Thank you."

The waitress walked away. I looked down at the plate between us. Then I looked up at her. Then I looked down at the plate again.

"Did you know Italians don't use butter?" I said looking back up.

"Just eat. Will you?"

We rarely go out for Italian food anymore. It avoids any problems.

Italians don't dip their bread in olive oil as they do in American restaurants. When I was a boy, no one dipped their bread in olive oil; this is an entirely new, entirely American thing. When traveling through Italy, the only time I am given bread prior to the meal is when I eat at restaurants that cater to tourists. Italians listen to their mothers and do not fill up on bread before a meal. Bread is served with the meal, but not as some sort of mini appetizer. As far as dipping bread in olive oil, the only time I have done this in Italy was when I was actually tasting olive oil. In those instances, it was a small cube of bread that was meant to be a delivery system for the oil, not a snack.

The Bread of Life

We, the Italian-Americans of my youth, bought our bread the same day we were planning to eat it. I remember my brother-in-law, Mario, coming home each day with a fresh loaf or two tucked under his arm. For a while, he and I drove a truck at night for a bakery. In the morning, as we headed for home, we would grab a few loaves – fresh and hot out of the oven. The next day, the bread was thrown away; on occasion, my mother would let it dry and use it for breadcrumbs. Although today, thanks to preservatives, Italian-Americans will keep bread around for days, Italians still avoid day old bread, except the Florentines.

When traveling to Italy, you need to be warned about the Florentines and their bread. It is tasteless. They don't add salt. Dante makes note of the difference in Florentine bread when, in *Paradiso XVII*, he writes, "you shall know the salt of another man's bread." This is accepted as his foretelling of his exile from Florence when one of the hardships of that exile is to be doomed to eat the salty bread made in the rest of Italy. As much as I may love Dante's writing, he and I part company when it comes to Florentine bread.

Although I have heard a number of excuses – I mean reasons – the first time I complained about Florentine bread, a friend told me that they make it tasteless so that the taste of the bread does not compete with the taste of the sauce for *fare la scarpetta*. Sounds like a flimsy excuse to me, but it does fit in well with the Italian aversion to mixing various flavors.

There is some method to the Florentine bread madness. Salt-less bread does not retain as much moisture so it does not mold as it gets stale. Once stale, it is used to make *pappa al pomodoro*, also known as Tuscan soup. This Tuscan soup, however, is substantially different to the Tuscan soup you get at the Olive Garden. In Italian Tuscan soup, stale hard bread is simmered with tomatoes, garlic, and onions. It is simple, inexpensive, and surprisingly delicious.

Bread and wine! Having explored some of the differences concerning food, let us turn our attention to drink.

What to Drink

One of the unique aspects of American eating habits is that we will often accompany our meals with a flavored beverage. Having dinner with an Indian friend once, he commented on the American custom of having something other than water with our meals. While that is changing, it seems most Americans, Italian-Americans included, will have an iced tea or coke with their meals. Coke in many parts of the United States is a catch-all word for any carbonated drink.

Italians, in keeping with the idea that you should not mix flavors, will typically drink water with their meal. There are generally two types of water that they drink: *naturale* or *frizzante*, which is to say flat or carbonated. When traveling through Italy, Americans are continually asked, "no gas or gasso?"

The only other acceptable drink with your meal (other than water) is wine. Having said that, the wine is *with the meal* not in anticipation of it. In Italian-American restaurants across the country, you are asked for your drink order at the beginning of the meal which is then served well in advance of the main course. In Italy, there are three distinct types of drink while dining. In advance of the meal, you have an *aperitivo* which is a light drink meant to whet the appetite. With the meal itself, you have your wine. Then at the end of the meal, you have a *digestivo* to aid digestion of the food.

As I have noted several times prior, Italians prefer to not mix foods (remember the fussy four-year-old). Wine, however, is seen as something that enhances food rather than detracts from it. The acidity of the wine prepares the mouth to truly taste the food. It is important, therefore, to match the right type of wine with the food you are eating. The flavor of one should not overwhelm the other but provide a balance. The idea of properly matching a wine to a meal may seem terribly ostentatious, but we are talking about the Italian love of food. What matters is the wine itself, not the label or the impression it will have on others. As noted earlier, it is common for Italians to make their own wines either individually or as a group, such as a family or neighborhood.

Finally, when it comes to what to drink with your meal, Italians never drink coffee with their food. They especially shun cappuccino after breakfast. Having a cappuccino after dinner is a well discussed Italian-American habit. A cappuccino is mostly uncooked milk and, as noted earlier, milk is seen as a food in itself; a food that inhibits digestion creating poor health. Having a cappuccino in the morning with a croissant is acceptable because the cappuccino is considered pretty much the meal. Having one to top off your lunch or dinner, or worse yet with your lunch or dinner, is like having milk with your meal. Italians, therefore, avoid it after breakfast.

The Diversity of Italian Food

As we can see, there is an ever-widening gulf between Italian and Italian-American food. Italians cringe at some of the concoctions that Italian-Americans have come up with such as Utica Riggies. Meanwhile, Italian-Americans see as pretentious the idea that someone should be denied a cappuccino after a meal or meatballs on their spaghetti if they happen to enjoy one. You would expect that communities which are geographically dispersed would evolve in different ways.

Ultimately, we need to come to the realization that there is no one Italian way of eating that is the definitive Italian way to eat. For all that has been said across these pages, we see throughout history that Italy and Italian culture has not been monolithic, a single thing which is the same everywhere. Even when we all inhabited that one peninsula, we had our regional differences. Why, when we are now spread across the world, should we expect to eat the same way in San Diego, Chicago, New York, Milan, and Bari? We need to embrace our differences while understanding that we are each a different ingredient in the salad that is Italian culture. Know that if you are drinking a cappuccino at the end of the meal, you are behaving as an Italian-American. If you are grabbing a quick espresso and a *cannolo* on the way to the office, you are behaving as an Italian. We are all part of that same great culture of *Italiani nel mondo*.

Except for pineapple and Canadian bacon pizza; you can't do that and be Italian.

Chapter 8: The Beautiful Language

I Speak German to My Horse

It is reported that the Holy Roman Emperor, Charles V, once said, "I speak Spanish to God, Italian to women, French to men, and German to my horse." How could it be otherwise? When I was young and single, I was romantically involved with an Italian girl. She was a Gina, see Chapter 6, *Italian Steel*. Instead of whispering *sweet nothings* in my ear, as described in the cliché, all I asked was that she whisper Italian to me. I didn't speak Italian at the time, which was fine since I didn't really care what she was saying. All she needed to do was softly and airily speak Italian and I would melt like gelato on a Roman August afternoon.

One of my favorite books about Italy and the Italian language is Dianne Hales' *La Bella Lingua*, to which the title of this chapter is an homage. It is a work similar to this book in that it also describes a love affair. Her love affair, however, began with the Italian language which, as she describes it, is "the world's most enchanting language."[94] Who can blame her for falling in love with Italy and the Italian language? It is truly *La Bella Lingua* (The Beautiful Language).

Is Italian truly that wonderful? You don't have to believe Hales; you don't even have to believe me. Simply listen to it. There is a cadence, a musical rhythm and rhyme that is integrated into common, everyday communication. The sounds of the language itself are pure and clean. While it is not my intent to be disrespectful to different cultures, simply compare Italian to some other languages. There are no clucks, guttural utterances, or sounds similar to clearing your throat as with many. Italian is spoken almost exclusively in the front of the mouth, giving it a quality one would expect of a language spoken by the angels.

Now, I would understand if you think I am getting a bit carried away, but I can support my argument. When Tolkien created the languages of Middle Earth, he created for each of the various races a language that was reflective of their personalities (which is not at all surprising since

---

[94] Hales, Dianne, *La Bella Lingua: My Love Affair with Italian, the World's Most Enchanting Language*, Broadway Books, 2009, inner cover

he was a philologist). The dwarves were miners of the earth so their language was crude and rough. The orcs, the bad guys if you will, had a language that was ominous with a lot of "o-r" sounds. They came from Mordor for example. The elves, however, were half-spiritual – part of this world and part of the heavens – immortal and angelic. They were closest to *Eru Ilúvatar*, the creator of all existence. The language Tolkien created for these people, *Quenya*, sounds so Italian, that a non-Italian speaker would easily mistake it for Italian. It is all spoken in the front of the mouth with many of the same consonant blends. Many *Quenya* words have similar sounding words in Romance languages such as Spanish, Portuguese, and Italian. I find the cadence of *Quenya*, however, most similar to Italian.

Fourth Ain't Bad

By some estimates, Italian is the fourth most-studied language, behind English, French, and Spanish. At first, you might argue that if Italian is such a beautiful language why isn't it the most studied language and not simply fourth. Well, look at the competition. Spanish is popular simply for the sheer size of the Spanish-speaking world. It has the second largest population of speakers, surpassed only by Mandarin Chinese. French has the 18th largest population, and Italian the 23rd.

In the United States, the majority of immigrants are Spanish-speaking, many almost exclusively so. Most schools in the United States offer Spanish classes simply for its utility. There is no motivation to speak Italian to communicate with some otherwise inaccessible part of the population, as with Spanish. I have never encountered someone from Italy in the United States who cannot communicate relatively well in English.

The popularity of French can be related to its colonial strength. Many of France's former colonies, such as Canada, have retained the use of the language. Its former colonies continue to use it for daily communication, causing the language to grow in usage in places such as Africa. Italian, however, did not remain an official language for Italy's former colonies after World War II. As you would expect, local use in these areas therefore declined.

English is the lingua franca of technology. If you work in the high-tech industry, you need to know how to speak English. It is as simple as that. Although anecdotal, most of my Indian co-workers do not share a common language. There are 22 national languages in India. When many high-tech workers come to the United States, the only common language they share with other Indians is English. On more than one occasion, when hearing a co-worker speak in her native language, I will look at one of my other friends for an explanation. Frequently, they will shrug and say something like, "Don't look at me. She speaks Hindi. I speak Maithili." Learning to speak Italian has no economic incentive, as with English. In Italy, they call Microsoft Windows, Microsoft Windows, not Microsoft *Finestre*.

People learn to speak Italian because it is beautiful. It is the language of Dante, Petrarch, Boccaccio, Verdi, and Puccini. In *Tosca*, Act II, Floria Tosca sings *Vissi d'arte*. She asks God how he could persecute her after she has lived for art and love. Although I can write the libretto here, the only way to experience the true beauty of this wonderful work is to hear it. While other languages could certainly convey the same concepts as those sung by Tosca, they could never capture the anguish and pain as was done by Puccini. While other languages have their poetry, each of which is beautiful in their own right, none can compare with the passion inherent in Italian. Not that I am biased in any way.

The Numbers on the Words

Let's begin with some basic facts about the Italian language. It is the official language of Italy, Switzerland, San Marino, and the Sovereign Military Order of Malta. Some have claimed that Italian is also the official language of the Vatican, while others claim that it is Latin. Neither is correct. The Vatican has no official language. Although Latin had been prevalent in the Catholic Church for centuries, over the past 100 years Italian has taken on a greater role. While many of the most important official documents of the Holy See are published in Latin, such as Pope Benedict's formal retirement statement, since 1929 the church publishes its laws and regulations in Italian. Pope Francis has accelerated this change. For example, in 2014 he broke with tradition and replaced the use of Latin with Italian as the language to be used by Bishops during the Vatican synod.

Italian is a relatively easy language to learn. Unlike English, Italian words are spelled phonetically. Unlike French whose last letter is silent, *sometimes*, in Italian, you pronounce every letter according to a few simple rules. Neither do you have consonant blends that radically change the pronunciation of words such as the *ph* in phonetic. Once you learn the basic rules of spelling, you could read Italian aloud just as well as any native speaker. The only caveat I would add is that, for some of us, rolling your r's requires a bit of practice.

While the English alphabet has 26 letters, Italians use only 21. They do not have J, K, W, X, and Y. Although there are times when you will see the letters J and K appear in names, these are not based on standard Italian, but are derived from regional Italian dialects. Italian words end in one of four vowels; *o, i, a,* or *e.* The exceptions are foreign imports.

The biggest challenge with Italian, as with learning most languages, is the grammar. Just as with other languages, there are *irregular verbs* which are verbs whose conjugation is not consistent with the basic rules of the language. Although these are among the most commonly used verbs, it still requires you to remember which are irregular. There are also aspects of the language that haven't a significant English equivalent, such as the conjugation of *reflexive verbs.* I won't go into the thrilling details here, but simply warn you that Italian does have its challenges, although far fewer than English.

While the English language is composed of approximately 171,000 words of which slightly more than 47,000 are considered obsolete, Italian is composed of more than 270,000 words. The only western language with more words than Italian is Portuguese with roughly 390,000 words. Although this may seem daunting, the average American's vocabulary is roughly 5,000 words when speaking and twice that when writing. Even the most educated have vocabularies of approximately 80,000 words. So, it isn't necessary to learn all 270,000 Italian words. A simple vocabulary of two to three thousand will get you through most conversations. With the addition of a couple thousand more, you can be as erudite an orator as any Italian.

Untranslatable Words

If you were to attempt to expand your Italian vocabulary beyond the simple equivalent of English words and phrases, you would find a rich selection from which to choose. Over the years, as I have studied the Italian language and traveled through Italy, I have picked up a number of words that do not easily translate to English. The following is a list of some interesting examples:

Abbiocco This is the caloric shock one feels after a long lunch. It is that delicious drowsy feeling you have after a nice large meal. The cure for *abbiocco* is a *meriggiare.* See below.

Apericena This is an aperitif served during the first course of a meal, typically accompanied with canapés.

Boh Don't know, don't care. This is perhaps one of my favorite Italian words. Simple, sweet, and short. The lack of effort required to say this word pairs well with its meaning.

Celodurismo A rough English translation: I have an erection. It is the contraction of the expression *ce l'ho duro* into one word. This is a term first coined by Umberto Bossi, the former leader of the ultra-conservative Northern League.

Ciofeca This is something of poor quality, something cheap and not well made.

Culaccino This is the reason my mother was always after me to use a coaster. It is the ring left from a wet glass. It can also be used to describe the end of a loaf of bread.

Faloppone We have all worked with a *faloppone*. It is the person who thinks himself much more than what he is, while never delivering on his promises.

Furbo A duplicitous or devious person; in English, we might say the person is Machiavellian. In Italian, however, there is a connotation of a bit of respect or admiration for the intelligence behind the person's craftiness.

Gattara A woman who owns an excessive number of cats; in the United States, they refer to such a woman as *the crazy cat lady*.

Gibigianna This is truly a beautiful term, it is light reflected on water.

Gengle A term for a single parent which is a combination of the word *genitori* (parent) and single.

Magari In the United States we might say "I wish." I have also heard the expression "From your mouth to God's ear."

Menefreghista A person who is apathetic, who just doesn't care.

Meriggiare A lunchtime nap, preferably in a nice quiet, shady location. The cure for *abbiocco* is a *meriggiare*.

Monello A scoundrel or rascal, also used to describe an urchin, a street child.

Oleologo A professional olive oil expert.

Pantofolaio Although it can be translated as a maker of slippers, it is also used to describe an idler or a person who lounges about the house. In the United States, we call this person a "couch potato".

Pentastellato An adjective of something which is characteristic of the Five Star Movement in Italy, a populace political movement started by the comedian and blogger Beppe Grillo.

Qualunquismo An apathetic attitude, specifically towards politics. While in other parts of the world you will find a distrust of politics, *qualunquismo* is an apathetic resolution to the state of the state.

Rocambolesco While you can translate this as fantastic or extraordinary, it is much more. It is extraordinary in a specific way; imagine a character swinging on a rope from one ship to another, knife between his teeth, and a fair damsel in his arms. The origin of the word is from Pierre Alexis du Terril who created the character Rocambole. It is used to describe an exciting adventure.

Italian Dialects

People often speak of Italian dialects, such as Tuscan, Neapolitan, or Calabrese. This is incorrect. Throughout Italy, people of various regions do not speak *dialects*, neither do they speak a common language.

To be clear, a dialect is a variety of a particular language which is distinguished by regional or group manners of speaking. Dialects can be described as sibling tongues, languages grown out of a common parent. Consider the differences in speech patterns between an Alabaman, New Yorker, and a Londoner. Each has a different way of speaking as well as differences in pronunciation and meaning. All these patterns, however, started from a common parent, English.

With Italian, however, there was no formal Italian language which was a parent to all the regional patterns of speech. Rather, each region developed independently from the *vulgar* Latin just as Spanish and French. Under the Roman Empire, there were basically two types of Latin, the classical formal Latin, which was the official language, and the common language, which was used by the people. This common form of Latin, the vernacular, is often referred to as *vulgar Latin*. The sense of the word *vulgar* here being something which is unrefined or lacking in sophistication and good taste. The Italian language spoken today began as the Latin spoken by the common Roman on the street.

As we have discussed extensively throughout this book, when the Roman Empire fell apart, the connection between the various parts of the empire broke down causing each of the regions to develop independently of one another. Communication between these groups, for the reasons described earlier, was poor. Each region or city-state saw themselves as separate from the others, each with their own heritage, customs, and culture. This was also reflected in the evolution of separate languages.

Languages are not static things; they are dynamic, changing over time. Even when you have a formal written language with specific rules, as we do today, grammar and word usage change over time. Think of the word, *thug*. At one time *thug* meant a violent person, a criminal. It brings to mind a heavily jowled, unshaven hoodlum with a bulldog-like face. Today, the word is seen by some as racist, referring to elements of the inner city. In the United States, use of the word *thug* in polite conversation is inadvisable.

After the fall of Rome, when people wrote, they wrote in formal Latin. Scientific works, literature, and even legal documents were all written in formal Latin. Many studied Latin simply to be able to write official documents for the aristocracy. There was no literary industry that created a common written Italian that could somehow preserve tenuous linkages of language with the past and other regions. Even if such a volume of texts did exist, the vast majority of the populace was illiterate.

This meant that what was proper – what meaning the language had – depended on what the speakers meant when they said it. It is similar to Lewis Carroll's Humpty Dumpty, "When I use a word, it means just what I choose it to mean." A vernacular, whose only rules are in popular usage of the street, changes much more quickly in much shorter periods of time. A word or phrase popular in one generation may fall out of favor in the next. Changes in the way people live or popular culture may give rise to new meanings to old words. Each region took its own path in the evolution of language, developing variations of Latin, not Italian. These became the local regional languages.

As I noted above, each region developed independently from the *vulgar* Latin just as Spanish and French developed. Therefore, it is more correct, although not common, to think of the various regional languages spoken throughout Italy to be at the same level on the hierarchy of languages as other Romance languages and not subordinate to some non-existent Italian mother tongue. For convenience sake, however, most people refer to what are really regional languages as dialects. For the sake of consistency, I will do the same.

When discussing the dialects of Italy, the Sicilians, as is usually the case, are something altogether different. As you will recall from previous chapters, the Sicilians do not even consider themselves Italian. The same holds true for the language they speak. The Sicilian language is considered by many to be a separate language from Italian altogether. While many Sicilians, my mother included, speak a language that is a mixture of Italian and Sicilian, the pure Sicilian language is more different from Italian than Italian is from Spanish or even French.

Consider how Sicily sits in the middle of the Mediterranean. It is no surprise the Sicilian language includes Arabic, Hebrew, and Greek. There are regions of Sicily that were settlements of Albanian refugees in the 15th century, specifically Piana degli Albanesi, Santa Santa Cristina Gela, and Contessa Entellina. They speak *Gheg* which is a hybrid of Sicilian and pre-Ottoman Albanian.

The Father of the Italian Language

Dante Alighieri is considered *the father of the Italian language* and, I believe, rightfully so.

In Chapter 2, *Italy What a Concept,* I discussed how Dante was one of the first to argue for a unified Italy, one in which the church and state were separate. He also argued, at the same time, for a common language for Italians. He referred to this as the *volgare illustre* (the illustrious vernacular). He proposed that the language be compiled from the dialects of Italy, retaining a common core while throwing out regional idiosyncrasies.

As noted above, serious works were written in Latin. In 1302, however, Dante wrote *De Vulgari Eloquentia,* in which he defends the eloquence of the vulgar, or common, language. While formal Latin may have been the official language of ancient Rome, he understood how the common tongue changes over time; a point made earlier. The defined language of a people should, therefore, adapt to changes in the way people think from one generation to the next as well as to fit changing times. He argued it was, therefore, illogical to chain all literature to a particular language or structure that was antiquated.

Dante proved his point by writing in Italian what is inarguably the greatest work of western literature, *The Divine Comedy.* By writing in this style, Dante made the poem accessible to the common Italian while demonstrating their language was worthy of such lofty topics as man's quest for salvation and the healing power of love. Look at what Dante did in the context of his time by writing in the common vernacular. When Jesus spoke in parables, he took common events in individual lives to demonstrate spiritual truths. *The Divine Comedy* did the same, taking stories that were *ripped from the headlines* of 14th century Florence to convey complex theological and philosophical truths in a way that was both understandable and relatable to the masses.

Some commentators, and others who become acquainted with Dante for the first time, will often comment that the Italian language is relatively easy for poetry since the words end in one of four vowels. This entirely misses the point of Dante's genius and is one of those arguments that drives *Danteists* mad. As you read Dante, you will see he does not simply rhyme on the last letter, but the last syllable of the word. He does this across the 14,233 lines of the poem. The structure of *The Divine Comedy* is a complex one. Dante breaks his poem into three books, or canticles, which are further subdivided into canti.[95] The rhyming scheme of these songs is in triplets referred to as *terza rima*. This is important. It shows the language of *The Divine Comedy*, the common language, is substantive enough to be the stuff of complex, yet beautiful, poetry.

Where Dante was mistaken was in his approach to the definition of a common language. You cannot stitch together portions of various dialects as if you are sewing a quilt. Ernst Pulgram noted in his book *The Tongues of Italy*, that to do as Dante suggested would give you an incomplete language. More importantly, the evolution of language does not occur as Dante recommended. Typically in language, a particular dialect emerges for a variety of reasons as superior to others, becoming the standard. The irony is Dante, in writing *The Divine Comedy* in his Tuscan dialect (albeit with some of the local peculiarities removed) did as Pulgram suggested.

Dante, Petrarch, and Boccaccio have been called the three jewels in the Italian literary crown. They created a body of literary work that raised the Tuscan dialect above the others. Pulgram has questioned whether Tuscan would have been selected as standard Italian if it were not for these three men. "I should venture to say that without Dante, at least Tuscan would have no greater chance than Roman or Neapolitan or Lombard. Indeed I should go so far as to suggest that if Dante had been a child of Naples and, providentially, Boccaccio and Petrarch also,

---

[95] Canti is the plural of Canto which means song. Each *chapter* of the work is a song. The first book is composed of 34 canti while the second and third are made up of 33.

Neapolitan and not Tuscan would have become Italy's national language."[96]

Later, in the 16th century, when men such as Pietro Bembo, an Italian scholar and poet of that era, argued the official Italian language should be based on the great literary works, they cited Petrarch and Boccaccio. Notice how Bembo did not reference Dante. To many of that era, Dante's achievement in appealing to the masses was a fault, not a strength. As one 14th century commentator put it, "Therefore I should exclude this poet of yours [Dante] from the company of literary men and should leave him with the girdle-makers, bakers, and that kind of crowd; for he talks in such a way that it seems he would rather want to be associated with that sort of people."[97]

In the years after Dante and his fellow Tuscan poets, debates raged as to the definition of the proper Italian language. I will not drag you through those debates here. Let it suffice to say that in 1582 *Accademia della Crusca* was established, also referred to as *La Crusca*. Still in existence today, it is the oldest linguistic academy in the world as well as the most important research center on the Italian language. *La Crusca*'s mission is to define and defend the Italian language. In 1612, *La Crusca* published the first Italian dictionary, the first dictionary of any of the Romance languages.

Despite establishing such an institute, the adoption of a standard Italian language was far from successful. Prior to unification, roughly less than ten percent of Italians spoke proper Italian. Estimates vary between 2.5% and 12.6%, but most prefer an estimate of around 9.5%. This is due, in part, to the high rates of illiteracy among Italians; in the 1860's, illiteracy rates were in the mid to high 70% range. At the time, for most Italians, proper Italian was primarily through the written word; remember, this was in the time prior to mass communication. Even in school, teachers did not use proper Italian. A 1910 study showed most educators used either a dialect or a hybrid of a dialect and proper Italian.

Other nations such as France and Spain have followed the example of Italians in establishing their own academies to watch over the purity of their languages. Ernst Pulgram notes that many of these others have

---

[96] Pulgram, Ernst, *Tongues of Italy, Prehistory and History*, Greenwood Publishing Group, 1978, pg. 60

[97] Pulgram, Ernst, *Tongues of Italy, Prehistory and History*, Greenwood Publishing Group, 1978, pg. 61

been much more successful in establishing their own standards. He writes, "It is remarkable that among the three most important Romanic countries, Italy was the first to produce a dictionary of a model language yet the least successful in propagating this language among its people."[98]

Fascism & the Italian Language

The dominance of dialects continued to the end of the 19th century. We do not see a substantive expansion of standard Italian until Italy begins to move from agriculture to manufacturing with greater centralization and access to public education. During the World War One era, about half of all Italians could speak proper Italian, although many in informal situations still relied heavily on their local dialect. Despite this modest success, there was still debate among Italians as to whether there should even be a common language. Some felt dialects were weeds that needed to be rooted out. Others celebrated dialects for their vibrancy and accessibility by the common man.

When Mussolini came to power, the debate was resolved by decree. Mussolini, as we have discussed, promoted his own nationalistic vision of *Italianità*. The fascist vision of Italy was of one nation, one uniform nation. It was "the nationalist promotion of an Italianità with Rome at its heart; a totalitarian intolerance of pluralism and an insistence on the subordination of the individual to the centralized authority of the state."[99] In such an Italy, there was no room for dialects. Schools were to teach in the official language of the state. While this was a repressive course of action, it did bring the Italian people together under one language. All signs and public notices were to be in Italian, proper Italian. There was also pressure to *Italianize* surnames and the names of places. *English-isms* in the naming of places was not to be tolerated.

[98] Pulgram, Ernst, *Tongues of Italy, Prehistory and History*, Greenwood Publishing Group, 1978, pg. 63

[99] Baranski, Zygmunt G., & West, Rebecca J., (Eds), *The Cambridge Companion to Modern Italian Culture*, Cambridge University Press, 2001, pg. 70

Italian-American Pidgin

In terms of the relationship between Italians and Italian-Americans, the story starts to get really interesting at this point. Most Italians came to the United States prior to Mussolini's rise to power. If they spoke standard Italian at all, it was only in formal situations; what was spoken in the home was the local dialect. Although the Italian government – prior to World War II – sponsored Italian schools, only a small percentage of second-generation Italian-Americans attended. The vast majority of Italian-Americans who did learn to speak Italian in the home learned to speak a dialect.

Complicating matters, most Italian-Americans began to speak an *Italian-American pidgin* which is not to be confused with *Italian Pigeon*, a dish prepared by my grandmother back in the old days. The *pidgin* to which I am referring is defined as an incomplete language which has been formed as a means of communication between two or more groups. This is a result of what we have been discussing throughout the chapter, the tendency for languages to evolve, adapting to their environment.

As discussed in a previous chapter, within the different Italian communities throughout the United States there was inter-regional communication, both within the community and at the construction site or on the factory floor. Relationships formed between immigrants from the various regions. While the first generation of immigrants may have initially retained their dialect, due to the interaction between various regional groups as well as the fading memory of how things were pronounced *back home*, our own Italian-American language – our *Italian-American pidgin* – took shape.

Italian-American pidgin not only facilitated communication between immigrants but with English-speaking employers as well. It began to incorporate English words that were common to the workplace, at times giving those words an Italian flare. For example, the word *backhouse*, which is another word for outhouse, in Italian-American pidgin is pronounced *boo-kowz*.

The following is a list of some Italian-American expressions and the correct Italian from which they originated;

Adutipazz – [ah-due-tea-pots] – you're crazy. From the Italian *ma tu sei pazzo* (but you are crazy).

Agida – [ah-jih-da] – aggravation. Most frequently, I heard my mother use this in the sentence, "you're giving me agida." From the Italian *acidità* (indigestion).

Ba fungul – [bah-fun-gool] – go f--- yourself. Deviations on this phrase include: *va fungulo* and *ma fungulo*. From the Italian *vaffanculo*.

Biangolin – [be-on-go-lean] – bleach. The actual Italian word for bleach is *candeggiare*. This expression, however, is derived from *bianco lino* (white linen).

Bicciuridu – [beek-oo-redo] – little baby boy. From the Italian *piccolo bambino*.

Bisgott – [bis-got] – a specific type of Italian cookie. Also, *bisgotti*. From the Italian *biscotto*. The literal translation of *biscotto* is "twice cooked." When preparing the cookie, it is first baked in the shape of a loaf then sliced. The slices are then baked again. Note, at times, people will say *biscotti* when referring to an individual cookie. This is incorrect. Biscotto is singular, one cookie. *Biscotti* is plural.

Braggiol – [bra-shoel or bra-joll] – rolled flank steak which is used as the basis for a meat sauce. From the Italian *braciola*.

Broschiutt – [bra-shoot] – Italian ham. From the Italian *prosciutto*.

Buttann – [boo-tahn] – whore. From the Italian *putanna*.

Cazz – [cots] – penis. You can also add an *o* at the end for *cazzo*. From the Italian *cazzo*.

Che cozz? – [kay-cots] – what the f--- are you doing?! From the Italian *che cazzo fai?*

Chefa? – [kay-fa] – what are you doing? From the Italian *che cosa fai?*

Cogliones – [coal-yo-nays] – testicles, balls. From the Italian *coglioni*.

Dutipazz – [due-tea-pots] – you are all crazy. This is similar to *adutipazz*. From the Italian *tutti pazzi*.

Fanabila – [fa-nob-a-la] – go to hell. There are several variations in both the meaning and pronunciation. It is also pronounced *afanabola* [ah-fa-nob-a-la] or *vafanabola* [va-fa-nob-a-la]. From the Italian *a fa Napoli* (go to Naples). Apparently, Naples to some Italians, is the proverbial equivalent of hell. Some Italian Americans see this as the equivalent of *ba fungul*.

Gabbados – [gaba-dos] – hardheaded. From the Italian *capa tosta*.

Gabagool – [gob-a-gool] – a spicy ham. From the Italian *capicola*.

Gabish – [gaa-beesh] – understand. From the Italian *capisci*.

Gaguzz – [gaa-goots] – idiot. From the Sicilian *cucuzza*. The literal translation is *pumpkin*. An idiot, therefore, is someone who has a pumpkin for a head.

Ganol – [ga-knowl] – an Italian pastry. From the Italian *cannoli*.

Gavone – [gaa-voan] – a glutton. This is also used to mean a person with poor manners, a low-life. From the Italian *cafone*.

Goombah – [goom-bah] – close friend. Also *goombadde* [good-bah-day]. From the Italian *comare*.

Gots an gool – [gots-on-gool] – creamed beef on toast. This phrase is also used to refer to making a mess of things, basically to *f--- things up*. This is a very loose translation from Italian. While *gots* is the Italian-American form of *cazzo*, there is no corresponding word that could link *gool* to toast. You might hear someone who is British use the phrase *make a dog's breakfast of it*; the British version is significantly less vulgar.

Gumad – [goo-mod] – mistress. If a man has a mistress, the mistress is referred to as a *close* friend in an ironic way. From the Italian *comare*.

Madone – [Ma-dawn] – a rough equivalent of "oh my God." Occasionally, people will add a *mia* at the end to form *madona mia*. Sometimes used in place of damn it. From the Italian *Madonna*.

Maliocch' – [maal-oak] – the evil eye. From the Italian *malocchio*. This will be discussed in more detail in the next chapter.

Mamaluke – [maa-maa-luke] – fool. From the Italian *mammalucco*.

Mannaggia – [maa-na-jah-ah] – although this is one of my favorite expressions when frustrated, there is no good direct translation. Typically, when I use this term, I drop the *ia* at the end, *mannaagg* [maa-na-jah]. When I don't drop the *ia*, non-Italian friends confuse what I am saying for the French expression *menage e trois*, which is something totally different. It is from what my Italian friends call *lingua antiquata* (antiquated language). The initial phrase was *male ne aggia* which roughly translates to *may they get trouble from it*.

Maron – [maa-roan] – another version of *madone* which is a rough equivalent of "oh my God." Sometimes it is used in place of damn it. From the Italian *Madonna*.

Marronna mia – [maa-roan-a-mia] – oh my god. From the Italian *Madonna mia*.

Menzamenz – [menz-ah-menz] – half & half. This is another favorite. It is a great response to *how ya doin?* It is especially appropriate when you are feeling good, but not great. From the Italian *mezza mezza*.

Menzamort' – [mezzo-morto] – half dead. Great response when you are hung-over or just not feeling well.

Minch' – [mink] – This is one with which you need to be careful. You can also append an *ia* to the end of the word, *minchia* [mink-key-ya]. When I was a kid we used this all the time, thinking it meant *holy cow*. Some Italians, however, take it to mean anything from *holy cow* to *holy f---*.

Oobatz – [oo-bahts] – a crazy or stupid person. From the Italian *un pazzo*.

Paesan – [pia-zahn] – a good friend. This is another favorite. When I see a good friend I will greet them with a cheerful loud *Eh! Paesan!* Try it with your Italian friends. From the Italian *paesano* which is literally fellow countryman.

Pasta fasul – [pasta-fa-zool] – an Italian bean and macaroni soup. Just like in the song, *when she says I love you just like pasta fazool, THAT'S AMORE!* When you go to an Italian restaurant you will see *pasta fagioli* on the menu. If you do, ask for *pasta fasul;* if the server is Italian, they will laugh. They will also think you are Italian and not try to slip anything Amarighan over on you. If they don't know what you are talking about, leave.

Pastine – [paa-steen] – a very tiny star-shaped pasta. These are wonderful. If you recall, in the previous chapter, I described how I use this for *pasta bianco* which eventually evolved into Fettuccine Alfredo in the United States.

Rigott – [ri-got] – Italian cottage cheese. From the Italian *ricotta*.

Schaldol – [Shca-doll] – escarole. Escarole is similar to spinach, but much heartier. It is the basis of Italian wedding soup, which is popular in the United States. It is also a slang word for paper money, both are papery and green. From the Italian *scarola*.

Shkeeve – [Shkee-vee] – This has no real direct English translation. Some may think of it as disgusting, but disgusting in my opinion is too strong a word. Imagine a person of very fair complexion with dandruff, unclean, and who always seems to have spittle in the corners of his or her mouth. That person is *shkeeve*. It does not necessarily always apply to a person either. Anything unpleasant, or which gives you the sensation you want to wash your hands if you touch it, is *shkeeve*.

Schifozz – [shki-foohz] – disgusting. This is a powerful word. It can refer to a thing, like what has been sitting in the back of the fridge in the container you haven't opened for the past six months. It can also refer to a person behaving in a disgusting manner. My mother mastered this word. She would use the original Italian *schifosa*. I can still hear her voice, after these many long years, talking about the housekeeping habits of a woman we knew. She would draw out the first syllable *Shkiiii*, then quickly pass over the second *fo*, with a strong emphasis on the final syllable *za*.

Schoff – [Shk-off] – a glancing slap to the head, usually to the back of the head. As used in the statement, *Billy, if you don't clean your room I am going to give you such a shkoff.* From the Italian *soffia*.

Sporcaccione – [spor-ca-chown-eh] – pain in the ass. This means more than just a bothersome person, however. The person is bothersome in that they seem to always cause trouble or an argument. This word has also evolved to the point where some Italian-Americans will use the more abbreviated form *scorch*. From the Italian *scocciatura*.

Stata zit – [stat-ah-zeet] – shut up. Also *stata geet*. From the Italian *stai zitto*.

Stungots – [Stoon-gots] – a stupid person. This is another great word. Although it is used in multiple ways, the way in which I have heard it used most frequently is *what a stungots*. It is the Italian equivalent of the Yiddish *schmuck*. From the Italian *stu cazzu* which is *what a dick*.

These are just a few of the colorful phrases with which I grew up. Just reading through the list brings to mind vignettes of my childhood. Generally, I have left words off the list where the Italian-American equivalent simply drops the last letter. For example, my father was *Calabres* in Italian-American pidgin, but *Calabrese* in Italian. You will also notice that *Italian-American pidgin* frequently replaces a *p* with a *b* and a *t* with a *d*, such as *spaghedi* instead of *spaghetti*.

Spaghetti can be a study in Italian-American pidgin all by itself. Sometimes, Italian-Americans will insert an *h* after at the beginning and drop the *i* at the end, giving you *shpagett*. If they do use a vowel at the end of the word, it is always plural, *spaghetti*. Even when referring to a single strand of spaghetti, they will use the plural form of the word, not *spaghetto* which is the more correct singular form.

While Italian-Americans rarely use the singular form of spaghetti, the exact opposite is the case with *lasagna*. In Bologna, they use the plural form of the word, *lasagne*. Lasagna refers to a single strand, or noodle.

214

They have a point. The traditional dish is composed of multiple noodles arranged in layers with filling in-between. If multiple strands of spaghetti is plural, shouldn't *lasagne* be used? Also, lasagne came from Bologna, so maybe they should get to tell everyone else when it is singular or plural. Regardless of the merits of their argument, most Italians and Italian-Americans use the singular form, *lasagna*.

When learning to speak Italian, these adaptations gave me a handicap that other students didn't have. At times, my Italian-Americanisms would slip into my speech. My instructors would patiently remind me in Italian, "Bill... Bill... please. In this class we speak Italian not Soprano," making reference to the speech patterns of New Jersey mobsters.

The English Invasion

English, as noted above, is the *lingua franca* of technology. The Internet, as well as its accompanying technologies, has accelerated the encroachment of English on languages around world. People in various countries communicate directly with one another using the idioms of the net and social media.

The invasion of the English language goes well beyond a few words being incorporated into the Italian vocabulary. During a recent visit to Rome, I was having trouble finding the bus to take me to the Appian Way. All roads may lead to Rome, but not all bus lines. So, after wandering around a bit, I asked someone passing by for directions. Not feeling very confident in my Italian language skills, I asked if he spoke English. "Of course," he said dismissively. His friendly demeanor quickly changed to irritation. It was clear I had insulted him.

I was to learn later that Italian colleges require an English examination. In order for a country to truly compete today, they require an English-speaking workforce. The type of examination is dependent on the particular major. For example, if you are an economics major, you are required to understand business English whereas a computer science major would be required to have more of a technology focus.

These examinations are quite serious; often students' futures are dependent on how well they do. When visiting Ravenna, a friend who tutored students in English was quite upset. Two of his students were having trouble in preparing for the test and he was concerned they would not be able to attend college if they did not do well.

As you can imagine, English is having an effect on the Italian language. The following list is a sample of English words that have found their way into acceptable Italian.

Crashare A computer crash.

Photoshoppare The name of Adobe's application has not only become part of the English language, as in "the image was photoshopped," it has also become an Italian verb.

Fangirlare Used to describe a girl that is an obsessive fan of a movie, comic book, music group, or any type of series; be it a book or television series.

Twitteratura Sometimes used to describe twitter posts with a poetic bent. It is a hybrid of Twitter and *letteratura* (literature).

Friendzonnare The infamous friend zone exists even in Italy! This is the place where all of us who are romantically interested in another person are banished with the words a good guy or friend. The target of desire does not want anything more than friendship. I think we all know by now that, when turning down offers of romance, we should refrain from using the phrase "Let's just be friends."

Lollare To Laugh Out Loud.

Skuoncare Skin care.

Spoilerare To give away the ending of a book or movie, as in "Spoiler alert. Rosebud is a …"

Shazzamare Similar to *photoshoppare*, this is the name of a popular app. In this case, it means to use the Shazam app to identify a piece of music.

Skillato Used to describe a skilled worker, used in place of the Italian *qualificato*.

The incorporation of English words into the Italian language has not gone without notice. In 2016, the Italian author, Annamaria Testa petitioned the Italian government, public authorities, the media, and businesses to use more Italian. The petition was subsequently signed by the president and board of the *Accademia della Crusca*. In it, the point is made that one should use Italian when possible, reverting to an English substitute only when there is no Italian equivalent. The petition uses specific examples such as: the use of *form* in place of the Italian *modulo*, or the use of *market share* in place of *quota di mercato*.

The petition asserts that Italian is the language of Italy. As such, the use of the language is a matter of transparency and democracy. When the government communicates in Italian, it is communicating in a way which is most clear to the Italian people. If the people are to participate in government, they must have a shared language through which they can exchange ideas.

The petition also goes on to say that there is a difference between speaking *Itanglese* and being bi-lingual. *Itanglese* is an amalgam of Italian and English. It is not English or Italian, it is a third Cronenberg language. Being bi-lingual is the ability to speak in two languages. While the latter is a virtue, the former is a vice.

Most importantly, the Italian language is loved by millions of people around the world. Remember, it is the fourth most popular language to be studied. It is the language of Italian culture, from Dante to Umberto Eco. It is the fabric of *Italianità*.

I share Annamaria Testa's concerns. If English becomes the language of the educated, if it becomes acceptable for the government to communicate in English rather than Italian, will the Italian language return to the language of the common people, the *vulgaria*? If Italian is replaced by English as the language of learning, where does that leave the average Italian who isn't necessarily bilingual?

Why do Italian Speak with Their Hands?

The stereotype of Italians is that we speak with our hands. This is one of those generalizations of Italians I admit to being true. Keep in mind, though, part of the beauty of the Italian language is that our entire body, our entire being, is used in communicating. There is no mistaking our intent. You need not even speak the language, you can understand just by watching.

Several years ago, my son and I were cycling through Northern Italy. Passing through Venice, we decided to do some sightseeing. It was in the summer and the city was crowded with tourists, clogging the restaurants, hotels, and streets. As we came to the Rialto Bridge, standing on a small side street was a gondolier. Holding his hat by its brim, muscles rippling beneath his tight striped shirt, he looked down at his feet. In front of him, half his size, stood a wisp of an Italian girl. The skirt portion of her flowered sundress danced as she angrily waved her arms and wagged her finger under the gondolier's nose. A stream of words flowed through her so quickly and so venomously, my heart grieved for the poor man. He did not dare raise his eyes to meet hers. He just nodded his head. She was mad.

"What do you think he did?" my son asked.

"I don't know what it was, but I am sure he won't do it again." To this day, I still wonder what on earth that gondolier did to make her so angry; there was no mistaking how that woman felt. Her entire self, from the tips of her toes to the tip of her tongue, was expressing her rage.

So why do Italians speak with their hands? An Amarighan once snidely suggested it was because our mouths were always full. Putting that aside, I have heard a number of theories. One study, at San Francisco State University, found a link between problem solving and gesturing. Patricia Miller, a Professor of Psychology, is quoted as saying, "Even we adults sometimes gesture when we're trying to organize our tax receipts or our closets. When our minds are overflowing, we let our hands take on some of the cognitive load."[100]

While Professor Miller's explanation is interesting, it doesn't explain why Italians do and Scandinavians don't. The best explanation I have heard to date is from a linguistic analyst friend. It is a matter of ambiguity concerning the use of the definite/indefinite article. "I cani abbaiano," can mean one of two things, "Dogs bark" or "*The* dogs bark." The two sentences have different meanings. Hand gestures give the speaker a way of providing further clarification.

Now, to understand and speak Italian, there are a number of gestures with which you should become familiar. Most of these gestures have survived in the Italian-American community; one of the few things we have retained from our cultural heritage.

Here are just a few.

All Purpose Form your hand into the shape of an upward-facing cone, shaking it slightly. For added affect you can use both hands. You can use this with expressions such as *ma che!* or *che cazzo!* It can also be used when you are just asking a question *che cosa?!*

Cuckold Make a fist then extend your index and little finger pointing them towards the sky.

---

[100] Lane, James, Why Italians talk with their hands (and Scandinavians don't), *The Babbel Blog*, May 7, 2014, https://blog.babbel.com/why-italians-talk-with-their-hands-and-scandinavians-dont/

Cunning Make a fist and extend the thumb. Then draw the thumb in a line from the ear to the corner of the mouth.

Fa bene Flatten your hand and, with the tips of your fingers, run it under your chin out forward, flicking it a bit at the end. Once completed, the flattened palm should be held briefly in front of you tilted slightly away from you with the palm facing inward. The actual meaning of *fa bene* is doing well. However, this is similar to the passive aggressive use the word *fine* in English. When you are in a discussion with someone and want to tell them to go ahead and do whatever they like (you don't care even though you really do) you will want to use this gesture. They will get the message.

Fanabila (*go to* hell) Hold your hand in a fist putting your thumb behind your front upper teeth. You might even flick the hand forward to add emphasis.

I agree Extend just your index finger and hold down the lower lid of just one eye.

I am hungry Hold your hand out flat and parallel to the ground. Then, in a slight back and forth motion, tap your stomach with the side of your hand.

I am watching you Extend just your index finger and hold down the lower lid of just one eye. While it is the same as the gesture for agreement, the meaning is really dependent on context.

Italian Salute One of my favorites. Swing your right arm up as if you are going to punch someone in the jaw, then with great flourish grab your inner elbow with the other hand. You don't have to say it, but a good *ma fungul* will help make the point. To perform this gesture well, you need to really show some power. The fist is held tightly and the slapping sound of your hand catching the elbow should come out. You really want to communicate a driving power to the gesture in a menacing way. There is nothing worse than an insipid Italian Salute.

Listen Tug on your ear.

Mafioso If you suspect someone of being in league with the Mafia, put your index finger in one ear, and hold the side of your nose with the index finger of the other hand. If the person is nearby, roll your eyes in their direction. It is best to try to be subtle about this, just for safety's sake.

Malocchio Make a fist then extend your index and little finger pointing them towards the ground. This is to ward off the evil eye.

Mannaggia (oh my god) Bite the side of your hand with it held out flat and parallel to the floor. Shake your hand a bit for emphasis.

Maron (damn it) Bite the side of your index finger with a closed fist. This is a general sign of anger.

No good Form your hand in the shape of a pistol and rotate at the wrist. This is most common in the area around Naples.

Pazzo (crazy) Tap your temple holding your hand like it is a pistol.

Perfect Make the OK gesture as in English, but then pull your hand across your mouth as if you are zippering your mouth shut.

Please Hold your hands flat and together as if in prayer, rotating them in unison at the wrist. This is not only useful when you are asking someone a favor, but when you are angry. For example, a mother might rhetorically say to her son, "Please! Tell me what the hell you were thinking when you …"

Sleeping together Take both your hands as if you are about to point at something, then hold your hands together with the index fingers side by side and rub the two extended fingers back and forth. This is another great gesture that clearly demonstrates what it is meant to represent.

Stata Zitt (shut up) Amarighans, when they want you to be quiet, will put their finger to their lips with a quiet Shhh! Amarighans are so funny. Italians and Italian-Americans will put the finger across the side of the mouth and angrily say with a glare *Stata zitt!*

Italian Opera

The language of any culture is one of its key characteristics. So much of the art of a culture is expressed through its language. Yes, I know this is obvious, but really think about it for a moment. In England and the United States, we speak English, although here in the States we do use the language a bit differently. Imagine the culture of these two nations without the music of Elvis, The Beatles, Van Morrison, or James Taylor. What effects would there be on our cultural heritage if we were cut off from this music? The same is true of our literature. Imagine what English would be like without Chaucer, or Shakespeare. Imagine the United States without Herman Melville, Mark Twain, or Kurt Vonnegut.

Now let's apply this same thinking to Italian culture, beginning with music. Keeping in mind that *Italianità* is the essence of being Italian – the spirit of Italia – there is nothing that more imparts *Italianità* than

Italian opera. The nature of Italian opera is the expression of Italian culture. In Chapter 2, *Italy What a Concept,* I discussed how *Va, Pensiero* from Verdi's *Nabucco* rallied the Italian people to the cause of Italian nationalism. Opera captures the spirit of Italians.

Italian-Americans, at times, have a ruthless attitude of which they are very proud. In the second act of *Tosca,* Puccini captures this ruthlessness well when Tosca, shortly after singing how she lived for art and love, stabs the villain Scarpia. In the opera, Tosca is a beautiful and celebrated singer who is coerced into a sexual encounter with the evil chief of police, Baron Scarpia. As she stabs him she sings:

> *This is the kiss of Tosca!*
> *Is your blood choking you?*
> *And killed by a woman!*
> *Did you torment me enough?*
> *Can you still hear me? Speak?*
> *Look at me! I am Tosca! Oh, Scarpia!*

What could be more ruthless, cold blooded, and vengeful? What could be more Italian? As he dies, she mocks him, "and killed by a woman!" What stands out to me in the piece, more than any other, is when she says "Look at me!" There is none of this knife-in-the-back, a blow from an unseen enemy. Tosca wants Scarpia to look her in the eyes. She wants to ensure he sees she is the killer. She wants the last thing he sees in this world to be her hatred.

Italian Literature

Our literature is as equally important to our cultural heritage as our music. As described in Chapter 2, *Italy What a Concept,* Italy's literary history includes the recovery and publication of the works of antiquity, but their contribution goes beyond the mere recovery of classical writing. Poets such as Dante and Guido Cavalcanti were poets of *Dolce Stil Novo* (Sweet New Style). Recognized as a step forward in the art of poetry, its practitioners broke new ground with multiple meanings to their verse, leveraging the use of metaphors and symbolism. This laid the groundwork for generations of western poets who were to follow.

The writings of Italians were not simply limited to poetry. Machiavelli, known as the *Father of Political Science* for *The Prince,* left behind a wide-ranging body of work. At one extreme, he wrote on such serious subjects as the history of Florence and discourses on the Roman Livy.

At the other end of the spectrum, he wrote a bawdy five-act play, *The Mandrake.*

Of course, reading the list, you might be thinking that this is all well and good, but what have they done lately. Modern-day Italian authors include Giuseppe Tomasi di Lampedusa who wrote the internationally renowned *Il Gattopardo* (The Leopard). There is also Umberto Eco. Eco is best known for his three most popular works: *Il pendolo di Foucault,* (Foucault's Pendulum), *L'isola del giorno prima,* (The Island of the Day Before), and *Il nome della rosa,* (The Name of the Rose), which was later made into a movie.

Neither should we forget the writings of Italian-American authors. Mario Puzo, known for *The Godfather,* also wrote *The Fortunate Pilgrim.* This lesser-known work presents a truer image of what Italian-Americans faced in coming to the United States. Rather than *The Godfather's* romanticized recollection and whitewashing of the past, *The Fortunate Pilgrim* presents what one family, and in particular the mother of that family, had to face in order to survive life in America.

Although I could list the Italian and Italian-American authors that have made significant contributions to the world of literature, it would not be very interesting. I fear I may have already tested your patience, so let me conclude with a key Italian-American author, Pietro di Donato. In an earlier chapter, I made reference to his work *Christ in Concrete.* It should be required reading for every Italian-American. Although the author is not as well known as Puzo, this work is much more significant to the Italian-American identity than *The Godfather.* At the time of its publication, it was chosen over John Steinbeck's *Grapes of Wrath* by the Book-of-the-Month Club, although Steinbeck's work was chosen over Donato for the Pulitzer Prize.

The Italian Language & Italianità

Earlier, I noted how the expression of the art of a culture is through its language; specifically, its music and literature. The importance of these elements helps provide the vertical integration to which I referred in Chapter 1, *The Awakening.* If you will recall, Robert Bly in *The Sibling Society* described vertical integration as establishing linkages with our past. We do this through the art of our culture; we are able to hear the music of composers and the words of authors who are long silent and the thoughts of our ancestors whose remains are now dust.

Chapter 9: The Donation of Constantine

Italy & Catholicism

Most people assume if you are Italian you are Catholic. It is a pretty safe bet to make, considering by most estimates that 83% of the Italian population is Catholic. Statistics provided by the Catholic Church claim 97% of Italians are Roman Catholic, or at least baptized as such. It is no wonder, therefore, that Italy is the country forever associated with the Catholic Church; and the Catholic Church, the *Roman* Catholic Church, is forever associated with Italy. Although these statistics do not indicate devotion, and the populations of other countries may have larger percentages of Roman Catholics, there is no other nation whose Catholicism so permeates not only their culture, but their way of being.

To understand the relationship between Roman Catholicism and Italian culture, all you need do is refer to *Lautsi v. Italy* which was a case brought against the Italian government at the European Court of Human Rights. From 2005 to 2011, in courts from the Veneto Administrative Court all the way up to the European Court on Human Rights, Mrs. Soile Lautsi challenged an Italian law which required the display of a crucifix in classrooms. The 1929 Concordat and Lateran Accords between the fascists and the Catholic Church required the display of a crucifix at the front of every classroom, as you will recall from Chapter 4, *What shall we do with the Dago*. Mrs. Lautsi argued that the display of the crucifix violated the clause of the European Convention on Human Rights which stated it is "the right of parents to ensure... education and teaching in conformity with their own religious and philosophical convictions." Not only was the crucifix a religious symbol, but a symbol most typically associated with a specific form of Christianity: Roman Catholicism.

Of course, a crucifix is a cross with the image of Christ nailed to it. All Christians display or wear a cross. Although Catholics will wear a cross, they are the only group of which I am aware who also display a crucifix. While Christians see the absence of a body as a representation of Christ's victory over death, Roman Catholics see the crucifix as a remembrance of Christ's sacrifice for us. Lenny Bruce used to say it was a good thing the Romans didn't use the electric chair or Christians would be running around wearing little electric chairs on gold chains. I can't help but wonder, if Christ were executed via the electric chair, as Lenny Bruce speculated, would Roman Catholics wear little chairs with Christ strapped to it? If so, what would we call it?

Despite the Catholic association with the crucifix, the Italian government argued it was more than a religious symbol. To the Italian people, it is a unifying image. Ultimately, the court sided with the Italian government noting the display of a crucifix does not constitute indoctrination, it is simply a passive symbol. What is significant is the government argued for six years that a crucifix should be displayed in every classroom because they felt it is part of their cultural heritage.

White & Black

Even the most cursory examination of Italian culture validates the position Catholicism is more than a religion to Italians but a cultural bonding agent. Every town has its patron saint, from Abruzzo's Saint Gabriel of Our Lady of Sorrows to Verona's Zeno. The center of each of these towns and cities is the piazza whose main building is a church or basilica. Not only were these churches the heart of the community, religious celebrations such as holy days or the days honoring the local patron saint were commemorated with a *festa*; they were celebrations which held fast the cords that bound the community together. These festivals featured a procession through the streets with a statue of a saint as well as various religious images of local significance. You will see processions of this type all throughout Italy to this day.

Two processions that are of particular interest take place during Holy Week in Sorrento. The first, the *White Parade*, takes place on the Thursday. It symbolizes the Madonna, Mary, searching through the city for her son. The procession is one of anticipation and hope. Lights and olive branches decorate the route of the procession as well as the churches along the way. During the White Parade, devotees carry a statue of Mary, taking her into each of the churches, while the rest of the procession waits outside, silently standing vigil.

There is a real irony to this procession. The men in the parade dress in white robes with pointed hoods that cover their faces. They walk through the streets carrying torches and crosses. If you are familiar with the southern United States, you could easily mistake them for the Ku Klux Klan (KKK). They are almost identical. The irony is that one of the groups targeted by the KKK is the Roman Catholic Church. Yet, the Klan stole their most iconic image from Catholicism.

Sorrento's second procession takes place on Good Friday. It is the *Procession of Death*, the Black Parade. This procession is more of a funeral march with macabre images of Christ's broken body and crown of thorns. Mary, as well as the participants in the parade, is dressed in black, replacing her traditional blue robes. The death of her son has crushed Mary's hope from the previous evening. This is Good Friday, a day when Christians confront the suffering on the cross which was the payment for our sins. It is the day when death was seemingly victorious.

These processions are something which is very Italian, an icon of *Italianità*, binding the local community. The Italian people use these special occasions to celebrate a joint heritage. Families that have been neighbors for generations repeat these traditions together, maintaining continuity with their mutual past. Although Italian-Americans may not be celebrating the same feasts or in the same cities as our ancestors, we have kept the tradition of processions and *festa* alive in the United States. Even today, you can find these celebrations in Italian communities across the country.

Festa

In my hometown, in the summer, each parish would have what we called a *feast* which was the equivalent of the Italian *festa*. It is one of the things I truly miss from my childhood. At some point, during the weekend, there would be the procession through the neighborhood. At the head of the parade would be the *honor guard* carrying the flags of the United States, New York State, and the pope. Then came the altar boys, the tallest of whom walked ahead of the rest carrying a cross. He would be accompanied by another altar boy who would wave a censer back and forth.

The highlight of the procession was the Knights of Columbus carrying, on a small platform, a statue of the saint being honored. Typically, the statue would be wearing something to which people could pin money, making an offering to the church. Often, at the end of the parade, was a small *marching band*. Calling them a marching band evokes an image much grander than they actually were. Generally composed of a few men with brass instruments, a drum or two, and a couple of guys with cymbals, their performances were not stirring Sousa-like anthems. As the procession passed through the neighborhood, it would collect people. We would all fall in line behind the band to march off to the church where we would join the feast.

Although these feasts were in honor of a particular saint, piety wasn't the chief concern. They were just fun. It was also a great way for the church to raise some money. Friday nights featured the *fish fry*; this was still in the days when we could not eat meat on Fridays. It wasn't until Saturday, however, when they started making the good stuff: sausage and Italian long pepper sandwiches. Cooked on massive gas-fed griddles in the midst of the feasts, you could smell the deliciousness as soon as you arrived on the church grounds. The men frantically chopped and fried, trying to keep up with demand, which they never could. I haven't a limb so dear that I would not gladly sacrifice to stand in front of that counter again impatiently waiting for my sandwich.

In addition to the food, there were a number of games and rides. Next to the church, would be a Ferris wheel and a small merry-go-round; rides for the little kids. They would also have a variety of carnival games such as *duck pond* and *ring toss*. It was one big party, enjoyed by everyone in the area, not exclusively members of the particular parish. Although some parishes would have better feasts than others, most of us would visit pretty much every festival in the city over the summer. Seldom did two occur on the same weekend.

During those feasts, we hadn't a care in the world. My memory of them was being as close to nirvana as I could imagine. We ate great food and ran around having a blast. My father was usually in such a good mood that I was allowed to stay at the feasts until they closed (even at the age of seven). Although our feast was a short city block from our house, it provided a feeling of great freedom.

Household Gods

Italian symbols of faith spread through people's homes, and each household maintained a family altar. Typically, you would find them in some corner of the house. My family's little altar was atop my mother's highboy dresser. There, grouped around a battery-operated red candle, stood a collection of statuettes: the Madonna, Jesus exposing his heart encircled in a crown of thorns, and Saint Agnes, the patron of our local parish.

My father was a truck driver, which meant he traveled for a living. So, the obligatory patron saint of travelers, Saint Christopher (with the baby Jesus propped up on his shoulder like Tiny Tim on the shoulder of Bob Cratchit) was a member of our family's celestial entourage. There was also a replica of Michelangelo's Pieta which my mother purchased at the 1964 New York World's Fair after seeing the original. Imagine going to bed every night under the watchful gaze of those pious eyes. Talk about performance anxiety! I am hesitant to contemplate what they witnessed over the years.

My mother maintained the altar in our home, which was the common practice. This is all part of the strength and independence of Southern-Italian women discussed in Chapter 6, *Italian Steel*. As Kay Turner points out in her book *Beautiful Necessities the Art and Meaning of Women's Altars*, these altars were maternal legacies for healing and ritual. It was at the home altar that many a mother sought intercession from the saints. Many mothers and grandmothers would start their day on their knees in front of the home altar saying the Rosary. Unfortunately, while there are still a few holdouts from previous generations, this seems not as popular a custom as it once was.

These religious symbols in the Italian home are reminiscent of the Roman *Lares* which were a group of gods who protected and influenced the lives of those in the household. This was typical of pagan religions that maintained some sort of deity in the home, often referred to as a *hearth* or *domestic goddess*. I have heard women jokingly refer to themselves as domestic goddesses, thinking it had some sensual connotation. In reality, *Lares* were most often deities associated with hearth and home, more about nurturing than sensuality.

Rosaries & Scapulars, Keys to Heaven

Italians and Italian-Americans carried the symbols of faith with them. Most cars had a rosary hanging from the rear-view mirror or a saint on the dashboard; again, Saint Christopher was a favorite with my family. We also wore various symbols of our faith. We discussed crosses and crucifixes earlier, but some of the most devout would wear or carry a rosary. The nuns at our school, who were the Sisters of Saint Joseph, would have large wooden beaded rosaries hanging from their black rope belts.

Italians and Italian-American Catholics also wore *scapulars*, which was another tradition unique to Catholicism. Originally, the scapular was a monastic robe, made of two pieces of cloth joined at the shoulders hanging down to the feet. It reminded the wearer of the yoke of Christ. Eventually, this robe evolved into two small patches of wool with a prayer or image of a saint embroidered on them, and they were worn as a sort of necklace directly on the skin.

A popular scapular is the *Brown Scapular*. In 1251, Our Lady of Mount Carmel appeared to Saint Simon who was minister general of the Carmelite order during the 13th century. She gave him the *Brown Scapular* promising anyone who died wearing it would not suffer the fires of hell. At times, I good-naturedly bait Irish Catholic friends, telling them I have no need of confession or the sacraments as long as I made sure I always wore my brown scapular. They argue it isn't simply the wearing of the scapular that would save your soul. The belief is that only a devout person who kept the faith would wear the Brown Scapular; at least that is how non-Italians see it. I don't buy it. That isn't what Mary said.

I actually do not wear a scapular, brown or any other color for that matter. As a boy, however, I wore a scapular for a short time. My teacher at Saint Agnes School, a nun, gave it to me after receiving First Holy Communion. She did so for each of the children. The following summer I took it off to go swimming, hanging it from the rear-view mirror of my father's station wagon. There it remained for as long as we owned the car.

Alternate Paths to God

Previously, we discussed how the rebellious attitude of Italians and Italian-Americans extended to the church in Chapter 4, *What Shall we do with the dago*. The home altars and scapulars were all part of this rebellion. Italians used them as a more direct route to God without the church as a go-between. Bear in mind, as discussed in an earlier chapter, many saw the church as simply another institution that lived off the sweat of the working woman and man.

A major alternative path was via the intercessions of Mary and the saints. Many non-Catholic Christians challenge the idea of *praying to saints*. They see it as a form of idol worship, but the very term *praying to saints* generally misses the point. A Catholic does not *pray* to a saint, what they are seeking is intercession of the saint on their behalf. You will hear Christians, Catholic or otherwise, speak of a *prayer line* where a network of Christians will pray for someone who makes a request from the group. This is basically how a Catholic sees the intercession of saints. Think of it as being friends with the boss's son-in-law and asking him to put in a good word for you.

Italians and Italian-Americans place a good deal of importance on the intercession of the saints. Often, people will have a patron saint who has a special significance because of some aspect of their lives, as my family did with Saint Christopher. It is through this special relationship that a person or group will request a saint to intercede on their behalf.

As I noted, the Irish leadership of the American Catholic Church had a real issue with the way in which Italians practiced their faith. As they saw it, *true piety consists in the daily fulfillment of the religious duties extracted of us by God Almighty and His Church.*[101] To them, having faith in a physical object was pagan. More importantly, they understood how this type of thinking challenged their authority. The Papal Flag has the keys of Saint Peter which are the keys to heaven given to Peter by Jesus. Peter, according to Catholicism, is the gatekeeper, but how important is a gatekeeper when a little patch of brown cloth could get you in through the back door!

San Giuseppe, the Patron Saint of Fathers

While all of the saints play an important role in Italian culture, the three big ones in the pantheon of glorified souls are the Virgin Mary, Joseph, and Francis of Assisi. We have discussed the Virgin Mary extensively in Chapter 6, *Italian Steele.* I would, therefore, like to focus on Saint Joseph. I have always felt bad for Saint Joseph. While fathers, in general, seem to be second in the hearts of their children to mothers, poor Joseph had an enormous challenge. How do you compare to a wife like Mary, *THE Madonna?*

The scripture does not say much about him after the birth of Christ, so people don't give him a lot of credit, but you have to admire his faith. A lesser man would have easily dismissed Mary as someone who *got caught messing around,* but Joseph was a man with a good heart. He initially intended to break off the betrothal quietly so as to not humiliate Mary. That says something of his kindness. It was within Joseph's right, by the standards of those times, to make a public spectacle of the girl, but he chose not to do so. Then, after the angel appeared to him in a dream, he accepted – on faith – his role in God's plan. Underrated by Christianity in general, people forget that God chose Joseph as he chose Mary. In my opinion, he is a man who is equal to Mary.

Two days after Saint Patrick's Day, March 19th, Italians throughout the world celebrate *La Festa di San Giuseppe,* The Feast of Saint Joseph. The

---

[101] Connell, William J., & Gardaphé, Fred, (Eds), *Anti-Italianism, Essays on a Prejudice,* Palgrave Macmillan, 2010, pg. 37

tradition on Saint Patrick's Day, at least in the United States, is to wear green and drink green beer until you are sick. On *La Festa di San Giuseppe*, however, we wear something red. Also, since the Middle Ages, Italians have used Saint Joseph's Day as a day to celebrate our fathers, both heavenly and earthly. In other words, it is Italian Father's Day.

As the head of the Holy Family, Saint Joseph has become the patron saint of all fathers, serving as the exemplar of Christian Fatherhood. Although there is nothing in the scripture that discusses the relationship he had with Jesus, Christianity tends to fill the void with speculation based on what is known of him. As he had a generous, kind heart towards Mary, we assume he was equally loving to his son, even more so considering the special circumstances of his birth.

Perhaps it is my overactive imagination, but in my mind's eye, I can see Joseph in his workshop with his son. I see the father's sawdust-powdered hands, placed on the hands that would someday be pierced with nails, showing him how to drive a carpenter's plane. I can imagine the father's pride he felt as he watched Jesus grow into an artisan in his own right. Of course, all of this is speculation, but I like to imagine these things even if I have no proof.

The Italian form of Father's Day has a difference in tone to the American version. While, in the United States, we gift fathers with ties and coffee mugs emblazoned with *World's Greatest Dad*, Italian father's day has a more holistic feel to it. It incorporates not only Saint Joseph as a model for fathers, but the role of the father within the family.

In Italy, celebration altars are set up to honor the Holy Family with Saint Joseph at the head. On the altars are offerings of limes, flowers, candles, and, of course, wine. In Sicilian celebrations, you will also find fava beans on the altars which are in memory of how Saint Joseph saved the people from a famine.

In some Italian towns, the community selects three members to represent the Holy Family: an older man, a young woman, and a little child. Accompanying the Holy Family are 12 men representing the apostles, and children dressed as angels. They are seated at a table of food specially prepared for the day. After a priest blesses the food, the celebration begins and everyone is welcome to eat as much as they like.

The food on the table carries a special significance. Loaves of bread are baked into different shapes such as carpenter's tools, a staff, the cross, as well as various animals and seafood to celebrate the beauty and abundance of the earth. You will not find any meat or dairy on Saint Joseph's Day. For example, rather than sprinkling their food with cheese, parmesan or otherwise, diners use breadcrumbs symbolizing the sawdust of Saint Joseph's profession.

A favorite pastry of mine is *zeppola di San Giuseppe*. Although you can get it any time of year, it is a special pastry eaten on that day. A *zeppola* is a cream puff topped with whipped cream and a black cherry.

You will also find various thick soups with escarole, broccoli, cauliflower, and the ever-present fava beans. My mother would make her special *Saint Joseph's Day spaghetti* to celebrate the holy day. She would boil broccoli in with the pasta along with some chestnuts. She would then mix it with a green split pea-based sauce. In keeping with the sharing spirit of the day, she would send me around the neighborhood with pots of the stuff for various friends. My mother made sure any of the older Sicilians in the neighborhood who might not be able to observe the day, were able to enjoy at least some part of the tradition.

Again, I come from a family which was half-Sicilian so Saint Joseph's day has a special added significance. Beyond the day being the day to honor one of the three big Italian saints, and beyond it being Italian Father's Day, Saint Joseph is the patron saint of Sicily. In the 12th century, a drought had struck the island causing a famine. As Sicilians prayed to the saint for rain, they lived off fava beans which were normally fed to the animals. When the rain finally came, the people promised Saint Joseph they would never forget how he had saved them. So, throughout the world, wherever Sicilians have settled, you will find *La Festa di San Giuseppe* celebrations.

One of these celebrations, which is especially interesting, takes place in New Orleans. When the plantation owners brought Sicilians to New Orleans, they worked shoulder to shoulder with African-Americans, as you will recall from Chapter 3, *To Your Scattered Bodies Go*. They shared with them all the Italian traditions of parades and festivals to honor their saints, especially Saint Joseph. What makes the New Orleans holy day special is that joining the Italian-American community in their celebration are the *Mardi Gras Indians*. The *Mardi Gras Indians*, however, are not Native-Americans, but African-Americans in Mardi Gras costumes based on Native-American dress. There are only two times a year you are able to see the Mardi Gras Indians on parade, Mardi Gras and *La Festa di San Giuseppe*.

What is heartening about this tradition is it is reminiscent of when the Italians first arrived in New Orleans. These were the days when there were close ties between the Italian and African-American communities. It was a time when Italian-Americans understood that an essential attribute of *Italianità* is an acceptance of all people; a transcendence of petty racial biases.

The Sacraments

Beyond the saints, Catholicism took an active form in Italian-American lives through the sacraments. The seven sacraments of the Catholic Church are: Baptism, Holy Communion, Confirmation, Confession, Anointing of the Sick, Marriage, and Holy Orders. Each of these mark the milestones of the journey of Italian lives. I have personal experience with the first four. Although married, I was not married within the church.

Coppola integrated them into *The Godfather* epic. Even the name, *The Godfather*, is based on the sacrament of baptism. He understood the unique role they played in linking us to our communities and ancestors thus making the sacraments integral to *Italianità*. The structure of the film synchronizes key events in the Corleone family history with the sacraments of the church.

The first of the sacraments is baptism. You don't wait too long after the baby is born to baptize it. Remember, according to the church we are all – except for the Virgin Mary – born with original sin on our souls which means unbaptized infants do not make it into heaven. If Dante is correct, they spend eternity in limbo with Virgil and all the other faithful pagans. We should make note that while the Catholic Church has not rejected limbo, they have not made it part of official doctrine either. The bottom line is if you want to be sure your kids get into heaven, you need to get with the program and get them baptized pronto.

On the day of the baptism, the parents dress the infant in a special baptismal gown which is often handed down from generation to generation. My sister's children wore the same satin gown my siblings and I all wore. In my family, the parents and godparents take the baby to the church while the rest of the family prepare for a celebration back home. After the last mass on Sunday, they hold the baptismal service with several infants being baptized at one time.

After the service, people gather at the home of either the parents or grandparents to celebrate the new arrival. Now, an Italian baptism is something you do not want to miss. Especially when done properly. The baptisms I have attended rival many an Amarighan wedding. During the diaspora, one of the criticisms of Italian immigrants was their extravagance when celebrating events such as a baptism, spending far more money on food and drink than the Amarighans thought proper. Most often, the food is homemade although on some occasions it is catered; in either case, there is plenty of it. Weather permitting, the men will gather in the backyard to drink wine and play *bocce*.

Baptism is one of those things Italians and Italian-Americans do well. It is something Amarighans really miss out on. Bringing a new life into the world is something important, something significant. It merits a celebration of the magnitude of an Italian baptism. The family and community are welcoming a new life into their fold. They are embracing that life, recognizing it as one of their own. The godparents specifically, and the extended family in general, are quite literally telling the parents of the child they are not there to simply celebrate, but to commit to supporting the family in caring for that new life. All of this is done through what Italian and Italian-Americans have built around the sacrament of baptism.

Confession & Communion

The next major milestone for Italians and Italian-Americans is the sacrament of First Holy Communion. Before you were allowed to receive communion, however, your soul needed to be cleansed through the sacrament of *Confession*. Today they refer to this sacrament as *Reconciliation*, which I suppose makes it somewhat more palatable to modern sensitivities. Confession, and the subsequent penance, cleansed your soul of sin and prepared you to receive Holy Communion.

So, the day before our First Communion, we lined up ready to tell the priest all the heinous deeds we had committed in the eight years of our existence. With folded hands and sealed lips, we slipped behind the curtain into the darkness of the confessional. We made certain to kneel on the panel that would trip the light that told the priest we were there. Then another panel would slide open, and there was a kind of corrugated plastic screen that hid our faces from the priest as we began the prayer taught to us by the nuns. *"Bless me, father, for I have sinned. This is my first confession..."* Then I ran through my list of sins.

I remember as I got to the end I was feeling a bit short; after all, this was my *first* confession. I needed to have done more than missing mass on Sunday or eating mortadella on Friday. So, I started making stuff up. I lied... I swore... I got into my old man's liquor cabinet... knocked off a bank... When I completed my list, he forgave my sins and I said my Act of Contrition: "Oh my God, I am heartily sorry for having offended

Thee. And I do detest all my sins for fear of the loss of heaven and the pains of hell. But most of all because they offend thee, my God..." So, after a Hail Mary and an Our Father, I was on my way with a nice shiny clean soul.

There are a couple of things I learned about going to confession. First, you needed to pick out your priest. If you happened to have gotten into your father's stack of *Playboys*, you wanted to go to the young, hip priest who would tell you it is perfectly natural to be curious about the human body and let you off with a Hail Mary or two. If you picked the wrong guy, you could end up with having to say a rosary and attend a novena. I also learned over the years that I did not need to develop a set of fictitious sins. I had plenty, even some to spare. They also became much more interesting as I got older. The irony is the more interesting my sins became, the less I went to confession until, eventually, I stopped altogether.

The next day we gathered early for our First Holy Communion. My father made a rare appearance at church, complete with a movie camera to film the event. The boys in their white suits and the girls in white ruffled dresses marched across Kossuth Avenue from the school to the church. I remember being nervous about receiving the Eucharist. The nuns warned us it would be dry and might stick to the roofs of our mouths. We were not to scrape it off with our tongues; that would be very bad. If the Eucharist did get stuck, we were told to find the nearest nun to take us for a drink of water to wash it down. And you never ever bit the Eucharist, NEVER. Christ's body was broken once for us, biting it would repeat the offence. Fortunately, I did not have that issue and communion went off without much of a problem.

Catholicism is substantially different to other forms of Christianity, differences that are monumentally important. The Catholic sacraments are both mystical and miraculous, yet the most mystical sacrament, in my opinion, is Holy Communion. Other Christian faiths go out of their way to point out that communion is simply symbolic, the host is not the actual body of Christ. Catholics believe, however, in transubstantiation where the substance of the Eucharist is converted into the actual body of Christ.

As children, we had a particular reverence for the Eucharist and all with which it came into contact, especially the hands of the priest. The nuns taught us that since the priest touched Christ's body – the body of the most Holy God – he was set apart from all other people. They genuinely were in awe of these men. Years later, when Sting sang of having a beast's eyes, a sinner's face, and a priest's hands, in the song *Moon Over*

Bourbon Street, I was struck by such an artful dichotomy. The contrast of the sinner beast with the holy hands of a priest amplified the sense of a conflicted soul that longed for goodness, but was aware of his own fallen state.

As of late, the Catholic Church has employed *Eucharistic Ministers* who assist the priest in handing out communion and congregants are allowed to touch – actually touch – the Eucharist. It is perhaps a pragmatic solution to the scarcity of priests. I can't imagine, however, what the good sisters at Saint Agnes School of my day would say concerning how communion has changed. Personally, I can't help but feel allowing the hands of a common person, Eucharistic Minister or congregant, to touch Christ's body is a form of desecration.

After our First Holy Communion came the party. In addition to the food, which was, as always, plentiful and delicious, the uncles and aunts came bearing gifts. Lots of nice envelopes with money stuffed into the fold of the card. Of course, with faux seriousness, various adults reminded me I wasn't a baby anymore, I needed to behave myself. As the priest told us, this was when we became part of the Christian community. Prior to communion, we were not responsible for our sins, we couldn't understand the concept, or so they told us. Once we passed through our First Communion, we were held responsible for our actions.

Confirmation

Confirmation is the act of confirming our Catholic faith; making a commitment to Catholicism. We are saying that, going forward, we will live out our lives as Catholics. So, we greeted the bishop of our diocese dressed in red. He gave us a slap on the cheek to symbolize Christian suffering and told us we had graduated to *Soldiers of Christ*. This is somewhat analogous to a Jewish Bar Mitzvah, although none of us stood in front of the congregation to pronounce on that day we had become men. It is interesting to note that, typically, religions that practice infant baptism, such as Catholicism, also have Confirmations. The other groups who delay baptism until the child can declare their belief themselves, generally don't have anything analogous to Confirmation.

Conduits of Grace

To many Italians and Italian-Americans, the sacraments and the saints are Christianity. They represent the two conduits of grace. The church controls the sacraments. For example, the church has both used and abused excommunication throughout history. In the 11th century, the council of Limoges, France, excommunicated the feudal barons of the area for battling one another in the midst of a famine. The church justly recognized that these men were wasting resources that were better applied to saving lives. Then there was the case of Bishop Pierre Cauchon who excommunicated Saint Joan of Arc. Twenty-six years later, Pope Callixtus III excommunicated Bishop Cauchon for what he did to Joan of Arc. I guess even when it comes to excommunication, what goes around comes around.

Excommunication could be used by the church to compel fasting, the paying of tithes, or even the observance of a feast. It was such a powerful weapon bishops became overzealous in its use. Eventually, the church came to realize bishops were getting a bit out of control, so, in 1545, The Council of Trent encouraged church authorities to exercise more moderation in its use. Heeding the council's advice, church officials began to establish much higher criteria for a person to be excommunicated.

Control of the sacraments also gave the church incredible political power. There have been instances when the pope has forbidden clergy from dispensing the sacraments to entire nations. If you were a devout Catholic in the Middle Ages, denial of the sacraments, especially Last Rights, was a real threat of eternal damnation. If the conflict between your ruler and the pope caused the church to take such action, you would quickly side with the church. If you were a ruler in such a situation, you would have both the church and the populace against you.

Where the sacraments lead to God through the church, the saints provide direct access to grace. Each of these paths to the divine play different complementary roles. While the sacraments primarily focus on salvation, the saints assist in answering prayers. As I mentioned earlier, it is not so much as praying to some minor deity, as it is asking a friend to intercede on your behalf.

The Italian focus on the mechanics of Catholicism created an image – to some – of a superficial belief, that there was no substance to their faith. Many non-Italian Catholics felt Catholicism to Italians was a matter of external observances with little focus on any inward transformation. These views are not far from the truth. Years ago, an acquaintance would berate me if he saw me eating meat on Friday. The prohibition against eating meat had long since been abandoned, but still, he persisted. The irony was that he had been married multiple times, was a serial philanderer with multiple children he had never met, and was known to beat both his wives and girlfriends. Yet, abstaining from meat on Friday kept him in God's good graces. At least, that is what he thought. He was somewhat representative of a lot of the old school Italian guys I knew growing up.

Nuns with Rulers!

This was, in part, what Catholicism was to me. Checking off items on a list of roles and responsibilities with no concern for inward transformation.

Catholicism was also Saint Agnes Church, the local franchise, whose bell tower loomed over so much of my childhood. It was standing in the back of that church, during mass, anxious to leave, but having to wait until after *collection*. Dutifully, I would deposit the family's pre-labeled envelope in the wicker basket so my father could see his name in the "Dollar Club" which was a listing of people who gave a dollar or more to the church the previous week. It was distributed each week with the bulletin. The envelope barely landed in the basket when my feet were rushing down the front steps free from the *celebration* of the mass for one more week.

For me, Catholicism was the brutality of the clergy. When I tell people I only attended Catholic schools prior to college, they usually chuckle something about rulers on knuckles. Rulers. How cute. We were beaten as children. Not only by nuns, but by the brothers and the lay teachers. One of the most vivid memories I have, is of a student in junior high school knocked out of his desk and onto the floor. The teacher stood above him screaming at the kid while he kicked him with the side of his foot. As I think back on those days, I realize how terrible it must sound in today's world, but back then we simply accepted it. The nuns and teachers beat the kids. The parents beat the kids. Hell, the kids beat each other. It was the way it was; we didn't know any differently.

As bad as the physical abuse may have been, it was the verbal abuse that was worse. A bruise will heal or a beating forgot, but the open humiliation and snide remarks lingered for far longer. The adults selected who were the golden children and who were the miscreants, the ones suited for derision. They had no qualms about singling out a student in front of their peers to mock them. Of course, the other students saw this was acceptable and replicated the behavior, targeting the misfit. Their comments worked on your soul like a varnish. It was a stain that seeped its way into the fibers of who you were, hardening your exterior. You came to believe what they said of you, living out the character they made you into.

You also learned to be mean like them. Like a son who learns to beat his wife from watching his father beat his mother, the object of humiliation retaliated by attempting to humiliate others. The same sneering jabs directed at you would be banked and withdrawn when you had your chance to poke another. If it sounds ugly, it was.

Challenging the Church

As I noted earlier, in the United States, the Italian expressions of faith – such as festivals and processions, saints and home altars – were so alien to the Irish Catholic hierarchy it seemed, at times, to be a conglomeration of Christianity and paganism. Their argument with the immigrants was understandable. First, Italian folklore creates a mysticism that combines elements of Christianity and the remnants of paganism. Then, the contentious relationship between the *contadini* and the church, caused the working class to seek a path to God that circumvented what they saw as a corrupt church that was in league with a suppressive aristocracy.

In the novel *Christ in Concrete*, Annunziata – the main character's widowed mother – encourages her son to have faith in Jesus. While she professes this faith, she goes to a spiritual medium in order to communicate with her deceased husband. Traditional Christianity sees such spiritualists as part of the occult. Dante placed them in the fourth *bolgia* of the eighth circle of hell. Most Italians – Dante being a notable exception – have no issue with it. She like many Italian women held onto the superstitions they practiced in Italy which included what some would see as elements of the occult.

I once raised this matter to a friend's mother who simply laughed it off. "Girls have always done this, it is no big deal." My own mother claimed spiritual powers such as being able to curse people and foretell the future because she was *born with a veil*. A child *born with a veil* is born with part of the amniotic sack over their face. When this occurs, Italians believe the child has some special spiritual powers.

Charms & Amulets

More than simple scapulars, Italians and Italian-Americans wear a variety of amulets to either bring luck or protect against the *malocchio*, the evil eye. The evil eye is by no means strictly Italian. This superstition can be traced back to 6th century B.C.E. Greeks, which is probably where the Romans acquired it.

Initially, the *malocchio* was a curse cast by an evil glare that brings about misfortune such as an injury or financial loss. Today, those who still have faith in in its power believe the person who casts the curse need not be physically present. Part of the motivation behind the secretiveness of Italian families, about which I had written previously, is a concern the envy of others will lead them to cast the *malocchio*.

The most common charm to ward off *malocchio* is the *cornicello*, also known as the *cornuto* or *corno*; many in the United States refer to it as the Italian Horn. It is the jewelry of Italian male stereotypes everywhere, along with braided gold chains. Admittedly I not only wear a gold *cornicello*, but I have that along with a *mano corno*, described below, hanging from the rear-view mirror of my car.

On more than one occasion, someone has asked why I am wearing a pepper. The *cornicello* is actually a bull's horn whose blessings include wealth and success, but it is primarily worn for protection against the *malocchio*. Although you will find women wearing it at times, the phallic aspects of the charm also make it a symbol of virility, so it is primarily worn by men.

Frequently you will see the *mano corno* worn either in place of, or in addition to, the *cornicello*. The charm is based on a hand gesture in which the index and little finger are held straight out while the other fingers, including the thumb, are folded into the palm of the hand. Italians refer to this as *facciamo le corna* which translates to "let's make the horns." Basically, it is the *rock-on* hand sign. When you make the rock-on gesture, you point your fingers upward, usually with your arms extended above your head, yelling *Woo-Who* as loudly as you can. When we *facciamo le corna*, we point to the ground in order to drive any bad luck into the earth, similar to grounding an electrical charge.

There are several meanings associated with the *mano corno*, but the most common I have encountered is protection against the *malocchio* or simple bad luck. In the United States, Amarighans say "God forbid" to prevent the occurrence of something unfortunate happening. So we use expressions like, God forbid I should lose my job the week before

Christmas. Italians, however, say *facciamo le corna*. We may say to a friend, "I hope I don't get sick during final exams next week" to which he or she would reply *facciamo le corna*. In other words, they are saying let's make this sign to drive away the bad luck.

You should be aware that the *mano corno* gesture, if pointed upward, means cuckold. If you make it at a man, you are saying his wife is unfaithful with the implication being he is not man enough to satisfy her or keep her faithful. For example, in 2002, Silvio Berlusconi created a bit of a controversy when he made *le corna* behind the back of the Spanish foreign minister. In Italian culture, it is far worse than *giving someone the finger*.

A more ancient charm, though virtually unknown in the United States, is the *cimatura*. Dating back to pagan times, the charm is in reference to the goddess Diana. It is shaped like a sprig of the rue herb which is divided into three stems. On the stems are symbols of the forms of the goddess Diana: Hecate – a key, Diana – a crescent moon, and Proserpina – a serpent. In Italian culture, rue wards off evil magic, as does the vervain flower which is another symbol commonly found on the *cimatura*.

Over the past 2,000 years, Christian symbols have been added to the *cimatura* such as a fish and the Sacred Heart. The rue being divided into three branches is also a reference to the Holy Trinity. As with the *cornicello*, the charm can be worn by either men or women. However, due to its reference to Diana, a female pagan goddess, it is typically a charm worn by women.

Another popular charm is the *gobbo*. At first, you might mistake the *gobbo* for a leprechaun, but upon closer examination, you will see he is a hunchbacked hobo. In one hand, he is carrying a horseshoe and with the other, he is making *le corna*. There are variations on the depiction of the *gobbo*. For example, some show him wearing a suit and top hat with a ladybug on top of the hat as well as a four-leaf clover pinned to his lapel. At other times, he wears a white Pagliacci-like clown outfit with a Venetian black mask. It is common for the lower half of *gobbo*'s body to be a *cornicello*.

Stregheria

The mysticism of Italian folkways extended far beyond the mere wearing of amulets. Southern-Italian mysticism was primarily feminine; defined, practiced, and driven by women. It was a response to a society in which men attempted to control both the home and societal institutions such as the church. Understand that, in southern Italy, Christianity was imposed on the population by the Roman Empire whose center of power was in the north. It was not a religion that developed naturally from within the people. As a result, Southern-Italians developed their own version of the faith.

In Chapter 6, *Italian Steele*, I described how despite the overt use of power by men, women were the actual sources of power since they controlled the daily operations of the home. The same was true of the church. While the Catholic hierarchy was dominated by men, women saw to the daily operations of the church, such as the maintenance of altars, the organizing of communal ceremonies, and most importantly teaching the faith to children. The lessons children were taught included alternate expressions of faith which were extensions of Southern-Italian folklore.

Through this tutoring, women were able to undermine male Catholicism's monopoly on spiritual power. This feminine power, which if believed, was deeper and stronger than that wielded by impotent priests. Women healers were able to seamlessly integrate Christian and pagan practices, co-opting Christian symbols to circumvent ecclesial authority.

An example of the merging of pagan practices with Christianity was the ritual of ridding oneself of the *malocchio;* a ceremony which was necessary if you were in possession of a defective *cornicello*. The process involves a bowl of water, olive oil, and salt. After blessing yourself three times with the *Sign of the Cross*, you do the same to the bowl. You then drip some olive oil from your thumb into the water. As you would expect, the oil forms into blobs on the surface. If the oil forms an eye shape the *malocchio* is present. The salt is then poured into the water in a *Sign of the Cross* pattern. As you pour the salt, you say a prayer asking God to remove the *malocchio*. Some say that you can only learn the prayer at midnight on Christmas Eve. Others maintain that while you can learn the prayer at any time, it is most effective on Christmas Eve. There are a number of variations on this process, but they all basically combine Christian symbols and Italian folklore.

The ritual of removing the *malocchio* is representative of *stregheria*, Italian witchcraft, which was administered by a local *maga* or *strega* (sorceress or witch). While this may conjure up, pun intended, images of Macbeth or Hogwarts, these women were seen more as wise women, sages, who were healers and keepers of the local traditions and lore. It is understandable that the church frowned on *stregheria*, which was also known as *La Vecchia Religione* (the Old Religion). It was the competition.

In Southern Italy, where life was a daily struggle, the people relied on *stregheria* as a practical means of survival. In addition to their magical powers, the *strege* were healers with the knowledge of centuries-old secret remedies. This gave them a source of power in the community that enabled them to live outside the normal restrictions placed on other women.

As with so many other aspects of our culture, after World War II, Italian-Americans left much of this behind in the drive to become Amarighan. While many of us continue to wear the *cornicello*, few understand its origin or significance. I have yet to meet an Italian-American that even knows of the *cimatura*, much less actually wear one. In Italy, however, many of the old superstitions, such as the wearing of charms, survive.

The exotic nature of these practices, as well as their association with paganism, make some Christian groups wary of them. Despite their cultural significance, more extreme Christians see them as satanic. As we consider some of these practices, it is little wonder, then, the Amarighans of the Catholic Church saw the Italian faith as having pagan elements. It did!

The Verdict on Catholicism

Today, Italians and Italian-Americans have similar attitudes towards the Catholic Church. As I noted at the beginning of this chapter, the Catholic Church claims 97% of Italians are Catholic. Yet, there is a difference between being Catholic, and *being Catholic*. Much like the crucifix at the front of Italian classrooms, for many of us, our Catholicism is more cultural than spiritual. We mark the milestones in our lives with the various sacraments, celebrate the days of various saints, and observe traditional meals on holy days. Yet, many, if not most, do not really believe the Eucharist becomes the actual body and blood of Christ or the pope holds the keys to heaven and hell.

It is difficult to truly estimate who is devout and who isn't. It is obvious, however, that the influence of the church is waning. As in Italy, many in the United States have left the Catholic Church for more cultish, colorful evangelical sects. They leave behind the connection with the past provided by church traditions and the sacraments. More importantly, the influence that the Catholic Church has on the Italian government has also weakened. The Italian government has long since lifted its restrictions on abortion, contraception, and divorce. It is interesting how the power of the Catholic Church in politics seems to diminish in Italy while in the United States it seems to expand.

Recently, while discussing the church, a relative asked me if I felt the church had been a net negative or net positive. This is a difficult question for me to answer, at least without bias. I understand my past makes objectivity something out of my reach. So, let me try to look at the facts of Catholicism's impact on the lives of Italians and Italian-Americans.

On the one hand, we have centuries of corruption, as we have discussed in this book. There have been moral failings such as the debaucheries of Pope Alexander VI who is infamous for hosting the *Banquet of Chestnuts* which was an orgy that would have rivaled any held by Tiberius or Caligula. There have been the church's political intrigues such as the role of Pope Sixtus IV in the Pazzi conspiracy, in which he plotted with the Pazzi family to assassinate Lorenzo and Giuliano de' Medici. As I have written earlier, the machinations of the Catholic Church are the history of Italy.

We need not even extend our examination of the church to centuries past. In Italy, many priests have openly had children with their mistresses. Then looming over all of this, of course, is the scandal of child abuse, made worse by the church when they protected the abusers rather than the children. In many instances, the church transferred these men to other parishes where they were again given access to children.

To list all that has been done by the church in the past 2,000 years creates a tally of an organization guilty of truly heinous sins. That, however, is only one side of the ledger. What makes these actions far worse is they mar, nearly obliterate, the deeds done by the hundreds of millions of Catholics who genuinely sought to live as Christ.

There are generations that led the monastic life dedicated to prayer and study. In addition to the cruelty, there was kindness such as the nun who gave me my first, and only, scapular. I talk of the beatings, but there were those who were caring and nurturing. There are also those missionaries who traveled around the world with the heart of Christ, caring for the sick and educating the illiterate. We need to look at this side of the ledger as well.

With each of the evils committed by the church, there is a great good acting as a counterbalance. There is the case of Pope Nicholas V. If

243

anyone is to be given credit for making Rome the center of western civilization it is Pope Nicholas V. When he became pope, Rome was an Ozymandias-like ruin, with much of the city uninhabitable. He took it upon himself to make Rome into a great city that would attract great minds and devout believers. To that end, he rebuilt the city, paving the streets and strengthening the fortifications. To ensure the city had an adequate water supply, he restored the Roman *Aqua Virgo* aqueduct which, like the city around it, had fallen into ruin.

The newly constructed aqueduct is today referred to as the *Aqua Vergine*. In 1629, at the terminus of the *Aqua Vergine*, Pope Urban VIII constructed a fountain. It is flocked to by tourists from all over the world who, with their back to the fountain, toss coins into the water with their right hand over their left shoulder. It was also where Anita Ekberg seductively danced for Marcello Mastroianni.

As we examine the history of the popes, we see many who are infamous for the worst crimes, but who are also responsible for some of the church's greatest contributions. For example, I mentioned earlier how Pope Sixtus IV was involved in the Pazzi conspiracy, yet, as pope, he founded a papal collection of art that became the basis for the Capitoline Museums and expanded the Vatican Library. He was also a patron of the sciences, giving leave to physicians and artists to dissect cadavers.

Perhaps we need to think of the Catholic Church in this light, to evaluate the entirety of its actions through the centuries. As I think of this balance, I think back to the first time I visited Saint Peter's Basilica. My wife and I stood in front of the high altar amazed by Bernini's ciborium, canopy. We were surrounded by great works of art in one of the most incredible structures in all of Christendom. Not only Christendom, the world! As I commented on how amazed I was, my wife reminded me that the methods used to raise the funds to pay for all the art and the opulence was what motivated so many reformers of the church throughout history. She reminded me how Luther objected to the indulgences that paid for the very art we were admiring.

So, what are we to conclude? Yes, it is true, at times, leaders of the Catholic Church acted in ways that were certainly far from the Christian ideal, to put it mildly. As shown in previous chapters, we see the damage done to Italy as a result of this behavior. What we don't see, however, is what Italy would have been without the church. What would Rome be without Saint Peter's or The Trevi Fountain? If there were no monasteries, would ancient writings have survived? Would the absence of Catholicism have prolonged the dark ages? We cannot answer these questions with any surety. Neither is life like a video game where we can hit the reset button to test another strategy. What we do know is the church has made momentous contributions to Italy both to its benefit and detriment. We know Italy would not be Italy without the Catholic Church.

Francis & the Future

Earlier in this chapter, I mentioned the three great Catholic saints are Mary, Joseph, and Francis of Assisi. While I have written of Mary and Joseph, I wanted to conclude this chapter with Saint Francis. I believe the current Pope Francis has chosen the name *Francis* because of the way in which the saint received his calling.

As the story goes, one day Saint Francis was seeking a place for meditation. Passing the church of San Damiano, he was moved by the Holy Spirit to seek God there, in a humble church which was on the verge of collapse. As he prayed, he heard a voice saying, "Francis, go and repair my house which is falling into ruin." Francis set about rebuilding the church of San Damiano, but before long it was apparent the voice was not speaking of that particular building. So, he took up a much broader mission of bringing a purer Gospel to the people. Saint Francis, perhaps more than any other saint, lived a life of humility and poverty. Through his example, as well as the order he had founded, a Gospel – free of earthly corruption – was preached to the world.

I am not ashamed to admit that when Jorge Mario Bergoglio announced he was to take the name of Francis as he ascended to the papacy, tears came to my eyes. There is a reason he is the first pope to take that name. Saint Francis is recognized as one of the truly great saints. Although it could be interpreted, by some, that selecting the name Francis was an act of great hubris, I see it as a bold statement on what the pope sees as his mission. He saw the church as in disrepair, and in need of another Francis to come and rebuild it.

The work of many good, kind Catholic men and women has stood in the shadow of the looming evil done by others. Like Saint Francis, Pope Francis seeks to rebuild the Catholic Church. Unfortunately, the Catholic Church is a centuries-old institution with incredible inertia. He is known to ask people to pray for him, and I do. I can think of no one who has a more difficult mission.

Chapter 10: The Beautiful People of Palermo's Prison

Who's Mimo?

The Mafia.

Of course, if you are going to discuss Italian and Italian-American culture, you are going to have to discuss the *Mafia*. Recently, I introduced myself to someone who, upon hearing my last name, simply responded, "*Mafioso*, eh?" It is common for someone to say something about the mob when they hear my last name. When I was young, I didn't know much about the Mafia, so typically I would say something like, "Yeah, so you better watch your step. I got some cousins that can make you disappear." For the sake of the record, the only things any of my family members make disappear are cannoli.

When my wife and I were first married, my brother gave me a newspaper clipping about Calabria. It seems, in that region, a Mafia boss died who happened to have the name Mimo Giovinazzo. Surprisingly, the name Giovinazzo is relatively common in Italy. The article went on to tell how the death created a power vacuum in which rival factions were carrying out brutal crimes in their war to gain dominance. In one incident, after beheading an adversary, the murderers used the head for target practice, tossing it in the air and shooting at it. At the time, I actually laughed at the article. The brutality of the crimes did not register with me as much as sharing the last name.

As a joke, I *faxed* (as I said, it was a few years ago) a copy of the article to my new wife. When I did this, however, I did not include a cover sheet identifying myself as the sender or my wife as the recipient. She worked in an office with roughly 60 people, so I thought the fax would simply be passed on to her. I expected to get a call from her later that afternoon, but work distracted me, so I forgot about it. Neither did I think of it that evening.

Several days later, I got a call from my wife who sounded upset, "Who is Mimo?"

I suddenly remembered the fax. "Who told you about Uncle Mimo?" I replied instantly, not wanting to waste the opportunity to tease her a bit.

"Bill," (out came her *Bill-you-better-not-be-fooling-around* voice), "don't tease me about this." So, I confessed to what I had done. She told me the article had been passed around her office. Finally, someone left it on her desk with a note asking for forgiveness if they had, in any way, offended her. Of course, the note was a tongue-in-cheek apology, but it was a nice touch.

As I have learned more about the Mafia's impact on Italy, I have repented of my past, flippant attitude. I have come to resent the Mafia. I resent how, when people think of Italians, one of the first things to come to mind is the Mafia. I resent how my people – who have contributed so much to western civilization – are known for our worst elements.

I began the last chapter discussing how Italians have earned their close association with Roman Catholicism. While many of us may not be devout, we are certainly culturally Catholic. As much as Amarighans may associate Italians with Roman Catholicism, the association with the Mafia is equally strong, although much less deserved.

To prove this point, let's trudge through some statistics. In 2001, Zogby International[102] conducted a poll in which they discovered that 78% of American teenagers between 13 and 18 years of age associate Italian-Americans with crime and/or the restaurant industry. To many, we are either Chef Boyardee or Tony Soprano. In another poll, conducted by Princeton's Response Analysis Corporation for the Sons of Italy in America, 74% of adult Americans believe most Italian-Americans have some connection to organized crime.[103]

These impressions have been formed, in part, by the popular media. Recall the discussion in Chapter 5, *What is an Italian*. The Italic Institute of America conducted a study of how Italians have been portrayed in films between 1914 and 2014.[104] In this hundred years of film, there have been 476 movies in which Italians have been portrayed positively versus 1036 in which they have been shown negatively. Of the total number of characters in these films, 34.9% were mob-related characters,

---

[102] Zogby International Survey, *American Teenagers and Stereotyping*, 2001

[103] *Americans of Italian descent: national public opinion research for Commission for Social Justice*, Response Analysis Corporation, Princeton, N.J.,1990

[104] http://italic.org/mediaWatch/filmStudy.php

33.6% were boors, buffoons, bigots, or bimbos, and 31.5% were positive.

Italian-Americans have been painted as blue-collar, criminal, and uneducated with little emotional control. This lack of control is expressed, according to popular American culture, in violent, argumentative, overly-sexualized behavior. The irony is less than .0025% of Italian-Americans are involved in organized crime, according to the U.S. Department of Justice. In addition, the U.S. Census Bureau reports two-thirds of Italian-Americans are white-collar professionals such as teachers, computer programmers, attorneys, physicians, and business executives. The reality is Italian-Americans are law-abiding, educated professionals who have helped form and advance the ideals of the United States.

The Mafia & the Media

Amarighans began associating Italians with organized crime since the late 19th century. Although the Mafia had been in existence since the mid-1800's, you see the first widespread use of the term in the United States in the 1890's. All you need do is refer to the murder of Police Chief Hennessy which we discussed in Chapter 3, *To Your Scattered Bodies Go*. The newspapers advanced the idea that the murderers were part of the Mafia. To this day, although there is no proof that the Mafia or even Italians were involved in the killing, many still maintain *the dagos did it*, as Chief Hennessy claimed.

Try to put yourself in the mindset of Amarighans in the 1890's. Italians were not yet integrated into American culture; they were seen as an exotic people with secretive, strange ways. Then you begin to read stories in the news about some covert criminal organization, the Mafia. You hear stories of their violent ways in Italy, and then in places in the United States. They seem to be wherever Italians settle. The dying words of a good American law enforcement officer, Chief Hennessy, only seems to confirm what you have begun to suspect. These people coming to this country are not good people. They are murderers and rapists. Italy is not sending us her best. Of course, the media capitalized on what events *seemed* to support and what many an Amarighan *felt*.

Although the Italic Institute of America study, cited above, reviewed the portrayal of Italians in film from 1914, Italian criminals in film have an earlier history. In 1906, Biograph (Thomas Edison's movie company) released *Skyscraper*, a 12-minute film about *Dago Pete*. In the film, Pete starts a fight in which he pulls a knife on a co-worker. Of course, Pete carries a knife; it is the *greaseball's* weapon of choice. Seeing what happened, the foreman fires Pete. In retaliation, Pete steals a watch and some papers setting up the foreman as the thief. In the last scene of the film, the foreman's daughter is able to show the real thief is, in fact, *Dago Pete*, who is subsequently hauled off to prison.

Dago Pete is a cartoonish character whose only motivation is to create havoc. The stereotype of the Italian criminal has evolved over the years, from *Dago Pete* whose villainous nature is drawn with broad strokes to more empathetic characters such as Michael Corleone and Tony Soprano who are forced into a life of crime. The Godfather himself, the patriarch of the Corleone crime family, seemingly had no choice in the role into which he was cast by the Fates. At least, that is the story told by the movie. He was a hard-working family man who was making an honest living when he unjustly lost his job. Although he was a criminal, he was kind to widows and puppies (literally, as shown in the film). How sweet.

Michael Corleone voices the underlying pathos of these characters in the oft-quoted lines, "Just when I thought I was out, they pull me back in." Tony Soprano didn't want to live a life of crime. Isn't that why he saw a shrink for Christ's sake? He was a serial philanderer who was able to murder family members and lifetime friends – anyone he saw as a threat – but, in the end, he was OK. He had a good heart.

Many Americans, especially Italian-Americans, feel empathy for Tony. They somehow relate to his inner struggles. Tony was an honorable man. So were they all, all honorable men... We can go through each of the icons of the modern *Mafioso*, from *The Godfather*, to *Goodfellas*, to *The Sopranos*.

The two sons of the Godfather represent two of the most common Mafioso stereotypes. The first is the bold, hairy-chested, womanizing Sonny. He is all emotion; driven by either lust or anger. His lack of self-control ultimately gets him killed. Admittedly, when I was young, the Sonny character had a real appeal, as he did for many Italian-Americans. He was a powerful animal, untamed by society. How's that for a cliché? Although he was unfaithful to his wife, he was good to his mother and protected his sister from her wife-beating *Calabres* of a husband. But, in the end, he was OK. He had a good heart.

The mirror image of Sonny is his brother, Michael. Michael was the smart one, purely Machiavellian. He was a faithful husband. When arriving in Las Vegas for a business meeting, Michael immediately dismissed the party girls. He was above such nonsense, he wanted to get down to business. He was cold and calculating. From the beginning of his entry into the *family business*, he was the strategist. He successfully orchestrated and executed the plot to kill the men who shot his father, including a police chief who until that point had been untouchable. Again, he was able to murder family members, leaving his sister a widow and her children orphans. He was even able to have his own brother killed. But, in the end, he was OK. He had a good heart.

Italian-Americans & the Mafia

Italian-Americans who object to the prevalence of the Mafioso stereotype should admit that we have only ourselves to blame. Too many of us have the attitude I once had, seeing the Mafia as a punchline to some joke. This is how most of us – second and third generation Italian-Americans – see the Mafia in general. Like most Italian-Americans, I laughed at mob references previously, and ignored the brutality.

A cavalier attitude towards the Mafia is a major difference between Italians and Italian-Americans. I have lost track of how many times I have had a conversation with someone, usually someone I don't know all that well, who will tell me in a conspiratorial voice, "You know I have a cousin in the Mafia." It is always an acquaintance, never an intimate; a cousin, or an uncle, or a friend of a friend. I try to cut these conversations off quickly. I make a simple point: people who are *in the* Mafia don't make it known they are *in the* Mafia. The people who go around talking about being *in the* Mafia (if they actually have anything to do with crime) are simply common criminals at worst. Most often, they are simple braggarts. You could almost guarantee they did not go through the initiation rites we will discuss later. Rest assured, if you had undergone this ritual and are running off at the mouth, you are not much longer for this world.

There is a real cognitive dissonance in Italian-American attitudes towards the Mafia. While there is this winking homage paid to the mob, since the end of World War II Italian-Americans have become uber-patriots. They see the Italian-American experience as an Uncle Sam-loving, flag-waving defense of truth, justice, and the American way. If you attempt to discuss with them the idea there were Italian labor leaders or anarchists that sought to violently overthrow the government, they get angry. Their patriotism causes them to shout down any thought that Italians who arrived on American shores did not sever all ties with

Italy; they learned English, waved American flags (exclusively), and eschewed all forms of protest or complaint. Yet, they happily embrace their relationship with the Mafia, criminals who truly subverted American values.

People who venerate the Mafia do not truly understand the Mafia. There is folklore wisdom warning you not to believe your own press. Italian-Americans haven't listened to this advice, at least when it comes to the Mafia. The mistaken beliefs of the Italian-American community concerning the Mafia are overwhelming. The first of the two most widespread is that the Mafia has an honorable origin. The Mafia is referred to as *The Honored Society* and its members as *men of honor*. It isn't and they aren't. I am told, "The Mafia takes care of its own" which is an overt lie as we shall see in the pages to follow.

The second myth, which I referenced above, is that the Mafia in the United States was the result of honest Italians faced with trying to make it in a society pitted against them. The image in the minds of Italian-Americans is of simple men forced into a life of crime to feed their families; again, this is an invented tradition straight from the movies. The victims of the Mafia were not Amarighans who were oppressing them, but their fellow Italian immigrants. As we look at the evolution of the Mafia, we will see how untrue both of these myths are.

What is the Mafia?

Let's begin by discussing the name of the organization. The actual word, Mafia, has its origin in a Sicilian play first performed in 1863. The play was written and produced by Gaspare Mosca, a political dissident during the occupation of the Spanish Bourbons, and Giuseppe Rizzotto, a career criminal who had spent half his life behind bars. The play was a farce set in Palermo's prison. Mosca would write the plot while Rizzotto would use his familiarity with Sicilian jails to write the dialog. Even this early play foisted the myth of *Mafioso* nobility, showing the main characters thrust into a quest for social justice.

The title of the play, *I mafiusi di la vicaria di Palermo* (The Mafia of Palermo's Prison) demonstrates how the meaning of words change based on their usage in society, as discussed in Chapter 8, *The Beautiful Language*. Prior to the play, *Mafioso* was a good thing, meaning something of beauty and grace. You described something which was excellent or attractive as *Mafioso*. As Mosca and Rizzotto were in the midst of writing the play, Mosca encountered two men arguing. As they were about to come to blows, one shouted at the other, "You want to make like a

Mafioso with me." This confrontation inspired the title of the play. A loose interpretation of its title could be something such as *The Beautiful People of Palermo's Prison*. The timing of the release of the play, along with the rise of the organized crime syndicate, was sufficient to change the meaning of the word. By 1893, the official definition of the word Mafia, according to the Italian dictionary, had become, "The name of a secret organization in Sicily that has as its aims to achieve profits through illicit means."

The word Mafia has evolved to become a blanket term for organized crime. So, you will hear people talk about other Mafias, such as the Russian Mafia or the Japanese Mafia. While these other crime organizations may have a particular code of honor, or some linkage with a past mythology, the application of the word to these groups dilutes the unique nature of the word's meaning. Make no mistake, this is not meant to venerate or romanticize the Mafia in any way. However, the Mafia is a particular thing, a particular organization with a specific history and culture. To call these other groups a Mafia, of any type, confuses that distinction.

When we speak of the Italian Mafia, however, we are referring to a collection of organizations, not one syndicate. There are three main subgroups, the *'Ndrangheta*[105] (Dragnet) in Calabria, the *Cosa Nostra* (Our Thing) in Sicily, and the *Camorra* in Naples. The word *Camorra* seems to roughly mean "gambling boss" from *capo* for boss or captain and *morra* – a Neapolitan game of chance.

'Ndrangheta is a relatively new term that came into use roughly 70 years ago. Prior to that time, they were referred to as *La Picciotteria* which translates roughly to young men with an attitude. We should note there is a fourth lesser group, the *Sacro Corona Unita* (United Sacred Crown), who operate in Apulia.

In his book, *The Italians*, Luigi Barzini notes that the Mafia is not as well organized as in the movies. There is no real central figure or leader from whom authority flows down to the lower levels of the organization. Authority within the Mafia flows up. I cannot help but be reminded of when Jefferson wrote, in the Declaration of Independence, "Governments are instituted among Men, deriving their just powers from the consent of the governed." It would be a stretch to claim the

---

[105] 'Ndrangheta is pronounced *in-drahn-get-tah*.

Mafia is any sort of Jeffersonian Democracy, but they do derive their *unjust* powers by the consent of the governed.

As we examine the structure of the Mafia we can see this decentralization. At the lowest level of the *'Ndrangheta*, for example, are family-based cells; people who are related in one way or another. These cells roll up into regions that are grouped into three main precincts. At the head of the precinct is the *capo crimine*, roughly translated as *crime captain*. The *capo crimine*, however, is not so much a governor who gives orders which the lower ranks must obey, but an arbitrator. He, in a sense, mediates between the subgroups when conflicts arise. Each cell acts, for the most part, autonomously. This loose, decentralized structure is somewhat reminiscent of the first government formed in the United States under the Articles of Confederation, when there was little centralized authority.

A Culture of Honor

Only the late 19th century *Mezzogiorno* could have created the Mafia. There are three main forces that came together that caused the Mafia to develop the way it did; the Southern-Italian culture of honor, the lack of popular support of the newly-unified Italian government, and the conflation of superstition and Christianity. Each of these factors did more than give birth to the Mafia, they provided a fertile environment for growth while giving it a distinctly Italian flavor.

As noted above, one of the big myths concerning the Mafia is that they are an honorable group of criminals. As mentioned, you will often hear the Mafia referred to as *The Honorable Society* or *The Men of Honor*. Honor plays a big role, you will even see this in the cheesiest of Mafia movies. This emphasis on honor is the result of the *Mezzogiorno*'s *culture of honor*.

The phrase *culture of honor* is a specific sociological term. In such cultures, there is a sense of obligation to protect your honor in response to any slight. In these societies, individuals establish boundaries of behavior where a violation of the rules of etiquette or respect will reap swift violent retribution. In responding violently, individuals demonstrate a willingness to retaliate to insult or threat. It is this willingness that gives evidence that the honorable man or woman is someone with whom you should not trifle.

Cultures of honor typically arise when there is a lack of formal law, and competitors can easily steal valuable resources. Most often, these cultures develop in nomadic or herding societies where the main sources of wealth are cattle, goats, horses, or sheep. It is easier to steal a herd of goats than it is an orchard or field of wheat. In areas where law enforcement is weak, we can see how this would lead to a violent society. In such situations, you would want to establish a reputation as a violent vengeful person. Think of it. You are a friendly neighborhood goat rustler and you come across my heard of goats on a hill. Knowing I shot a guy in the head for looking the wrong way at my daughter would cause you to think twice about stealing my goats. If I shot a guy for a look, what would I do to *you* for the theft of my livestock?

Most often cited cultures of honor are the Middle East, the southern United States, and inner-city gangs. Interestingly, the Middle East has had a significant influence on the *Mezzogiorno*, starting as far back as 827 CE when Muslim invaders established the Mazara settlement in Sicily. For nearly 200 years, Sicily had been an Islamic foothold in Italy. In addition to a relatively short rule, Islam also influenced the *Mezzogiorno* through trade. An influence which is seen in Sicilian architecture and heard in the Sicilian language. It should, therefore, not be surprising to see they also inspired a culture of honor on the island.

The practices of Middle Eastern honor societies and those of the *Mezzogiorno* crime syndicates are at times identical. Most people in the United States associate *honor killing*, murders that are meant to be a punishment in the name of family honor, with Muslims and the Middle East. Most often these murders are in response to some sexual crime such as adultery or homosexuality. According to a United Nations study in 2000, there were approximately 5,000 *honor killings* per year with most of them occurring in Islamic regions of the world; most, *not* all.[106]

Honor killings are also a practice within the Mafia, although most Italian-Americans don't realize this. The actual lives of *mob wives* are far from what is seen on American *reality television*. Women are chattel, where fathers marry off their daughters to establish ties between themselves and other factions. The women who are unfaithful to their husbands, even those husbands who have long been dead, are killed by their closest male relative, just as it is done in the Middle East. The bodies of these women are typically incinerated or dissolved in acid.

---

[106] Zoroya, Gregg, Honor Killings: 5 Things to Know, *USA Today*, June 9, 2016

Even their bodies must be eliminated to re-establish family honor.[107] Is this what *the* Mafia *takes care of their own* means?

In addition to the historical influences of the Middle East, recall how Italy got its name: the land south of Napoli became known as *Viteliú* or *calf-land*. This is cattle country. We should also make note that while Sicily, for example, was known for citrus, the *Mezzogiorno* was a difficult region for farming. A large portion of the society were herders. The 'Ndrangheta in Africo, Calabria, for example, got its start by cattle rustling.

We have discussed multiple times throughout this book how the newly unified Italian government was seen in the *Mezzogiorno* as another foreign invader. It had no credibility with the common man or woman. After generations of foreign occupation, the *contadini* considered those who cooperated with the government, any government, as collaborators and traitors. As you will recall from Chapter 6, *Italian Steel*, this generated among *contadini* families a *bunker mentality*. As noted in that chapter, the sociologist Sabetti, labeled this as *moral familism*, a loyalty to your family above the rest of society. When Sabetti described the *contadini* behavior as a rational response to the poverty of the south as well as a seemingly uncaring government, he was describing what motivated families to develop into criminal syndicates.

As we can see, all the ingredients necessary to create a culture of honor exited in the *Mezzogiorno* in the late 19th century. First, we have the cultural influences from the Middle East which made an impression on the population, a large percentage of which were dependent on the herding of livestock. Second, through much of their history, the *contadini* of the south were an occupied people who did not recognize the legitimacy of the government of a unified Italy, making it weak and powerless. The resulting culture virtually required any organized crime syndicate to create an image of honorability.

Omertà

Moral familism provided the framework upon which hung the *omertà*, the Mafia's code of silence. The basic cell of the Mafia is the family, who are the people with whom your loyalties lie. As the Italian adage tells us, a fish with his mouth shut does not get caught. Keeping your mouth

---

[107] Perry, Alex, Blood and Justice, *The New Yorker*, January 22, 2018

shut was a way of life. This is why you know, as I said at the beginning of this chapter, anyone that goes around saying they know this guy or that guy in the Mafia is a blowhard.

This also worked to keep the victims of the Mafia quiet. In the *Mezzogiorno*, if you went to the authorities you were seen as a traitor to your people, a rat. You were also considered weak because you could not deal with the problem yourself. If you are being shaken down for protection, you keep quiet. Going to the police would only make matters worse. For all you knew, the police were probably in on it anyway. This gave the Mafia great leeway. If someone was murdered or their business was bombed, when the police asked questions no one knew anything, even the victims.

The Italians brought this same code of silence with them to the United States. When the Black Hand, a street gang often confused with the Mafia, started to extort local businesses, few, if any, went to the authorities. The police were Amarighans. They weren't going to help. The Mafia, as well as the Black Hand, knew the local populace would not go to the police. Just as in Sicily, in the Little Italy communities throughout the United States, the Mafia was able to act freely knowing the local Italian population would not go to the authorities.

This attitude continues even to this day. Several years ago, I was visiting some friends on the east coast. As we were having breakfast, the daughter who was reading the morning newspaper, shook her head mumbling, "Everyone saw that coming." When I asked her what had happened, she told me the previous evening a man had been shot in a local bar – one of those windowless little corner mom & pop hangouts popular in east coast working class communities. According to her, the man's wife had been caught skimming money off the profits of an illegal gambling ring in which she was involved.

Since the death, the husband had been vocal about going to the police to tell them everything he knew. Finally, the people he was threatening began to take him seriously so they had him killed. He had been sitting at a bar, drinking, when a man wearing a ski mask walked in, shot him in the back of the head, and walked out. When the police started to question the few *witnesses* that were still there, no one saw anything. Everyone happened to have been in the restroom at the time.

Maidens & Knights

Honor is embedded into the Mafia's cultural myths. For example, there are a number of myths concerning the origin of the Mafia, and each substantiates the lie that the Mafia is somehow an honorable clandestine society. The origin myth with which I grew up was that the Mafia began when a couple of Napoleon's soldiers raped a Sicilian girl. The local community, in seeking to avenge the girl, began a system of patronage that evolved into the Mafia. Others claim it began with monks during the Sicilian Vespers. This was when, in 1282, the Sicilian people evicted French occupiers from the island. Others suggest the Mafia began with a secretive society known as the *Beati Paoli*: a medieval society which was reportedly composed of an order of knights who, in protest against the Inquisition in Sicily, fought for the poor and common people.

The story I prefer, not for its accuracy but color, is of three Spanish Brothers. According to legend, the story of *The Honored Society*, the Mafia, begins in 1412 in Toledo of Spain. There were three brothers – *Osso* (bone), *Mastrosso* (Master Bone), and *Caragnosso* (heel bone) – who were members of the *Guardugna*, a military association. The *Guardunga* had a strict code of behavior which included a variety of customs and rituals.

As fate would have it, the sister of these three men was violated and then murdered. Incensed by this dishonor, as well as the violence done to their beloved sibling, the three men took bloody vengeance on the perpetrator of the crime. Subsequently, they were imprisoned on the Sicilian Island Favignana which was part of Spain at the time. They were sentenced to 29 years, 11 months, and 29 days.

The time they had spent in prison was not wasted. After years of study and contemplation, the three men defined a code of honor which included rituals and customs that became the basis for the *Honored Society*. Once freed, the three men traveled to various regions of Italy to spread the way of life they had defined. *Osso* stayed in Sicily while *Mastrosso* went on to Naples and *Caragnosso* left for Calabria. Thereby, they become the fathers of the *Cosa Nostra*, *Camorra*, and *'Ndrangheta*, respectively.

The University

The Spanish Brothers myth is a wonderful fairytale, loaded with knights and violated maidens, and honor codes, and tradition, but in the end, it is a myth. Yet, within every lie, there is a truth and within every truth, there is a lie. As the story tells us, the Mafia began in the prisons of the *Mezzogiorno*, which is correct. They were, however, off by about 450 years.

In the beginning, the vast majority of the *'Ndrangheta*, the Calabrian Mafia, were young men. Some were artisans, others were simple laborers or goat herders. They were callow youth who all had one thing in common, they had all been to jail. When these young men emerged from prison, they were immediately adopted by the *'Ndrangheta* and put into leadership roles. It was in the prisons that the young *Mafiosi* learned their trade. The jails of the *Mezzogiorno* were the Mafia's universities. Coincidently, many east-coast Italians I know, who did have a run-in with the law, refer to their time in prison as *going to the university*.

In the late 19th century, gangs controlled the prisons of the *Mezzogiorno*. The time spent in prison by these young men was a time of bonding, indoctrination, and training. When they came out, they were already integrated into the *Honored Society*. As we look into the history of other countries, such as Russia and South Africa, we see prisons as training centers there as well. What makes the *Mezzogiorno* unique is from whom they received much of their training.

Many of the Mafiosi were in prison during the *Risorgimento*. Along with them were political prisoners fighting for unification who also happened to be Freemasons. We discussed the role of Freemasons as well as the subgroup the *Carbonari* (Coal Burners) in Chapter 2, *Italy What a Concept*. From them, the Mafia learned the mechanics of secret societies such as the use of rituals and how to organize. As you look at some of the rites of the Mafia, such as the initiation ritual, you will see how they leveraged what they had learned – incorporating it into their own secret society. In a sense, you could almost say the Mafia is the freemasonry of crime.

The Mafia also made the right connections in prison to establish a sufficient customer base for their special type of *expertise*. Having established a relationship with the Mafia, and once freed, the political prisoners hired them as muscle for the *Risorgimento*. Which was fine for the Mafia; they had no political conscience. It was also fine to turn on those same revolutionaries to become paid informers to the government (which is something they did quite happily). These were the people of the south, loyalty was to your family.

In the Beginning

We see the first documented signs of the Mafia in western Sicily in the 1860's, at about the time Garibaldi liberated the island from the Bourbon occupiers. In 1863, Niccolò Turrisi Colonna, Baron of Buonvicino, authored the study *Public Security in Sicily*. In this report, Colonna described the practices of the Mafia that are still followed today such as the *omertà* and the internal courts that dealt with members who broke their code of honor. In the years following Colonna's study, the Mafia grew in infamy. Everyone in Sicily was talking about the Mafia and accusing everyone else of being a member. It created such a stir that two Tuscans, Leopoldo Franchetti and Sidney Sonnino, traveled to Sicily to study its society and culture. The resulting report, *Political and Administrative Conditions in Sicily*, is considered, even into the 21st century, to be one of the most authoritative on how the Mafia came into existence.

When Franchetti and Sonnino traveled to Sicily to research *Political and Administrative Conditions in Sicily*, they sought out Niccolò Turrisi Colonna. The locals warned them that Colonna was in league with the Mafia. In the years between Colonna's report and the visit by Franchetti and Sonnino, Colonna brought Mafia elements into local government. During the time after the *Risorgimento*, including the period of the diaspora, the Mafia was far from on the side of the *contadini*, as some of the myths would have you believe. While many of the bandits in the hills of Italy fought the aristocracy, the Mafia were entirely mercenary, gladly taking pay for being the enforcers for the rich landowners and corrupt southern government.

Franchetti and Sonnino's study pointed out that the *Risorgimento* in Sicily intended to replace the feudal system of the past with a modern Republic. They wrote of how the role of government has been to maintain a monopoly on violence, waging war and punishing criminals. In the south, the government failed in this responsibility and the Mafia filled the void. Franchetti called the Mafia, *l'industria della violenza*, (the industry of violence). The commodity in which the Mafia traded was extortion. As John Dickie describes it, the extortion racket regime is the basis for criminal territorial authority in the *Mezzogiorno*. Since the state cannot protect the citizenry, the Mafia does. Of course, they also create the need for it by ruthlessly making anyone who resists a victim of their violence! This is the financial base from which the Mafia operated and still operates. Even to this day, small business owners are the subject of violent retaliation for not paying protection money.

Like ticks on a dog, the Mafia came to the United States with the immigrants of the diaspora. They brought with them the same business practices they had developed back in Italy, including extortion. Story after story comes out of Little Italy of the bombings of shops because the owners were not willing to pay. At times, you will hear Italian-Americans talk about how the Mafia had, at least at one time, a code of honor which prevented them from harming families or children. They say they were professionals whose actions were only part of the business. This is ludicrous. There are many kidnapping stories of Italian immigrant children by the Mafia. Even after the ransom had been paid, the children were never seen by their families again.

Of course, as we have said before, the victims of these crimes did not go the police. The Mafia preyed on our own people. It wasn't a matter of surviving prejudice in the new world, or some warped notion of professionality, the Mafia were simply ordinary criminals, sociopaths.

The Mafia & the Church

In addition to the culture of honor and the lack of a government with strong authority, the third factor that helped shape the Mafia was how superstition was conflated with Christianity in the *Mezzogiorno*. As discussed in the previous chapter, Italians place much greater emphasis on the role of saints in the dispensation of grace than non-Italian Christianity, including other Catholics. In the initiation rituals, we can see how this reverence for saints was mingled with what the early *Mafiosi* learned in prison from the *Carbonari*. In 1984, Tommaso Buscetta described the ritual:

> *The recruit is taken to a secluded location (which may also be a private home), in the presence of three or more men of honor of the family and then the oldest informs him that the goal of "this thing" is to protect the weak and eradicate abuses; afterward one of the candidate's fingers is pricked and the blood is spilled onto a sacred image. Then the image is placed in the hand of the novice and set on fire. At this point the novice, who must endure the burning by passing the image from one hand to the other until it is completely extinguished swears to be loyal to the principles of "Cosa Nostra", solemnly stating, "May my flesh be burned like this sacred image if I do not keep faith with my oath." In broad outline, this was the way the oath is taken, and only at that point, the man of honor is introduced to the head of the family. Before that he is not supposed to*

know who the boss is, nor is he supposed to know of the existence of the Cosa Nostra as such.[108]

Over the past 150 years, there have been different descriptions of the Mafia's initiation rites. Others have described the rite to include a pistol and knife placed on the table in front of the novice. While others describe the novice as being asked a series of questions prior to the commencement of the ceremony meant to determine their willingness to become part of the secret society. Although there are some variations, the basic points in Buscetta's description seem to be present in all of them.

Note the inclusion of a sacred image, typically a saint, as well as the spilling of blood onto the image. This is all part of the Christian mysticism that permeates the *Mezzogiorno*. Those familiar with the rites of Freemasonry will notice similarities between the two as well. As noted by Diego Gambetta, "The Mafia ritual has the distinct flavor of a simplified version of the rituals of the *Carbonari* ... and, more remotely, of the Freemasons. The initiation ritual of the *Carbonari* involves knives, blindfolds, blood, fire, and the invocation of a saint – Saint Theobald, protector of the sect."[109]

The relationship between the Mafia and Christianity, or more specifically Roman Catholicism, goes beyond the initiation rites. The two seem to orbit one another. The gravitational influence of each organization pulls the other in one direction or another. *Mafiosi* see themselves as honorable protectors of society, which, in Italian culture, includes being good Catholics. They support various feasts and saints. When there is a procession in honor of the town's patron saint, the local *capo* is sure to be seen at the head of the procession, walking next to the priest. There is a sense among the bosses that their authority within the *Honored Society* is somehow supported by the church.

Considering the actions of the church, the belief it has somehow blessed the mob is not at all unreasonable. Since the beginning of the Mafia, during the tumultuous years of hostility between the Catholic Church and the government of a unified Italy, the church found a ready ally in the Mafia. They were an alternate source of authority in the south. You

---

[108] Gambetta, Diego, *The Sicilian Mafia: The Business of Private Protection*, Harvard University Press, 1996, pg. 266

[109] Gambetta, Diego, *The Sicilian Mafia: The Business of Private Protection*, Harvard University Press, 1996, pg. 149

will be hard-pressed to find, in the early years of the Mafia, any protest or complaint on the part of the church. For the most part, the church either tacitly blessed the Mafia or simply did not address it. A number of priests were implicated in the anti-Mafia campaigns and trials of the late 1920's. As the church began to settle its differences with the Italian government, their tolerance of the Mafia weakened to the point where, in 1993, Pope John Paul II condemned the crime syndicate. The real breakthrough, however, came when Pope Francis traveled to Calabria in 2014, where he excommunicated members of the mob.

Italians & the Mafia

Ultimately, we see Italian-Americans have little reason to venerate the Mafia. I learned firsthand that admiration for the Mafia is one of those things which Italians and Italian-Americans do not have in common. Few Italian-Americans are not fans of the movie *The Godfather*. Images of Michael Corleone and Sonny are common in Italian restaurants. It is an unwritten law that *Speak Softly Love* is played at Italian-American weddings. So, when I happened to mention the film to an Italian friend, she became uncharacteristically angry. "I hate that movie. I won't watch a Coppola movie because of it." She was one of many Italians I know who feel the movie romanticized the Mafia to the extent that it washed away the truly evil characteristics of the organization.

Italians have encountered the Mafia in a very real way. They understand the Mafia is, in part, responsible for the lack of progress in the south. They see the violence, and understand that *Mafiosi* are not beautiful people or honorable men, but thugs who deserve the contempt of all Italians throughout the world. Letizia Battaglia, a Sicilian photographer, has noted while Americans love *The Sopranos*, they don't realize the Mafia is dangerous, more like ISIS. Letizia has been photographing Sicily for more than 60 years. When she speaks of her work, she says her "archives are filled with blood." In remembering the violence of the Mafia, she has said "the best judges, the best policemen, the best people were killed. Some were friends."

Perhaps I can tell more of how the Mafia came to power in the United States or I could even discuss the cultural differences between the Italian and American Mafia. I could go into the details of how the Italian Mafia look on the American Mafia as uncouth barbarians. I could even talk about how the Italian Mafia made Lucky Luciano the victim of a con. I could go into these topics, but I won't. I resent the Mafia and the association they have with the Italian people. I resent that, when writing a book about Italian culture, it could not be complete without discussing an organization of murderers and extortionists.

Let me summarize this simply. If you love Italy and the Italian people, you will hate the Mafia as an Italian hates the Mafia.

Epilogue: Italianità

In the first chapter, I spoke of how, like Dante, my awakening was the beginning of a journey. It was a journey to discover *Italianità*, which I likened to a flowing river whose path had been buffeted by the forces of history.

Although this river has many branches, they are all part of the same river; it is important to keep this image in mind. Each of these branches represents the various groups of Italians around the world, each with their own version of Italian culture. Although one group might dismiss another as not truly being Italian, because they drink cappuccino in the evening or call it sauce instead of gravy, we are all still Italian. If we are to truly own our heritage, however, and if we are to truly own our cultural identity, we must become aware of these differences, and incorporate them into our overall understanding of what it means to be Italian.

To Italians

Many Italians, however, have an issue with this broad, inclusive view of the Italian community. They ask how Italian-Americans can call themselves Italian when they don't speak the language, eat the same food, or even appreciate Italian cultural icons. I would remind them of the diversity of Italy itself. For much of our history, many have claimed, as did the European statesman Count Klemens von Metternich in 1841, that Italy was merely a geographic expression. I would remind those that would exclude Italian-Americans from *Italiani nel mondo* that diversity, differences in speech, in food, and in customs, is inherent to our heritage.

How many Italians claim the Roman Empire as part of their heritage? Mussolini's pitch to the Italian people was that he would restore Italy's Roman greatness. Rome, however, was just one part of what is now Italy. A Calabrian is about as Roman as an Alabaman is a New Yorker. Just as both the Alabaman and the New Yorker are Americans, so too are the Calabrian and the Roman Italian, despite their cultural differences. We can extend this same thinking to Italians and Italian-Americans.

Most importantly, I would say to my Italian friends, remember we claim an Italian heritage out of love. Yes, we have an incomplete, overly-romanticized image of Italy but it is a love of Italy and all things Italian, including its people, that motivates us.

To Italian-Americans

To my Italian-American friends, I would say that we should admit there is some truth to Italians' criticism of Italian-Americans. How can we say we are Italian when we haven't an understanding of Italian culture? There are elements to Italian culture of which all *Italiani nel mondo* should be aware. Italian-Americans need to rediscover these things, to reclaim what previous generations have lost.

First, we need to learn the language. Speaking the language provides access to so much of our culture: opera, literature, poetry, and film. Now, I am not suggesting that you necessarily become fluent, although if you can all the better. We should, however, have some familiarity with some of the basics. At least come to an understanding of how the expressions used within the Italian-American community relate to how they speak in Italy.

Second, I recommend we develop a better appreciation for pillars of Italian culture, some of the things I mentioned in the previous paragraph. Try to develop an appreciation for Italian opera. You don't have to start by listening to an entire opera. You don't become a runner by starting with a marathon. Start simply with a few arias or snippets of some of the great Italian composers. Even if you discover you don't really enjoy opera, at least gain an appreciation for the role opera has contributed to our history and cultural evolution.

In terms of literature, many of the great Italian authors have been translated into English. You need not limit yourself to Dante, Petrarch, or Boccaccio either. There are a number of modern Italian authors that have been translated into English, including Giuseppe di Lampedusa, Umberto Eco, and Italo Calvino; all of whom are great authors.

Finally, I would encourage you to travel Italy. I know many Italian-Americans who are like I used to be. They long to go to Italy, but for one reason or another they never quite seem to get there. Now I understand that many of us simply cannot afford the expense. The first time I traveled to Italy, it took a good deal of financial planning on my wife's part as I have described. If you can go, however, follow my nephew's advice from chapter 1: *go for Christ's sake.*

While there are many tours throughout Italy, I would avoid tours that pile 30 or 40 people on a bus, careening from one tourist trap to the next. I remember sitting outside a restaurant near Lake Como as one of these monsters belched black diesel clouds as it squeezed through the narrow streets. One tourist pressed his wide-eyed face against the glass, turning his nose into a snout, as he tried to catch glimpses of the town he had hoped to experience.

When I travel through Italy, I prefer to do it on a bike.

I have toured Italy multiple times on a bike, which has taken me beyond the typical tourist-worn paths; places where the buses couldn't go. On my first bike ride through Italy, I was cruising along the edge of the Po river, just south of Venice, when I passed through a town that was barely more than four corners. I stopped in the *bar*, remembering that a bar in Italy is quite different to those in the States, for a snack. As I ate, I was able to speak with one of the people who lived there. He rarely saw Americans, and I am not sure which of us was more excited by the conversation. It was one of the high points of the trip to hear about his 50 plus years in that small town.

There are a number of bicycle tour companies that will take you to just about any part of Italy you would like to go. Most of these tour companies provide everything you need, as well as support while you are on the ride itself. They book the hotel rooms, arrange dinners, and point out local points of interest that would escape the average tourist.

To reclaim our heritage, we must connect with our past. Recall how chapter 1 discussed Robert Bly's description of a sibling society, a society where the integration between all generations is a flat horizontal structure; a society whose culture has little or no connection with the past; a society that has lost touch with the traditions of their ancestors. To be truly a branch of the River *Italianità*, we must connect with our past. Learning the language, understanding the art, reading the literature, listening to the music, traveling to Italy, each of these things provides us with *vertical integration*, a link with those Italians who came before us.

So, what is Italianità?

So, after coming all this way, are we any closer to understanding *Italianità*? Can we really define the essence of being Italian and Italian-American? After all the diversity of Italians that I described above, what one thing is there? Well, let's step back and think about what we have learned on our journey.

As I think back, I come to an understanding of *Italianità* which should have been obvious. *Italianità* is not about Italian and Italian-American culture. It is quite the opposite. Italian and Italian-American culture is about *Italianità*; expressing those essential attributes inherent in *Italiani nel mondo*. Culture is the collective output of a group's intellectual accomplishments: painting, sculpture, literature, music, and food. *Italianità* is much more than these artifacts. *Italianità* is in the hearts of *Italiani nel mondo*. Culture is an expression of what is in those hearts. Despite the various differences between Italian and Italian-American cultures, between regions in Italy, or even between different groups in the United States, there is this heart that we all share.

So, when we look at Italian and Italian-American culture, what do we see expressed? First, there is strength. As we have seen, for centuries Italy has been dominated by foreign powers, as well as our own institutions, but we have remained strong. When you listen to Verdi's *Va Pensiero*, you hear the voices of a people who have been oppressed but not broken.

This same strength can be seen in Italian-Americans. It was proven as we took a leadership role in the American labor movement. It was proven by our grandmothers, mothers, and aunts who worked long hours in sweatshops when the rest of America thought it improper for women to work.

Second, there is defiance. Remember how Tosca tells Scarpia to look her in the eyes as he dies, jeering that he had been killed by a woman as he bleeds out. Remember how as Ezio, in *Attila*, sings, "You can have the world, but leave Italy to me," the Italians would shout back, "Viva Verdi!" in defiance of the Austrians.

Italian-Americans feed off defiance as the Olympian gods feed off ambrosia. It is the *what-you-looking-at* attitude, the willingness to cut off your nose to spite your face. It is the labor activists in the *Crusade for Bread and Roses* who, after tearing apart factory machinery, threatened with death anyone who would dare attempt to restart the works. It is the *vaffanculo* look in the eye of an angry Italian-American woman.

Third, Italians have a resolute eye to the future. So much that is written of Italy is about its past but it is so much more than that. Although Italy, like many other nations, is faced with its challenges, the strength and vision of the Italian people are more than able to overcome them. Listen to the national anthem when they sing, "Brothers of Italy, Italy has awakened ... we have been for centuries stamped on and laughed at because we are not one people because we are divided. Let's unite under one flag, one dream." When I hear these words, I envision Volpedo's painting *Il Quarto Stato*. I see the *contadini* marching forward into the future.

Italian-Americans also have this faith in the future, this vision of a better tomorrow. Leaving the security of their motherland, traveling to a place where they did not speak the language, working in horrible conditions, subjected to prejudice, they labored in the hope of a better life for themselves and their children. This vision is one that Italians and Italian-Americans share.

Most importantly, *the* essential attribute of *Italianità* is *abbondanza,* that is to say, abundance, plenty. I do not mean by this material wealth. By *abbondanza* I am referring to the Italian sense of living life with an existential joy. It is a life-affirming attitude that seizes being; a cognizance of the sheer joy of simply being alive. It is a fervor that savors existence whether it is the boisterousness of the *Mezzogiorno* or the *bella figura* of the north. What all Italians have in common, Italians or Italian-Americans, is a passion for life itself. This is *Italianità*, the essence of being Italian.

How could it be otherwise? How could Italians have produced the art that we have created had we not been consumed with the beauty that surrounds us? If we had not been in awe of the majesty of the divine? How could we have written the poetry and literature had we not burned with the revelations that could inspire others? How could we have given birth to a culinary tradition that has conquered the world had we not found delight in even the most common of meals shared with friends and family? How could we have composed the music, and operas had we not wished to stir hearts with this joy? Even those operas that end in death relish the exquisite truth that even life's sorrows must be savored as a part of living.

So, this is *Italianità*; it is the unique combination of strength, defiance, and vision, infused with a passion to live life abundantly. While these attributes may express themselves in different ways in all the different permutations of Italian and Italian-American culture, they are our foundation. They are the essence of being Italian and Italian-American. They are *Italianità*.

Index

References

America's Changing View of Mussolini and Italian Fascism by Mark Weber

American Teenagers and Stereotyping by Zogby International Survey

Americans of Italian descent: national public opinion research for Commission for Social Justice by Response Analysis Corporation

Anti-Italianism, Essays on a Prejudice by William J. Connell & Fred Gardaphé (Eds)

Are Italians White? How Race is Made in America by Jennifer Guglielmo & Salvatore Salerno (Eds)

Being a Character: Psychoanalysis and Self Experience by Christopher Bollas

Beyond the Melting Pot by Daniel Patrick Moynihan & Nathan Glazer

Blood and Justice by Alex Perry

Bowling Alone: The Collapse and Revival of American Community by Robert D. Putnam

Christ in Concrete by Pietro di Donato

Christ Stopped at Eboli by Carlo Levi

Clelia, Il Governo dei Preti, Fratelli Rechiedei by Giuseppe Garibaldi

Communism, Fascism and Democracy: The Theoretical Foundations by Carl Cohen

De Monarchia by Dante

De Vulgari Eloquentia by Dante

Democracy in America by Alexis de Tocqueville

Dubliners by James Joyce

Elements of Theology by Proclus

Emigrazione transoceanica e mutamenti dell'alimetazione calabrese tra Ottocento e novecento by Piero Bevilacqua

Enneads by Plotinus

Fascism Part I: Understanding Fascism and anti-Semitism by R.G. Price

From Sicily to Elizabeth Street: Housing and Social Change Among Italian Immigrants, 1880-1930 by Donna R. Gabaccia

Garibaldi by Denis Mack Smith

Honor Killings: 5 Things to Know by Gregg Zoroya

How Italian Food Conquered the World by John Mariani

Il Canzoniere by Petrarch

Il Nostro Tempo e La Speranza by Corrado Alvaro

Inferno by Dante

Istruzione e sviluppo economico. Il Caso italiano, 1861-1913', in Gianni Toniolo's L'Economia Italiana by Vera Zamagni

Italian American Youth and Educational Achievement levels: How are we doing? by Vincenzo Milione, Ciro Rosa & Itala Pelizzoli

Italian Cuisine: A Cultural History by Alberto Capatti & Massimo Montanari

Italian Food Rules by Ann Reavis

Italian Immigrant Radical Culture by Marcella Bencivenni

La Bella Lingua: My Love Affair with Italian, the World's Most Enchanting Language by Dianne Hales

La Questione Sociale by Cristina Melone

Legacy of Hate: A Short History of Ethnic, Religious and Racial Prejudice in America by Philip Perlmutter

Letter from Theodore Roosevelt to Anna Roosevelt, March, 21, 1891.

Lettera aperta: Ai preti della Chiesa di San Michele di Paterson by Christine Melone

Living the Revolution: Italian Women's Resistance and Radicalism in New York City, 1880-1945 by Jennifer Guglielmo

Making Italian America: Consumer Culture and the Production of Ethnic Identities by Simone Cinotto (Ed)

Metaphysics by Aristotle

My Life by Giuseppe Garibaldi

O Labor of America: Heartbeat of Mankind by Arturo Giovannitt

Pietro di Donato, A Melus Interview by Dorothee von Huene-Greenberg

Power and Privilege: A Theory of Social Stratification by Gerhard Lenski

The Better Angels of Our Nature: Why Violence Has Declined by Steven Pinker

The Cambridge Companion to Modern Italian Culture by Zygmunt Baranski & Rebecca West (Eds)

The Divine Comedy by Dante

The English Village Community and the Enclosure Movements by W.E. Tate

The Gulag Archipelago by Aleksandr Solzhenitsyn

The Italian-American Table: Food, Family, and Community in New York City by Simone Cinotto

The Italians by John Hooper

The Italians by Luigi Barzini

The Labor War at Lawrence by Mary K. O'Sullivan

The Lawrence Strike of 1912 by John McPherson

The Migrants Report, Italians in the World by Giancarlo Perego

The Moral Basis of a Backward Society by Edward C. Banfield

The Pursuit of Italy by David Gilmour

The Sibling Society by Robert Bly

The Sicilian Mafia: The Business of Private Protection by Diego Gambetta

Tongues of Italy, Prehistory and History by Ernst Pulgram

Travel & Tourism Economic Impact 2017 Italy by World Travel & Tourism Council

Truly Italian: Quick & Simple Vegetarian Cooking by Ursula Ferrigno

Una Storia Segreta: The Secret History of Italian American Evacuation and Internment During World War II by Lawrence DiStasi (Ed)

Were You Always an Italian? Ancestors and Other Icons of Italian America by Maria Laurino

Why Italians talk with their hands (and Scandinavians don't) by James Lane

Why Sinatra Matters by Pete Hamill

Aphantasia: Experiences, Perceptions, and Insights by Alan Kendle

Close your eyes and picture a sunrise.

For the majority of people, the ability to visualize images – such as a sunrise – seems straightforward, and can be accomplished 'on demand'. But, for potentially some 2% of the population, conjuring up an image in one's mind's eye is not possible; attempts to visualize images just bring up darkness.

Put together by lead author Alan Kendle – who discovered his Aphantasia in 2016 – this title is a collection of insights from contributors across the world detailing their lives with the condition. It offers rich, diverse, and often amusing insights and experiences into Aphantasia's effects. For anyone who wishes to understand this most intriguing condition better, the book provides a wonderful and succinct starting point.

The Savvy Traveller Survival Guide by Peter John

Travel is one of our favourite activities. From the hustle of bustle of the mega-cities to sleepy mountain towns to the tranquillity and isolation of tropical islands, we love to get out there and explore the world.

But globe-trotting also comes with its pitfalls. Wherever there are travellers, there are swindlers looking to relieve individuals of their money, possessions and sometimes even more. To avoid such troubles, and to get on with enjoyable and fulfilling trips, people need to get smart. This book shows you how.

What Business Can Learn From Sport Psychology: Ten Lessons for Peak Professional Performance by Martin Turner and Jamie Barker

How are the best athletes in the world able to function under the immense pressure of competition? By harnessing the potential of their minds to train smart, stay committed, focus, and deliver winning performances with body and mind when the time is right.

This book is about getting into a winning state of body and mind for your performance – whatever that might be – sales pitches, presentations, leadership, strategic thinking, delivery, and more. You will develop the most important weapon you need to succeed in business: your mental approach to performance. This book reveals the secrets of the winning mind by exploring the strategies and techniques used by the most successful athletes and professionals on the planet.

Write From The Start: The Beginner's Guide to Writing Professional Non-Fiction by Caroline Foster

Jam-packed with great advice, this book is aimed at novice writers, hobbyist writers, or those considering a full-time writing career, and offers a comprehensive guide to help you plan, prepare, and professionally submit your non-fiction work. It is designed to get you up-and-running fast.

Write From The Start will teach you how to explore topic areas methodically, tailor content for different audiences, and create compelling copy. It will teach you which writing styles work best for specific publications, how to improve your chances of securing both commissioned and uncommissioned work, how to build a portfolio that gets results, and how to take that book idea all the way to publication.

CPSIA information can be obtained
at www.ICGtesting.com
Printed in the USA
BVHW040157150521
607271BV00001B/63